CHANGING TIDES

Previously Published in
The American Society of Missiology Series

American Society of Missiology Series, No. 31

CHANGING TIDES

Latin America and World Mission Today

Samuel Escobar

Maryknoll, New York 10545

Copyright © 2002 by J. Samuel Escobar.

Chapters 1-5, 7-9, and 11-13 were translated by Phillip Berryman from *Tiempo de Misión: América Latina y la misión cristiana hoy* (Santafé de Bogotá, Colombia: Ediciones Clara; and Ciudad Guatemala, Guatemala: Ediciones Semilla, 1999); they were furthered edited and adapted by the author for an English-speaking audience.

Published by Orbis Books, Maryknoll, New York, U.S.A.

Manufactured in the United States of America.

Manuscript editing and typesetting by Joan Weber Laflamme.

Library of Congress Cataloging-in-Publication Data

Escobar, Samuel
   [Tiempo de mision. English]
   Changing tides : Latin America and mission today / Samuel Escobar.
      p. cm. — (The American Society of Missiology series ; no. 31)
   Includes bibliographical references and index.
      ISBN 1-57075-414-4 (pbk.)
   1. Missions—Latin America. 2. Missions, Latin American. 3.
   Missions—Theory. I. Title. II. Series.
      BV2831.3 .E8313 2002
      266'.0098—dc21
                                        2002000623

I dedicate this book to my children
Lilly Ester and Alejandro
faithful companions during these years
of missionary pilgrimage over the roads of the Americas.

Contents

PART THREE
MISSIOLOGICAL PERSPECTIVES ON POPULAR PROTESTANTISM

Preface to the ASM Series

The purpose of the ASM (American Society of Missiology) Series is to publish—without regard for disciplinary, national, or denominational boundaries—scholarly works of high quality and wide interest on missiological themes from the entire spectrum of scholarly pursuits relevant to Christian mission, which is always the focus of books in the Series.

By *mission* is meant the effort to effect passage over the boundary between faith in Jesus Christ and its absence. In this understanding of mission, the basic functions of Christian proclamation, dialogue, witness, service, worship, liberation, and nurture are of special concern. And in that context questions arise, including, How does the transition from one cultural context to another influence the shape and interaction between these dynamic functions, especially in regard to the cultural and religious plurality that comprises the global context of Christian mission?

The promotion of scholarly dialogue among missiologists, and among missiologists and scholars in other fields of inquiry, may involve the publication of views that some missiologists cannot accept, and with which members of the Editorial Committee do not agree. Manuscripts published in the Series reflect the opinions of their authors and are not understood to represent the position of the American Society of Missiology or of the Editorial Committee. Selection is guided by such criteria as intrinsic worth, readability, and accessibility to a range of interested persons and not merely to experts or specialists.

The ASM Series, in collaboration with Orbis Books, seeks to publish scholarly works of high merit and wide interest on numerous aspects of missiology—the study of mission. Able presentations on new and creative approaches to the practice and understanding of mission will receive close attention.

The ASM Series Editorial Committee
Jonathan J. Bonk
Angelyn Dries, OSF
Scott W. Sunquist

Preface

By now it is clear that Latin America will play a major role in Christian mission in the new century now beginning. Protestant churches in the region are showing great missionary drive. Half of the world's Catholics now live in Latin America, and their missionary leaders see them as a major potential resource for the future. It is therefore not surprising that Christian reflection in these lands has focused on key questions about the mission of the church. The region has been a kind of laboratory of experiences and thinking, and it is incumbent upon us to understand what is happening and to interpret it. Developments like the self-generated growth of grassroots churches, the process of social change generated by religious conversion, the adoption of Protestant methods by Catholic missionaries, and the missionary impulse of Latin American exiles elsewhere in the world make it urgent for us to observe and make an effort at interpretation.

This book is part of an effort to interpret these developments from the standpoint of Christian mission. I do not know whether I have achieved my purpose of making it a coherent book with structure and connection rather than simply the collection of articles in which much of it first saw the light of day. Readers who know my work will recognize that some sections or chapters were first produced for congresses or consultations during the past ten years. Theological reflection in the Latin American Protestant churches has not taken place in the academic ivory tower, but in events where activists and theologians pause to look at the road traveled with a self-critical eye and proposals for doing better.

I have made use of the work of biblical scholars, historians, and sociologists, and I hope I have done justice to them in the notes, where I credit them for what I have received. I am not a specialist in any of these fields, but I attempt to use their contributions to respond to questions that arise from the study of Christian mission.

I thank my colleagues in the Latin American Theological Fraternity and the American Society of Missiology (ASM) from whom I have learned so much through the years and who have prompted a major portion of these reflections. Special thanks to René Padilla in Buenos Aires, Ian Darke in Costa Rica, William F. Dyrness in Pasadena, California, and Darrell Whiteman, editor of *Missiology*, who encouraged me to write and publish material that I have included in this book. Pew grants administered by the Overseas Ministries Study Center allowed me to organize consultations in which some of these pages were first conceived and discussed. I thank specially Gerald H. Anderson for his friendship and encouragement through the years.

With the exception of chapters 6 and 10, this is a translation of *Tiempo de Misión,* a book that was published in Spanish jointly by Ediciones CLARA-Semilla, the Anabaptist publishing houses in Colombia and Guatemala. My special thanks to Juan Francisco Martinez, who now teaches at Fuller Theological Seminary, for his fraternal encouragement and his patience as an editor of the Spanish version. The order of the chapters has been rearranged and some sections have been amplified and updated for the English edition. Part of chapter 6 was published as an article in *Missiology,* and part of chapter 10 appeared as a chapter in the book *Emerging Voices in Global Christian Theology,* edited by William F. Dyrness. Chapters 3 and 11 have been enlarged and updated for this edition.

I feel honored by the decision of the editorial committee of the American Society of Missiology series to select this book to appear in a series that represents so well the ethos and spirit of the ASM. Without the encouragement of Bill Burrows at Orbis Books, *Changing Tides* would not have been a reality. For some time now I have carried on a conversation with Phillip Berryman about many of the issues I tackle in these pages, and I thank him for being a *traduttore* and not a *traditore. Muchas gracias* to Bill and Phil!

May God use these reflections to encourage and help Christians who have set out in obedience to the missionary call of Jesus Christ.

List of Abbreviations

ABU	Alianca Biblica Universitaria [Brazil]
ASM	American Society of Missiology
CEHILA	Commission for the Study of the History of the Church in Latin America (Spanish acronym)
CELA	Latin American Evangelical Conference
CELAM	Consejo Episcopal Latinoamericano (Latin American Bishops' Conference)
CLADE	Latin American Congresses on Evangelization (Spanish acronym)
CLAI	Consejo Latinoamericano de Iglesias (Council of Latin American Churches)
COMIBAM	Cooperación Missionera Iberoamericana (Iberoamerican Missionary Cooperation)
COMLA	Congreso Misionero Latinoamericano (Latin American Missionary Congress)
CONELA	Confraternity of Evangelicals of Latin America
FTL	Fraternidad Teológica Latinoamericano (Latin American Theological Fraternity)
SVM	Student Volunteer Movement
WEF	World Evangelical Fellowship

PART ONE

THE CHANGING FACE
OF CHRISTIAN WORLD MISSION
TODAY

1

Christian Mission Today

It was in Manila, in the Philippines, in 1989, the same year that the Berlin Wall fell, that we all first realized how much and how fast the world was changing. Several thousand of us had gathered as Christians in one of those huge multicultural, multiracial congresses where you meet many new friends but it is hard to find your old ones. Those of us from the Third World[1] were very curious to find out about the Russians and Eastern Europeans. Among them was a Russian engineer who had become an evangelical preacher. He was going around looking for an African physician whom he had known twenty years previously in Moscow. That African student had spent months telling the Russian the story of Jesus and challenging him to become his disciple. Twenty years later the Russian wanted to thank that third-world missionary who had shared the gospel with him. The high point of the meeting was a spectacular and moving embrace.

The advance of the gospel today, as in the past, owes a great deal to encounters in which some ordinary human beings out of need or calling go beyond the boundaries of their own world and venture into the world of "the other." For almost twenty centuries the gospel of Jesus Christ has been crossing all types of borders, going from one country to another, from one culture to another, from one social class to another. Today Jesus Christ is invoked and his word is read in almost all languages and dialects. The message of Jesus has attained a universality greater than that of any other person in history.

Historians, anthropologists, and sociologists study migrations of communities or peoples, movements of cultural penetration, and changes of religious affiliation. What they find hard to explain is the drive that moves believers to share their faith, especially when they gain nothing thereby and sometimes have to bear persecution. We Christians believe that in this constant crossing of borders, the Holy Spirit is pressing the church to fulfill the mission for which God formed it, and so it achieves the aim of redeeming love, revealed and carried out by Jesus Christ. In a broad sense, the term *mission* has to do with the presence and testimony of the church in a society, how the church is a community whose members incarnate one type of life according to the example of Jesus Christ, the worship that the community renders publicly to God, the service to human needs undertaken by the community, and the prophetic function of challenging the forces of evil that destroy persons and societies.

3

The more specific concept of *mission* that serves as our starting point in this book has to do more precisely with this drive of the Christian church to carry the message of Jesus Christ to the four winds. When the church becomes fully aware that it has been formed and sent into the world with a purpose, it feels impelled to fulfill its mission. The very word *mission* comes from the Latin root *mittere*, which means "to send." In recent times there has been a rediscovery of the meaning of *presence* and *service* in the world, which must characterize the Christian mission. There has likewise been a rediscovery of the particular meaning of the proclamation that is an absolutely essential component of mission. Historian and theologian Justo González has stated it eloquently and clearly:

> The history of the Church is the history of its Mission. This is because the Church *is* its mission. The church is not born when the Lord calls some fishermen, but when he calls them to make them "fishers of men" (Mt. 4: 18-22; Lk. 5:1-11); not when a group of Christians shuts itself up in a chamber "for fear of the Jews," but when Jesus Christ tells these Christians "as the Father has sent me, so I send you" (Jn. 20:19-23); not when the disciples have the mystical experience of seeing tongues of fire over their heads, but when this experience is translated into a witness that overcomes all language barriers (Acts 2:1-11).[2]

Century after century the Spirit causes women and men to come forth from the people of God seized with a passion for evangelization and to set out and cross all kinds of borders to carry the story of Jesus of Nazareth, the gospel of salvation, to other human beings who do not yet know him. The church that carries out its mission is always a pilgrim community, a people on the way, sent out to the four winds under obedience.

The witness of the evangelist John tells us that at a high point of his ministry Jesus said, "And I, when I am lifted up from the earth, will draw all people to myself" (Jn. 12:32).[3] John observes that with these words Jesus was referring to his death. Thus, from the cross on which he was exposed to the gaze of all, like a criminal, Jesus was going to be like a magnet attracting all human beings. Later this risen Jesus, to whom all authority in heaven and on earth has been given, tells the apostles, that is, those whom he has "sent," that he wants to have disciples in all the nations of the earth. Hence he sends them with a full agenda: to announce, teach, and baptize (Mt. 28:18-20), and he promises that he will be with them continually through the Holy Spirit.

The geographical borders that the apostles will have to cross on the initial mission are explicit in the missionary mandate from the Master as concentric circles with a universal scope: Jerusalem, Judea, Samaria, and the ends of the earth (Acts 1:8). By the second missionary generation represented by the apostle Paul, the borders also take on a specific cultural dimension. Having preached throughout the eastern region of the empire "from Jerusalem and as far around as Illyricum" (Rom. 15:19), Paul proposes to go to the "ends of the earth," faraway Spain where the continent ends. Likewise the apostle affirms the universality of his call in terms of the multiple cultures of the world whose borders he crosses; he is in debt to the cultured and the uncultured, to the learned and the unschooled, to Jews and Gentiles (Rom. 1:14).

The reason for this constant movement is that the very nature of Christian faith makes it missionary. Paul says that "faith comes from what is heard, and what is heard comes through the word of Christ" (Rom. 10:17). The truth that saves and gives meaning to life is not a truth that every human being brings into the world, like a spark that may be fanned into a flame by religious practice or philosophical knowledge. The truth that saves is a word that another human being, a *witness*, transmits to us. It is not something discovered by introspection, but a witness that is received. Whoever attains salvation upon receiving the testimony is obligated to incarnate this word and to reflect the light received by also becoming light.

The new life is a word that enlightens. "The Lord is my light and my salvation; whom shall I fear?" (Ps. 27:1) sang the Israelites, and Jesus said, "I am the light of the world. Whoever follows me will never walk in darkness but will have the light of life" (Jn. 8:12). Thus as God is light and Jesus is the light of the world, the disciples are to give light. In the Sermon on the Mount, Jesus declares: "You are the light of the world" (Mt. 5:14), and explains that this has to do with the practice of the truth, with a life of "good works" that bring others to glorify God. In Paul's words, this proclamation wells up out of an immense sense of gratitude—"I am a debtor to all" (Rom. 1:14)—and this leads him to exclaim, "Woe to me if I do not proclaim the gospel" (1 Cor. 9:16).

The history of Christian mission is not only the story of the vicissitudes along the way while crossing geographical borders. It is also the story of venturing to cross from one culture into another, struggling against the ethnocentrism and racism innate in the human heart. It is the story of the ongoing and surprising discovery of "the other." Jews discover "Gentiles" beyond Jerusalem, well-educated Greeks discover the "barbarians" beyond the border of the Roman Empire, Spaniards discover the "moors" beyond the border of medieval Christendom, Europeans discover "Indians" and "Asians" across the ocean. At its best moments, Christian mission starts out from this new experience of a new people in which borders vanish because "there is no longer Jew or Greek, there is no longer slave or free, there is no longer male and female; for all of you are one in Christ Jesus" (Gal. 3:28). Those who belong to this people can genuinely say, "From now on, therefore, we regard no one from a human point of view" (2 Cor. 5:16).

The incarnation of the word,[4] which grounds God's saving work, tells us that the Word is translated into a visible reality that our eyes can see. The message of this incarnate Word can be translated into all human languages. Indeed, the basic documents, namely the gospels, are already a translation, because we do not have them in the Aramaic that Jesus spoke, but in the everyday Greek that was more widely spoken in the first century. This "translatability" of the gospel shows that it is a message that can reach maximum universality; that is, *this message is intended to be translated and shared.*

Thus the gospel drive that presses the church toward fulfilling its mission also brings the people of God to a constant contextualization process. The text moves from context to context. Today, at the beginning of a new century, we are more aware than ever that missionaries are vessels of clay, bearers of the glory of the gospel, who are themselves weak and likely to break. As Paul said very well: "But we have this treasure in clay jars, so that it may be made clear that this extraordinary power belongs to God and does not come from us" (2 Cor. 4:7). When this text is taken in its context in the second letter to the Corinthians, the apostle's specific intention becomes clear as he describes the missionary task as an enterprise carried out by persons who are fragile and weak, subject to contingencies like perils, suffering, and persecution. The memory of these lines of Paul knocks down any imperial pretension and reaffirms the model of mission in the style of Jesus Christ, a style completely different from that practiced by the Constantinian church allied to oppressors and conquerors, who used mission to subject other human beings to domination.

NEW FRONTIERS

We find ourselves today in a world in which the gospel has crossed *almost all geographical borders* and the church is present in the most remote corners of the earth. From one angle it can be said that transportation and communications technologies have made the planet a global village. Email carries a news report from Moscow to Medellín in a few seconds, and any Japanese tourist covers in eight hours the journey from the Canary Islands to some point in the Caribbean that it took Columbus six weeks to do in 1492. Through computers a Guatemalan bishop can know in seconds whether the Holy Office in the Vatican approves of a certain liberation theologian or not. Over an invisible network of waves and wires a new and nervous culture with its own language of satellites, computers, statistics, deadly weapons, rapidity, and viruses is taking hold quickly and efficiently throughout the world.

From another angle, however, it can be said that the cultural and social gaps separating one race from another within a single society may have increased to the point that in the same city some groups separated by only a few yards do not communicate with one another. That is what happens among blacks, Hispanics, and Jews in New York City, or between Serbs and Croats in the Balkan Peninsula. Although some churches send missionaries from New York or Los Angeles to the other side of the world, their own members are sometimes unable to pray or be in solidarity with their brothers and sisters in Christ just a few blocks away.

Moreover, migrations have brought into the heart of Europe and the United States refugees from around the world who are now posing the challenge of a new cultural and religious pluralism unfamiliar to the wealthy countries. At the same time, the collapse of Marxism in Eastern Europe has exposed the age-old barriers of racial prejudice that is reaching the proportions of a destructive tribalism and that had not been destroyed but only repressed by the ideology of dialectical materialism. In such a world, what new borders must Christian missionaries cross today?

A NEW FACT AT THE TURN OF THE CENTURY

At the beginning of this century a Christian observer stands facing something completely new in the history of Christianity. The numerical balance of forces of the Christian presence in the world has been radically altered. By contrast with the early twentieth century, when large churches and missionary strength were growing in Europe and North America, today the practice of the Christian faith is declining rapidly in Europe while the churches of Africa and Latin America are growing vigorously. The numerical growth of Christian churches in Africa is the most dramatic case. It is estimated that in 1900 there were nine million Christians in Africa, whereas today there are over 300 million.[5]

It is acknowledged that missionary drive has shifted to the South. Even though the African and Latin American churches are poor and are facing dramatic challenges as a result of the social and economic crisis in their regions, they are sending missionaries to other parts of the world. It is also startling to see how certain young Asian churches, such as those in Korea, have burst into the missionary world with unusual strength. The European and North American churches remain rich and enjoy special privileges in their societies, but they seem to be incapable of resisting the eroding impact of modernity, secularism, and pluralism. Their members show little or no interest in sharing their faith. They seem to have become resigned to closing their places of worship, giving up all efforts to shape the societies of which they form a part, and gradually disappearing.

Specialists in missionary research such as Catholic Walbert Bühlman and Protestants Andrew Walls and Lesslie Newbigin have been noting and analyzing the entry onto the scene of the churches of the South. Bühlman describes this new process as the emergence of the "Third Church." In 1986 he wrote:

> I have maintained that the Third Church is approaching, church of the Third World but also church of the third millennium. Roughly speaking, we can say that the first Christian millennium, with the first eight councils all held in the East, stood mainly under the leadership of the First Church, the Eastern Church; the second millennium stood under the leadership of the Second Church, the Western Church, which shaped the Middle Ages and, from the time of the "discovery" of the New World, undertook all missionary initiatives. Now the coming third millennium will evidently stand under the leadership of the Third Church, the Southern Church. I am convinced that the most important drives and inspirations for the whole church in the future will come from the Third Church.[6]

This factor can no longer be ignored in any reflection on the future of Christian mission. With the meeting of the International Missionary Council in 1928,[7]

European Protestants became aware that the old Europe was losing its spiritual fiber and could no longer be regarded as the "Christian civilization" that it had always claimed to be. In Catholic circles in 1943 two French priests, Henri Godin and Yves Daniel, launched the cry of alarm with their work *France: Pays de Mision?,* in which they recognized that vast sectors of the French population, particularly workers and students, were ignorant of the Christian faith or had abandoned it.[8] This realization has only grown and become more acute. The missiologist Lesslie Newbigin[9] was on very good grounds when he said that so-called western Christian culture is the one most resistant to the gospel, while other cultures show themselves to be much more receptive. Bühlman explains the shift of the strength of the churches to the South and points to one cause that also suggests its missionary potential:

> The West is becoming more and more an aging community and church. But in the Third World as a whole, 42 percent of the population is under 15 years of age. The church there is a church of youth, hope, the future. These peoples are also still very poor. The church there has the opportunity of becoming the church of the poor and for the poor, not merely on paper but in deed and in truth.[10]

Bühlman is not exaggerating; a sustained look is enough to show the validity of what he says. For example, the churches that have grown most in Latin America are grassroots churches of the Pentecostal type. It is at this grassroots level that growth has been greatest. The older forms of Protestantism helped create a middle class, but many of them are declining in both North America and Latin America. In the United States in my own denomination, American Baptist, there are places where the average age of members is 60 or over; there are no children or young people. These churches will soon be closing. Yet in this same denomination the Hispanic, black, Vietnamese, and Chinese churches are growing. These ethnic minority churches are generally poorer than the Anglo-Saxon or European-descended majority, with different styles, worldviews, liturgies, schedules, foods, and the like. Hence it is sometimes difficult to get along together within the denomination.

It is not easy for missionary strategists, theological educators, and candidates for missionary work to deal with the consequences of this new balance in Christianity. It used to be said that Christianity was a western religion—that is no longer the case today. If we could see a picture of all the faces of Christians in the world today, most of them would not be white, but rather black, yellow, bronze, a whole range of colors, with whites a minority. "What color is God's skin?" goes a song. In answering that question, we turn not to an ideal but to reality.

Andrew Walls in particular draws attention to the fact that the major theological issues and missiological debates in this century are not going to be those posed by European and North American universities and seminaries. Rather, they are going to arise out of the life of the churches that are embarking on missions along the new frontiers. The Eurocentric worldview, which is so influential in the way history is written or the theological agenda is defined, will have to change. We must therefore realize that the majority Christianity today is not that of the theology of the pastoral textbooks that are taught in theological seminaries. Today's Christianity is different from what was in the minds of the Protestant missionaries who came to Latin America early in the twentieth century. The Christianity of this century will be of another color and another type.

Only within the framework of this new world situation of Christianity can what happened in Latin America during the twentieth century be understood. Anyone posing the question of the future of Christian mission must comprehend this reality, for the followers of Christ in Latin America will play a very important role in that mission. Understanding the current missionary reality has been possible thanks to the dedicated work of missionaries and scholars who have combined activism with reflection. The systematic study of Christian mission is an interdisciplinary approach that we call missiology. This book is written from an evangelical viewpoint, and hence a chapter is devoted to sketching out the missiological task and identifying the prevailing missiological approaches in the evangelical world, this sector of Protestantism that continues to produce most missionary activity.

2

Mission Today: Practice and Reflection

As we enter a new century, there are over four thousand agencies devoted to sending out Christian missionaries, and over 425,000 people working outside their countries of origin as Christian missionaries.[1] This total may be grouped into three main sectors: Catholic, Orthodox, and Protestant. Within the Protestant sector the most vigorous missionary force is that of the so-called evangelical churches, which are theologically conservative, pietistic in spirituality, and very zealous about evangelization. This sector includes the missionary strength of the Pentecostal churches. Protestants in the so-called historic churches showed strong missionary activity in the first half of the twentieth century, but it dropped off for various reasons. After World War II, missionary activity from the United States intensified, especially from independent missions and parachurch entities. Today evangelicals and Pentecostals constitute the largest missionary force within Protestantism, and the missions coming from the Third World are also from churches of this kind.

What has been said thus far has to do with what we may call official mission in the sense that it is organized deliberately with people who are fully devoted to such activity. But the church's missionary activity is much greater because there are millions of Christians who spontaneously strive, wherever they are and in their own manner, not only to live as disciples of Christ but also to transmit their faith to others. When I visited Australia in 1988, my hosts in the Church Missionary Society, a mission of Anglican volunteers, told me that they had a task force studying the possibility of starting a mission to serve Spanish-speaking immigrants. Near the end of my tour I also had a chance near Sydney to meet with a group of Spanish-speaking believers who had immigrated to Australia. There were around fifty people, including Argentineans, Chileans, Nicaraguans, Mexicans, and Peruvians. Some had emigrated for political reasons; others were seeking a better economic future. They were working as professional people, merchants, and skilled craftsman, but none was a pastor or missionary. Yet they had already founded nine Spanish-speaking churches in southwest Australia! Within the new wave of Latin American, Asian, and African immigrants in the United States and in some European countries there are thousands of people with evangelical convictions who are active church members and are actively evangelizing and forming disciples. A process of church revitalization is plainly underway and the churches benefit from this new activism.

During the second half of the twentieth century, missiological thinking has sprung up alongside evangelical missionary activity. One of its constant features is the effort to understand how Christian mission developed in New Testament times, in keeping with the Protestant conviction that the Bible is the authority for the doctrine and practice of Christian belief. However, in going back to consider the biblical text, the historical moment made it necessary to raise new questions that reflected the social transitions of the century, especially the waning of European colonialism and the rise of new nations in the Third World. There was a desire to correct and adapt missionary practices to new ways of engaging in mission more in keeping with the biblical teaching, "according to the model of Jesus Christ." The Lausanne Covenant (1974) and the movements preceding and following it are a good expression of this new attitude.[2] The Latin American Congresses on Evangelization (CLADE I—Bogotá, 1969; CLADE II—Lima, 1979; CLADE III—Quito, 1992; and CLADE IV—Quito, 2000) have been its nearest equivalent in Latin America.[3]

One characteristic of this missiological reflection is that it reflects the evangelical conviction about the church's missionary obligation but also a *critical* stance toward the way it has traditionally been carried out. Such necessary criticism is not always well received by large missionary organizations. One reason is that after World War II many third-world countries achieved independence from European colonial domination, and that was the very framework in which reflection critical of those forms of missionary practice shaped by the European or North American colonial mentality arose. The contrast between this mindset, with its associated missionary practices and the missionary model of the New Testament began to be recognized. The servant form as a model for a missionary faithful to Jesus Christ was rediscovered, and ways to correct the older practices were sought.

This correction seems to have turned out easier for European than for North American evangelical missionaries, partly because in 1945 the United States emerged from World War II strengthened, and it extended its economic and political hegemony in the world while Russia was consolidating the Soviet Empire in Eastern Europe. The result was the Cold War, and many Christians began to see the world divided between the good (westerners) and the bad (Communists). Often enough one could see the missions being promoted on the grounds that the world had to be saved from Communism. Consequently, everything that seemed to imply social criticism came to be regarded as subversive or Communist, and labeled as such.[4] This has notably hindered missiological reflection and self-criticism of the enormous North American missionary endeavor. That is the very reason why the development of evangelical missiological reflection is so urgently needed.

THE NATURE OF MISSIOLOGICAL REFLECTION

Missiology is an interdisciplinary approach to the reality of mission. It draws on the biblical sciences in the sense that the Bible shows us a norm for how Christian mission is to be carried out. It also draws on what history has to offer, because the way in which the missionary command of Jesus Christ has been fulfilled over the centuries in different contexts has to be taken into account. The social sciences are also useful because they help us to analyze the different social and institutional mechanisms as well as the types of social relationships established as Christianity expands.

REFLECTION IN THE LIGHT OF THE WORD

Each new generation of missionaries inherits models from its predecessors, but it is challenged to correct, invent, or rediscover certain principles *in the light of the word of God.* The work of the biblical sciences contributes to the missiological task understood as "reflection on practice." When we read carefully the correspondence of Saint Paul, for example, we see how he reflected on his own missionary practice.[5] The apostle often explains how his action seeks to be conformed to the model of Jesus Christ. Missiological studies on epistles such as 2 Corinthians show that the apostle contrasted his own missionary style with that of the Jewish missionaries who preceded him, and he did so with a grounding in Christology.[6]

The structure of Luke-Acts also assumes a reflection on practice. The content of this two-volume work shows how the mission of Jesus and that of the apostles were driven by the Holy Spirit, and how the missionaries continued to respond to new situations with acts of obedience illuminated by the word of God. More than a simple chronicle of what happened, this work is written for a generation of believers who needed to know how the Lord and the first generation of believers had carried out their task in response to the imperative of the word of God and the impulse of the Holy Spirit. It was a work that sought to inspire obedient action and to inform that action with revealed truth.[7] I find especially meaningful the familiarity evident in the style of Luke-Acts with social structures and historic moments of the ancient world that influenced the development of Christian mission, its rootedness in the basic lines of the Old Testament text, and at the same time the certainty that what was driving missionary action was the power of the Spirit.

The new century obviously requires a return to the biblical models of mission. We are going through a radical change of era in culture, politics, and economics. Moreover, the growth of popular forms of Christianity in the southern hemisphere has changed the religious map of the world. The models of the traditional mission inherited from the mindset of Christendom and the colonial age are now unworkable, even though many missions are still practicing them. It is time for a paradigm change that can only come from a salutary return to the word of God. As David Bosch said, "Our point of departure should not be the contemporary enterprise we seek to justify, but the biblical sense of what being sent into the world signifies."[8] The new perspective requires firm surrender to the missionary imperatives that are part of the very structure of our faith, and at the same time a serious work of research and biblical interpretation.[9]

MISSIOLOGY AND HISTORY

This book is a missiological reflection from an evangelical basis and perspective. Taking into account that Latin America is still considered a Christian continent and that not long ago the five-century anniversary of its "evangelization" was celebrated, we must honestly ask what we can learn as evangelicals from the history of the missions and particularly from the Catholic missionary enterprise of the sixteenth century. Let us bear in mind that in recent decades the Catholic missionary enterprise has been researched and studied from a variety of perspectives. In addition, the Protestant missionary presence for more than a century is also available for analysis and comparison. The application of modern historiographical criteria and the opening to self-criticism among some historians and liberation theologians are reflected in the work of CEHILA and the valuable collection of national and regional studies that it has published.[10] Conservative historians also provide a great deal of information, albeit with little critical spirit, in their apologetic effort to once more uphold the goodness of the civilizing endeavor of Spain and Portugal.[11]

Here the evangelical perspective stands in need of correction. For traditional evangelical scholars, the starting point for interpreting the sixteenth-century Catholic mission has been the pioneering work of John A. Mackay in *The Other Spanish Christ*,[12] followed by the work of W. Stanley Rycroft in *Religion and Faith in Latin America*.[13] In his outstanding if argumentative historical overview, Mackay demonstrated his familiarity with the spiritual history of Spain and the Spanish character, and also made a limited use of the socialist analysis of the Peruvian writer José Carlos Mariátegui. In *Historia de las Misiones* by Justo L. González[14] we have an effort to look at the Spanish enterprise more objectively, following a line similar to that of the great historian Kenneth Scott Latourette. González deals with Catholic and Protestant missionary work within a broad framework of historical continuity. The same criterion is followed in two more recent works by Protestants, the monumental work of Hans Jürgen Prien, *La Historia del Cristianismo en América Latina*,[15] and the work of the same title by Pablo Deiros, intended for classroom use.[16]

Thus we now have enough material to obtain a more objective picture, one that, while remaining critical from an evangelical posture, pays much more attention to the issues involved in missionary methodology and to the theological focus that characterizes missiology. Initially, some scholars influenced by liberation theologies proposed a somewhat simplistic revisionist history of the Protestant missionary enterprise using Marxist criteria.[17] Moving beyond the simplifications of the polemical history of the past, authors like González, Prien, and Deiros have sought to delve into history and interpret an incredible wealth of missionary events that were unknown sixty years ago, when Mackay wrote his well-known book. Certain absolutely necessary questions have thereby been raised, enabling us as evangelicals to be more objective about our own history. Such objectivity is especially necessary if we Latin Americans are going to set out to participate in the missionary task globally and if we are going to do so in an original manner and taking advantage of the lessons from previous missionary practice.

Moreover, at any special moment of missionary advance a missiology is formulated, and it presumes a certain *view of history*. Michael Green, for example, tells us that the Christian thinkers of the second and third centuries interpreted the existence of the Roman Empire as the work of God, who was preparing the world for the extension of God's kingdom.[18] Examination of this view of history shows that it not only offered a look back to the past, but it also went on to become a utopian thought for imagining the future in terms of the spread of the Christian church. The Belgian-Brazilian historian Eduardo Hoornaert has shown how the classic *Ecclesiastical History* of Eusebius of Caesarea was shaped by a Constantinian vision that saw acceptance by the empire as a glorious historical moment for the church. Says Hoornaert, "Doubtless Eusebius' view is that of a particular segment of the Christian leadership of the era, one that entertained great enthusiasm for the political relationships arising under Constantine, and one that would have readily 'understood' Eusebius' projection of these relationships to a divine plane."[19] Eusebius therefore tells the story from that perspective.

At other times there was a messianic outlook. Such was the case of the Iberian peoples in the sixteenth century. Enrique Dussel has pointed out the Iberian messianism that saw the defeat of the Arabs in the peninsula as a sign of God's blessing and choice to complete the task of evangelizing the world "discovered" by Columbus's voyages.[20] Mackay had also noted the fact eloquently and with good documentation in his classic work.[21] A view of history also provided backing and a framework for missionary action for nineteenth-century English-speaking missionaries. The ideology of the British empire colored the British missionaries' worldview and understanding of history;[22] in the case of those from the United States, it was the ideology of Manifest Destiny.[23] These visions were marked by ethnocentrism and national pride, which served to convert them into ideologies that justified the expansionist power of an empire.

It has been pointed out that liberation theologies are primarily missiologies. This can be accepted inasmuch as they begin by raising the issue of the social role of the church in the world. In this sense, the more recent missiologies produced by Catholics follow Vatican II closely, especially the constitution *Gaudium et Spes*. In the case of missiology linked to liberation theologies, a distinctive note was that they presupposed the Marxist utopia. Indeed, these theologies arose at a time when Latin America seemed to be heading toward socialism, coming closer to utopia. Particularly in Gustavo Gutiérrez there is a strong sense of interpretation of the march of Latin American history as a march toward socialism. In *The Power of the Poor in History*[24] Gutiérrez locates this reflection within a whole philosophical framework, which, while it critiques the Enlightenment, also seems dominated by its spirit. The collapse of the Marxist utopia has forced liberation theologians to do some rethinking. Some of them seem to be coming closer to a classic Christian eschatology.

The proposal by the philosopher Francis Fukuyama about the "end of history," which expresses well the state of mind of one sector of intellectuals in the United States, will force theologians to revise the utopian framework of their theological reflection. For Fukuyama, today's western, capitalist, democratic society is "the end-point of mankind's ideological evolution," and therefore we stand before the "end of history." This is actually a "sad age" when the ideological struggles that were a challenge to greatness and daring are becoming simply an endless resolving of technical problems.[25] Indeed, as we will see below, there is a kind of missiology from the United States that has been presenting the missionary task as nothing more than solving technical problems. What is dangerous about this situation is not so much its vision of history but rather the type of anthropology that it incorporates, that is, the human being as a bundle of technical problems, the human being as a statistic, as a marketing item. Perhaps nowhere has this anthropology been better expressed than in the so-called Church Growth school's implicit theology of mission.

Evangelical missiology must return to the biblical vision of history and must also interpret the historic moment represented by the current missionary situation. In our reflection we have tried to see the meaning of the emergence of the churches in the non-white and non-western world, what Bühlmann calls the coming of the Third Church, as a sign of our time. There is no need to adopt the Marxist utopia to recognize in this emergence of a global church a significant point in history. Missiologists like Andrew Walls, Walbert Bühlmann, and Orlando Costas, each in his own way, have tried to show the implications of this new moment. What we need is for the evangelical theology that is emerging in the Third World to capture this significance and to express it out of its own experience and within its own contextual rationality. The dehumanizing features of a "management" view of mission must be counteracted by recovering the fullness of mission.

MISSIOLOGY AND SOCIAL SCIENCES

The issue of the relationship between Christian faith and the social sciences has been raised in Latin America in academic circles where religion is studied. The issue is not purely academic, however; ultimately it is about how to understand one's living out of Christian faith, and the life and witness of one's own church. The issue is posed in Latin America from several angles, each of which enables us to focus on different aspects of the reality, although ultimately it brings us to the same fundamental questions. For example, we have the arguments over liberation theology, some forms of which have attracted more notice, particularly because of the Vatican's criticisms of the use of social sciences by certain theologians. Gustavo Gutiérrez's "Theology and the Social Sciences" best exemplifies this way of posing the issue.[26]

Another example is the selection of keys for interpreting the history of the churches. Thus, for example, political scientist Scott Mainwaring, in studying the relationship between Catholicism and politics in Brazil, seeks to find an eclectic approach that incorporates elements from American functionalism, Latin American Marxism, and classic sociology.[27] Finally, studies seeking to understand Catholic popular religiosity began in the pre-Medellín (1968) period and have gone through several phases since then, sometimes enwrapped in dispute. The critique of the ways of approaching the phenomenon—modernizing, secularist, or Marxist—arises out of pastoral concerns, but it also brings us to basic questions about the relationship between the people's faith and their interaction with social structures.[28]

In Protestant circles the issues are also raised from different perspectives, although not always with full clarity. In this study we would at least like to contribute to raising issues specifically and to indicate the routes over which research and reflection might continue. The questions come primarily from three angles. First, there is the need to understand the attacks against Latin American Protestantism, both in its popular manifestations and its missionary-originated expressions. These attacks come from Catholic and Marxist anthropologists and sociologists, who generally disguise their hostility as scientific objectivity. The frequency and extension of these attacks through the media suggest that they are part of a pastoral strategy by bodies of bishops.[29]

Second, we have the case of the Church Growth theories and strategies, which are the result of the application of the social sciences prevailing in North America to the church's missionary task. Church Growth *[iglecrecimiento]* studies the social factors that foster numerical growth and seeks to propose a successful strategy based on these factors, marketing techniques, and management-by-objectives methodology.[30] Finally, we have the effort to understand the social sciences, their function and limitations from the standpoint of evangelical theology. This would make it possible to evaluate the questions raised above and apply criteria more appropriate to the missionary and pastoral task, as has happened in the field of pastoral psychology.[31]

Here the importance of an approach that pays special attention to the missiological factor becomes clear. As has been noted, missiology is the result of an interdisciplinary effort in which the contribution from the social sciences intensified in recent years. The study of the social behavior of Christians by the sociology of religion has forced theology to enter into dialogue with the sociology of religious behavior. For example, French-speaking Catholicism in Europe was forced to review its sense of mission when sociological statistics showed that France was more pagan than certain African countries to which the French were sending missionaries.[32] The first book of American sociologist Peter Berger (1961) showed that sociological studies proved that the most devout evangelicals in the United States were the most backward from a social standpoint. That is why he called it *The Noise of Solemn Assemblies*, using the ironic expression of

Amos 5:21 that condemns religiosity combined with injustice.[33] Likewise, in order to understand missionary processes, missiology has been forced to dialogue with cultural anthropology and sociology.

In Latin America the method and content of reflection on Christian mission have placed emphasis on understanding it by means of the *tools of observation, analysis, and interpretation* provided by the social sciences, especially anthropology and sociology. As we have seen, both liberation theology and the Church Growth school of missiology have made use of the social sciences to one degree or another, so in their discourse we encounter the prevailing anthropological and sociological categories. That imposes on us an initial reflection in which we try to define the scope and limitations of approaches to mission that use the social sciences in order to try to define what, strictly speaking, a theology of mission would be. In such clarification we must distinguish between the role of the social sciences and the role played by revelation.

Here we may note three clarifications made by Roger Mehl, a theologian and sociologist of the French Reformed church, that help us to establish what he calls "the possibilities and limits of a sociology of Christianity."[34] First, the social sciences must admit their limits. Mehl says that "sociology has no right to assume that it reaches religion in its essence, and even less does it have the right to claim that it is in a position to furnish an exhaustive explanation of religion. It cannot reduce religion to the social, as Durkheim so rashly did. It must recognize its limits."[35] It is here that evangelical missiology questions the reductionism of studies that approach the phenomenon of mission with the atheistic bias of Marxism or with the anti-Protestant bias of Catholicism. One approach denies the validity of the missionary impulse that springs from faith, because it denies the existence of God as object of that faith; the other denies the legitimacy of the Protestant missionary effort because it regards it as sectarian and hence inferior.

Mehl states a second principle that the missiologist must keep in mind: "Sociology can study only the visible, objectively-ascertainable aspects of religion." He adds, citing Binet, "Analysis only reaches the external acts; it is incapable of apprehending the motivations of these acts which alone give the acts their true meaning."[36] This is the place to critique many sociological explanations that are hostile to Christian mission, starting from the assumption that the latter is nothing more than the superstructure of the economic process, and explain the facts in terms of the partnership between empire and mission.

Third, the missiologist must keep in mind that sociology "does not describe an ideal church. It describes the church in its empirical reality, which is not always in accord with the norms to which this church claims to refer. But every society, and the churches in particular, do indeed refer to norms, and this effective reference is not without influence on their comportment."[37] Missiologists must recognize the facts proven by sociologists. They can be helpful for proposing correction and pointing out the distance between the missionary ideal presented by the Bible or the theology and reality of the missionary enterprise, whose embodiments may contradict its ideal.

MISSIOLOGICAL CURRENTS IN THE EVANGELICAL FIELD

A consideration of the vast missiological literature produced in evangelical circles makes it possible to see how much progress has been made using the Bible, history, and the social sciences in missionary practice and in systematic reflection about it. Without going into the broad field of practice and reflection among Catholics and ecumenical Protestants, I limit myself here to sketching the main missiological trends in evangelical circles. I have grouped them in three approaches to missionary practice and missiology reflection, using the terms that in my view seem to define them: *post-imperial* missiology, *managerial* missiology, and *holistic* missiology. I will now briefly describe each.

Post-imperial Missiology

This has been developed especially in Europe, and in Great Britain in particular. It comes from circles in which there is a great deal of missionary activity, along with careful work in the area of biblical scholarship and theological reflection. Its primary feature is recognition that the colonial age is over and that missionaries cannot act as though the West were still Christian and as though colonialism were legitimate. This reflection moves in three directions. First, it pursues a renewed search for biblical models to correct and shed light on missionary practice. Michael Green's work is representative here. Second, we find a critical interpretation of mission history, using data from sociology and social history, but without falling into Marxist reductionism or excessive deference to sociology. The works of Stephen Neill,[38] Max Warren,[39] and Andrew Walls[40] may be situated here.

It may be said that an evangelical sector that takes this missiological reflection seriously has produced new forms of mission in society and cooperation with national churches within non-colonialist frameworks. This missiology conserves the spiritual zeal and sense of calling of traditional missions along with serious work in biblical scholarship to formulate a concept of mission that combines proclamation with service. Its weak point lies in what we could call the move from theology to pastoral activity, that is, in the development of methodologies of missionary and evangelizing action to embody biblical principles. The reason is partly the fact that evangelical churches in Europe do not embody vigor and vitality, that is, there is no rich and manifold practice offering models.

Managerial Missiology

This school of missiology has been developed especially in the United States. Its basic postulate is that Christian mission can be reduced to a "manageable enterprise" through the use of information technology, marketing techniques, and managerial leadership. Movements such as Dawn, AD 2000 and Beyond, Church Growth, and Spiritual Warfare are expressions of a missiology whose main features are as follows: First, there is an emphasis on quantity that seeks to reduce everything to statistics. The aim is to visualize the missionary task with precision, thereby giving rise to concepts such as "unreached peoples," "homogeneous units," "open fields," "10-40 window," or "Adopt-a-People."[41] Even this school's demonology and its idea of "spiritual warfare" give pride of place to statistical data. In this field there is an effort to catalogue the resources available and to quantify them.[42] The missionary process is then reduced to very precise steps taken by means of "management by objectives."

Second, this missiology is distinguished by its pragmatic emphasis, which *reduces the concept of mission to forms of proclamation that can be quantified.* Theological work or consideration of context are not considered important, since it is taken for granted that definitions created in North America are transferable to any place in the world. There is no room for mystery or paradox. Hence, if the biblical norm does not seem pragmatically possible, it is thrown out in the name of the criterion of practicality.[43] Along with that goes a static perception of society, due to the influence of some North American schools of social science. Reality is taken as a fixed datum, and no attention is paid to the changes that are needed or that may come as the result of the transforming dynamism of the gospel.[44]

This missiology manifests the zeal and sense of urgency that are proper to the evangelical tradition, as well as the desire to evaluate missionary action realistically. It is attractive especially because of its methodological proposals, which are offered by using sales techniques. Because of its volume and material and technical resources, it fell into the trap of becoming a goal in itself, placing everyone else at its service. In other words, in marketing customers are of interest only insofar as they allow the company to make money and grow. The managerial focus gives rise to the suspicion that its proponents see mission as an activity that makes it possible to grow and crown its missionary centers in the United States with success.

Holistic Missiology

Holistic missiology has been developing particularly out of the way matters have been posed in the Third World, but in dialogue with kindred groups in Europe and North America. One of its fundamental assertions is that serious questions have to be raised not only about *how much* missionary activity is needed, but *what kind* of activity reflects biblical teaching and responds to the context. This missiology, to begin with, starts from a situation of dynamic evangelizing and missionary activity. Not for a moment does it deny the urgency of mission, but by the very experience of the young churches of its proponents, it has a critical and corrective emphasis. It agrees with the search for the biblical models of post-imperial missiology, and it therefore rejects the excessive pragmatism of managerial missiology.

Second, making use of a biblical model as its foundation, it stresses contextual issues. The ethnic, social, political, and ecclesiastical reality of the Third

World, of the young churches, and of the immigrant minorities of North America and Europe make context imperative and lead it to question managerial imposition, since it sees there remnants of the former colonialism. Hence, due to the connections of its environment, it believes that it is urgent to rediscover the transforming dynamism of the gospel by raising questions on the effect of missionary action out of a comprehensive view of the human being and society. This note is more urgent in Latin America, given the background of Iberian missionary action in the sixteenth century and a nominal Christianity in a continent of dire poverty and injustice.

The weakness of this approach has been its lack of a systematization that could make it accessible at practical levels of ministry. Moreover, it has not paid sufficient attention to the development and study of already existing models. Its rejection of the exaggerated focus on methodology of managerial missiology needs to be replaced by a criterion of the application of theology to the creation of models. Three features ought to characterize Latin American missiology. Missiology as a reflection on the missionary act in the light of the word of God draws nourishment from the *perception* and *participation* in missionary acts of obedience to the Lord of mission. It cannot be limited to being armchair observation. Missiology is *systematic* reflection, and insofar as possible its structure should be provided by the structure of biblical revelation itself. Missiology is *critical* from the standpoint of the word of God. Because it grasps the missionary situation and compares it to the revealed norm, it cannot limit itself to a simple *methodology* for work, nor to the ideological justification for existing practices.

In the twenty-first century a great deal of mission will be from the South. Hence, it will be mission "out of poverty" and "from the periphery." There are valuable elements in the three missiologies described that ought to be taken into account in visualizing the future. The idea of "mission from six continents to six continents" demands that we seek new structures, models, and methods. The impulse of the Spirit must bring us to humble and open reflection in the light of the word of God. It is this seeking for the biblical integrity of mission that guides our reflections in the rest of this book on Christian mission in Latin America today and from Latin America to the world in the century just begun.

PART TWO

MISSION *IN* LATIN AMERICA

3

Latin America:
Mission Land

A CONTRADICTORY MISSION SITUATION

When we look at Latin America from the standpoint of Christian mission, we encounter some surprising and contradictory facts.[1] Catholicism arrived in this region as a missionary wave five centuries ago, and 50 percent of all Catholics in the world live in Latin America. Yet only 2 percent of the worldwide Catholic missionary force comes from Latin America. On top of this imbalance is the fact that in order to survive in this region, the Catholic Church needs a continual influx of missionaries from other continents. Thus, for example, of the 4,164 Catholic missionaries who left the United States in 1996, 1,799 (43.2 percent) were going to Latin America.[2] An even larger contingent of European Catholic missionaries is in Latin America.

In the case of evangelicals the proportion of foreign missionaries in Latin America is smaller, albeit still high. According to the most recent statistics, of a total of 33,074 Protestant missionaries leaving the United States, Latin America receives 8,772, that is, 26.5 percent.[3] This high percentage is paradoxical inasmuch as among evangelicals there is a great deal of talk of the spectacular growth of the indigenous churches in Latin America, which would seem to make a large missionary presence unnecessary. It also contrasts with the common claim that there are great needs for missionary work in regions of Asia, Eastern Europe, and the Middle East, where very often what is needed is a basic pioneering work of evangelizing and establishing churches. The percentage of missionaries who go to Latin America is disproportionate in comparison to the areas in the world most in need.

As if to complicate the picture even further, in Latin America at this turn-of-century moment the people's religiosity has increased, and within an atmosphere of growing pluralism, religious movements of all kinds, such as Spiritism, New Age, different types of Eastern religious pursuits, and the resurgence of pre-Hispanic religions, have been spreading. In Christian circles there is a continual switching among religious denominations. A Belgian Catholic missionary who was an advisor to the bishops of Bolivia drew attention to this fact, "According to statistics, every hour an average of 400 Catholics goes over to Protestant sects."[4]

As a new century begins, the framework for so much religious movement in the continent is a globalization process with its contrasting two faces. On one side is the impact of the market and ever-faster modernization, in which the mass media arouse the passion to consume ever more attractive and varied goods. On the other is a way of life that can only be described with strong adjectives: a fierce concentration in large cities, desperate internal migration, a monstrous foreign debt, the dramatic emergence of marginal sectors, and widespread poverty. All of this is in full view of coldly indifferent and hardened governing classes in a continent whose population is still considered Christian. If it is true, as the apostle Paul says, that "the whole of creation has been groaning in labor pains until now" (Rom. 8:22), these cries are taking on a somber tone in the context of Latin America.

Yet the name of Jesus is proclaimed aloud and very clearly in the streets and squares of the great megalopolises, as well as in remote villages. In both places there are simple people and cultured intellectuals ready to risk their lives for what they regard as the demands of their faith in Jesus Christ as Lord. Some churches are declining in number and influence, but other churches are growing. The Bible is being translated and is circulating in hundreds of indigenous languages and dialects. Among the hundreds of thousands of Latin Americans who go to other places in the world in voluntary or forced exile, there is a small but significant number of Protestants who take their enthusiastic faith and spread it wherever they go. The missionary situation of Latin America is bursting with contrasts.

LATIN AMERICA AS MISSION FIELD

When Protestant missions from Europe and North America began to send missionaries to Latin America in the mid-nineteenth century, the Catholic church rejected their presence, claiming that the region was Christian and was already evangelized: it did not need missionaries. Most of the older European Protestant churches adopted the same position and decided not to send their missionaries to Latin America. In 1910 a large missionary conference was called in Edinburgh in order to consider the state of Christian mission and the possibility of joint actions in the future.[5] The slogan chosen for the meeting expressed an evangelical sense of urgency: "the evangelization of the world in our generation." The older and more prestigious Protestant missions attended the meeting, which is now regarded as the starting point for the modern ecumenical movement. However, the organizers were bound by the position that Latin America was not a mission field, and hence they did not invite any of the Protestant missions that were then working in the region or any of the Protestant churches that were established by that time.

The well-known Mexican journalist and Bible scholar Gonzalo Báez-Camargo interpreted this exclusion as a sign of the prevailing mindset among Protestants in 1910, which was still shaped by Victorian-era complacency and paternalism. They saw the human race as divided into a "Christian world," which included Europe and the Americas, and a "non-Christian world," which encompassed Asia, Africa, and the Pacific islands. "In other words," says Báez-Camargo, "there were grouped on one side and on the other a bloc of Christian civilized 'sending' countries, and a bloc of non-Christian uncivilized, 'receiving' mission fields."[6] Báez-Camargo believes that this global classification was too naive and paved the way for blatant inconsistencies, such as placing Latin America in the first bloc and excluding from Edinburgh Protestant missionaries who had been working there for over a half century. It condemned them and the hundreds of thousands of Latin American Protestants existing by 1910 to be permanent outcasts from the ecumenical movement.[7]

In the intense missiological debates around this issue Protestant missionary statesmen from Great Britain and North America usually described the spiritual condition of Latin America in somber tones. The appeal to send Protestant missionaries was accompanied by a description of social, moral, and spiritual conditions that were considered as a call to action. Robert Speer, the widely known American Presbyterian mission statesman, wrote in 1913:

> The first test of religious conditions is to be found in the facts of social life. No land can be conceded to have a satisfactory religion where the moral conditions are as they have been shown to be in South America. If it can be proved that the conditions of any European or North American land are as they are in South America, then it will be proved also that that land needs a religious reformation.[8]

Speer was an enthusiastic member of the group of North American and European missionary leaders who were not in agreement with the criterion adopted at Edinburgh. They formed the Committee of Cooperation in Latin America and supported a missionary congress of Protestant bodies that were working in the region, which was held in Panama in 1916. That meeting was a milestone for the Protestant missionary effort in these lands. It was preceded by a careful study of the situation, based on information sent by missionary correspondents throughout the continent, and that material served as the basis for ten working groups.[9] The three volumes that sum up the studies of the congress give us a clear idea of the scope of the Protestant mission in these lands and the results that it had achieved. The congress also reflected the self-critical attitude of the participating missions which recognized the flaws in their work and were looking for new forms of cooperation and coordination.[10]

Speer's observation reflected an evangelical conviction about the relationship between faith and ethics, between religion and morality, that is also found in other authors of missionary literature in those days, "Christianity is not opinion or ritual. It is life and that life must utter itself in moral purity and strength. No amount of theological statement or devout worship can avail to take the place of ethical fruitage in social purity and victory over sin."[11] For Speer, the

situation was not a matter of concern only to Protestants but also to Catholics in
North America.

We find the same approach in John A. Mackay, a Scottish Presbyterian who
was a missionary in Peru since 1916 and later on in Mexico before becoming
president of Princeton Theological Seminary. Well known for his friendship
with several liberal and socialist leaders of Latin America, Mackay had come to
the conviction that most of them rejected the Catholic religion out of moral
motives related to social justice.[12] Twelve years after the Panama congress, at
the initial meeting of the International Missionary Council (1928) in Jerusalem,
Mackay made very clear the legitimacy of a Protestant missionary presence in
Latin America:

> Sometimes those who are interested in Christian service in South America
> are apt to be regarded as religious buccaneers devoting their lives to eccle-
> siastical piracy, but that is far from being the case. The great majority of
> men to whom we go will have nothing to do with religion. They took up
> this attitude because religion and morality had been divorced throughout
> the whole history of religious life in South America.[13]

Interpreting what happened in this meeting in Jerusalem, Báez-Camargo holds
that it represented a significant change of mindset. In analyzing the change, he
notes that people had become aware that it was impossible to speak of Christian
mission without taking into account the social context in which it was taking
place. "So the assembly launched itself into an earnest study of social and economic questions as they affect missionary work. It also aimed at awakening and
strengthening of the sense of the Christian's responsibility for social justice."[14]
In Jerusalem it was also noted that a wave of secularism had invaded the countries both sending and receiving missionaries, and according to Báez-Camargo,
acknowledgment of this fact had major consequences for both missiology and
theology:

> This proved to be a revolutionary admission, for it meant that, after all,
> the formerly self-designated "Christian world" was also a mission field
> itself. It meant again—and this was still more important—that the King-
> dom of God cannot be defined in terms of mere territorial accretion, but
> that the whole of life everywhere must be brought under the Lordship of
> Jesus Christ.[15]

Thus, starting from convictions established by Protestant missionary practice in Latin America, serious questions were raised about the Christianizing
process that had accompanied the Iberian conquest in the sixteenth century.
This perspective is well summarized by the Argentinean Methodist theologian
José Míguez Bonino, who would later be the only Latin American Protestant
observer at Vatican II. Míguez says,

Latin America was never "Christian" in the sense that Europe or even North America can be said to be so. What took place here was a colossal transplantation—the basic ecclesiastical structures, disciplines, and ministries were brought wholesale from Spain, and were expected to function as a Christian order: a tremendous form without substance.[16]

That was why it was possible to speak of this Latin American missionary field, which turned out to be fertile terrain for the growth of evangelical Protestantism. The 160,000 Protestants in 1916 had grown to around fifty million in 2000. A Catholic observer said in 1989:

If current growth rates continue, Latin America will have an evangelical majority in the early 21st century. Actually, in terms of church participation, "practicing" evangelicals may already outnumber "observant" Catholics.[17]

Among Protestant missionaries there was a tendency to consider Latin America a territory needing basic evangelization, a field of pioneer experiences where the New Testament model could be applied almost literally. In their more enthusiastic moments such missionaries expressed the hope that something unprecedented could happen, and they used the New Testament era as a reference point. Thus, for example, in 1916 Brazilian evangelical leader Erasmo Braga, after describing how first-century Christianity had signified "the end of paganism," came to this conclusion: "The lesson of history authorizes us to hope that under the impact of the simple and sincere gospel message, as the apostles preached it in ancient Rome, the 'end of paganism' will also take place for Latin America."[18] This vision was re-echoed in 1973, almost sixty years later, in the words of Roger Greenway, a Christian Reformed Church missionary, who in the 1970s devoted special attention to studying the evangelization of large Latin American cities. Greenway said:

If revitalized churches whose leaders have been trained in church growth-oriented schools can be turned loose in the burgeoning cities, then a multiplication of churches will occur *such as the world has not seen since the first century*."[19]

The numerical growth of Protestants in recent decades has led Catholic observers to refer back not to the first century but to the sixteenth. Bishop Boaventura Kloppenburg, for example, has noted how in terms of changing religious affiliation, what is happening in Latin America surpasses what happened during the Protestant Reformation in the sixteenth century. In the twentieth century the Catholic church lost more faithful to Protestant churches than it lost in the age of Luther and Calvin.

DEVELOPMENT OF A CATHOLIC APPROACH

In traditional Catholic missiology the geographical element is a defining key. Missionaries are sent to territories where the church is not yet established and mature, in which missionary work means evangelizing pagans and planting the church. That was not the case of Latin America, of course. Consequently, the idea of mission land was used for territories where native minorities lived in remote and isolated areas, where they had not been assimilated into the general national culture in countries such as Bolivia, Peru, Colombia, or Venezuela. In some of those countries there were agreements between the Vatican and the government giving the Catholic church an exclusive right to carry on missionary activity in those territories. Such agreements offered legal coverage to the actions of Catholic opposition against Protestant missionaries and believers. In the case of Colombia, opposition became violent persecution.[20] The practice and the concepts evolved during the second part of the twentieth century due to new concepts about mission, to some teachings from Vatican II, and to the rise of a self-critical attitude among Catholic theologians and missiologists.[21] As we will see later on in our study, Protestant missionary activity was also influential in the change of Catholic missiological thinking.

Only after World War II did Catholics awaken to the missionary situation of their continent. In 1955, at a meeting of bishops from the whole continent held in Rio de Janeiro, CELAM (Latin American Bishops' Conference) was formed. One of its first actions was to issue a call for Catholic missionaries to come from other regions to help a church that felt threatened by the spread of Marxism and Protestantism among the masses. How did the Catholic hierarchy explain the need for missionaries to this continent that it had previously portrayed as Christian? Catholic missionary efforts from North America and Europe were presented as a necessary investment that would then make it possible to mobilize a Latin American missionary force toward other places in the world. Such was the perception of Pope Pius XII when he wrote in 1955:

> We are confident that the benefits now received will later be rendered back a thousandfold. There will come the day when Latin America will be able to give back to the entire Church of Christ all that it has received; when, as We hope, it shall have put to use those ample and powerful energies which seem only to await the hands of the priest, that they may at once be employed for the honor and worship of God and the spread of Christ's kingdom on earth.[22]

Five years later and in this same spirit, Monsignor Agostino Casaroli, Pope John XXIII's special representative, gave a widely reported talk to superiors of the major religious orders in the United States. He asked that each North American religious province send ten percent of its religious, priests and sisters, to Latin America as missionaries. The response was enthusiastic. In fact, Father John Considine, perhaps the most famous American promoter of the missions, had written a book asking that forty thousand missionaries be sent to Latin America by Catholics in the United States. The goal proposed by Considine in 1946, and made official by the Latin American Catholic Bishops in 1955, and reinforced by the Pope in 1960, was never met, but a great deal of enthusiasm was generated and many men and women from the United States and Canada came to Latin America as missionaries. From Europe also came waves of French, Belgians, Irish, and Swiss, who joined the Germans, Spaniards, and Italians who had been working with Latin American Catholics for a long time. These Catholic missionaries from Europe and North America were very influential in understanding critically the situation of Latin American Catholicism and in the awakening of a Catholic social consciousness that then issued in liberation theologies.

The second bishops' meeting at Medellín (1968) and the third at Puebla (1979) registered the impact of this influence, although the full scope of the effect on Catholicism of the missionary labor of Catholics who came from Europe and North America in this period has not yet been well studied by Latin American missiologists or church historians.[23] The study of the issue of missions in Latin America has been much influenced by foreign missionaries who have settled in Latin America, such as Juan Gorski,[24] Roger Aubry,[25] Manuel M. Marzal, S.J.,[26] Franz Damen, and others. The 1955 awakening led to an effort at self-criticism and to a growing recognition that the Latin American population in many places needed basic evangelization. Angelyn Dries has studied how Catholics in North America changed their mind about the nature of Latin America as a mission field. At first, mission-minded Catholics in the United States felt the need to counteract the negative assessment of the religious situation that came from Protestant missionary writers. Catholics thought that these critical writings were misrepresenting Latin American realities and were not paying attention to the rich cultural and artistic realities of Latin America. Dries writes, "While the actual numbers of converts to Protestantism were relatively small in the early 1930s, Catholics became concerned that Protestant missionaries were becoming interpreters of Latin American religious culture to the North American public."[27] The National Catholic Welfare Council had a Latin American Committee that dealt with this kind of issue. This committee had written to Latin American bishops asking them about the type of information that was to be conveyed to the American public. Reporting about the answers Rev. Raymond McGowan wrote, "Most of the replies stressed the necessity of putting before the American public that Latin America was not a field for missionary work and that such incursions do not tend to increase good feeling between the Americas."[28] Dries remarks that according to this view "the southern hemisphere was, therefore, not to be seen as a 'mission country' but as an extension of Spanish Catholicism in the American setting."[29]

Militants of the lay movement Catholic Action had a different opinion from that of the bishops. Some of the most progressive Catholics came from the ranks of that movement, and their conclusions about the state of the Church in Latin America were more self-critical. In 1953 they held an inter-American congress in Chimbote, Peru, where three hundred delegates came to sobering conclusions. One of them was that

> It can certainly be affirmed that Latin America is a continent that has received the message of the Catholic faith but that it requires at the same time a profound restoration in order to approach the full Christian ideal, today still quite distant. Such a restoration demands an apostolic attitude of missionary penetration, much more than it requires an attitude of conservation of a badly understood traditionalism.[30]

The conclusions of the Chimbote congress became known in the United States through a book written and published by the Maryknoll order. As in many other instances, this publication shows how progressive and reform-minded Catholics from Latin America became connected with Catholic missionaries from North America, a connection that proved to be fruitful.

By the late 1950s American missionary practice as well as winds of renewal from Rome that were to flourish later in the Second Vatican Council brought the development of new perspectives on the nature of the missionary task in Latin America. For instance, the Maryknoll order had to move to Latin America missionaries from China who had been displaced since the time China came to be controlled by communism in 1948. Promoters of mission came to understand that missionary work in Latin America could not be limited "merely to convert the pagans but to influence the Catholic life of the two continents."[31] They came to the conclusion that "even had the war not precluded increasing our personnel in the Far East, the field in Latin America is essentially missionary in character."[32] This new understanding reflected also a correction of old assumptions about the civilizing thrust of missionary work. "We go to South America not as exponents of any North American civilization but to preach the Catholic faith in areas where priests are scarce and mission work is needed. As far as the elements of true civilization are concerned we expect to receive as much as we give."[33]

The following decades saw a wave of intense Catholic missionary activity that was to have a transforming effect not only on the receiving church in Latin America but also on the sending church in North America. In evangelical missionary literature one does not find the same open admission expressed by Dries that "the experience of missionaries in Latin America more than any other region shaped a new theological vision for missionaries and U.S. Catholics in the 1960s, 1970s, and early 1980s."[34] Dries points out that missionary experience in Latin America set the tone for the theological agenda in the United States, brought new emphasis to ecclesiology that was to be reflected in Vatican II, and prepared the Catholic church for the wave of Hispanic immigration that would come to the United States. This is what came to be understood as "mission in reverse."

During a CELAM meeting in 1983 the pope proposed the idea of "a new evangelization for Latin America." This idea was developed and made more specific in the fourth CELAM assembly in Santo Domingo (1992). The term *re-evangelization* is avoided because that would amount to an acknowledgment that the missionary work of the sixteenth century failed. Instead, the term adopted was *new evangelization,* which seeks to renew and deepen evangelization in its fervor, methods, and expression. The assumption is that the work done in the sixteenth century was not a failure but needs to be rekindled:

> We have been evangelizing in Latin America for some five centuries. Today we are living through an important and difficult moment in that process. It is true enough that the faith of our peoples finds clear and unmistakable expression. But we also note that it has not always reached full maturity and that it is threatened: by secularist pressure, by the shocks accompanying cultural changes, by theological ambiguities in our milieu, and by the influence of proselytizing sects and foreign brands of syncretism.[35]

Using categories from Vatican II and Paul VI's document *Evangelii Nuntiandi,* the notion of *evangelization of culture,* has been developed. Roger Aubry says that the Catholic missionary task of the future will be concentrated on those sectors where people are undergoing social transition. He points out particularly how in the course of migrating from the countryside to the city, the masses have abandoned the Catholic church. "We note that the attachment to the church of these persons or groups affected by social change is very weak, and that their faith is too frail to be a vital resource for responding to these new circumstances."[36] Segundo Galilea, one of the most prolific students of this issue, refuses to call the Latin American continent a "mission land," and yet he recognizes that there are vast sectors that need an initial evangelization.

> Today there are groups of Latin Americans who need to be evangelized in an even more restricted sense: to start with, non-believers, Amazon Indians, student, intellectual, ideological, and militant groups. Baptized people have often left the church and religion. Some are "post-Christian."[37]

In relation to the question of Latin America as mission land, the assembly of CELAM in Santo Domingo (1992) went back to positions that were held before Vatican II. This assembly seemed to be marked by the assumption that evangelical missionary work is a foreign conspiracy. The tone was set by the opening address of Pope John Paul II, who challenged the bishops to "defend" their flock from "rapacious wolves." It was a clear allusion to the growth of evangelical churches, usually described as "sects" in Catholic documents. The pope added:

> We should not underestimate a particular strategy aimed at weakening the bonds that unite Latin American countries and so to undermine the kinds of strength provided by unity. To that end, significant amounts of money

are offered to subsidize proselytizing campaigns that try to shatter such Catholic unity.[38]

The tone and assumptions of these remarks, reminiscent of Catholic reactions at the beginning of the twentieth century, are no longer acceptable for other Catholic missiologists and scholars, especially those with pastoral experience in Latin America. Dominican scholar Edward Cleary commented critically on the pope's speech and added: "Ten years of study has convinced me that there is not a strong relation between money spent and results. The great advances seen in Protestant growth in Latin America are not the results of dollars from the United States."[39]

Research and observation have led some Catholic missiologists to similar conclusions; the evangelical churches that are growing faster are the ones that do not depend on connections outside their countries. These scholars acknowledge that Latin America lives a crucial moment in the history of Christianity, a moment that demands an effort to know objectively the reality of the Protestant advance and the challenge it represents. Latin America is an illustration of how the older churches in Christendom show signs of decline and fatigue, while facing the presence of vigorous minorities committed to evangelize. It is important to remember that there are also other regions of the world where established or mainline churches are facing the same situation. It is the case of some state churches in Europe and of so-called historic or mainline denominations in places like the United States, Canada, and Australia. However, the growth of Catholicism or new denominations in the United States and Australia has not evoked the kind of passionate reaction that the growth of evangelicals has evoked among some Roman Catholics in Latin America.

MISSIONARIES FOR THE EVANGELIZATION OF LATIN AMERICA

On the contemporary evangelical side, American missiology has coined the term *unreached peoples* to refer to communities and groups of people who have never heard the gospel. The evangelical missiologist William D. Taylor writes that "Latin America offers a whole world of unreached peoples." He is referring first to the immense process of migration from countryside to city, indicating the urgency of evangelizing, planting new churches, and training leaders. Taking Mexico City as an example, he says that "help is needed from the outside, but it should be sensitive and cooperative missionary help that is willing to enter into partnership relationships with existing Mexican churches instead of merely starting an uncounted flock of new."[40] Taylor includes among the unreached the "untouchable" upper classes and economic elites, people in neighborhoods with makeshift housing, university students and professors, the military in their enclaves, and peasant leaders, as well as those at the bottom of the social spectrum, the slum inhabitants, those who live in garbage dumps, and those locked into hopeless, grinding poverty. He asks whether there is still room in Latin America for European and North American missionaries to come, and he answers with a ringing assertion:

> Yes of course. *But*, he or she must be a missionary who comes devoid of even latent paternalism, one ready to learn from Latin ministry partners, one who has talents and training but is also humble, one who will learn the language with the highest proficiency possible, and one who will understand and come to love the history and cultural mosaic that makes Latin America what it truly is and can become by God's grace.[41]

Catholics are also asking what kind of missionary is needed for the future. It is the Americans who have been most acute and exact in their evaluation. In his short history of the missionary effort, Gerald M. Costello speaks bluntly of the crisis and desertions of many priests and nuns during the critical 1960s. He describes the transformation that took place in American Catholic missionaries as a result of their experience in Latin America: "Then a new mission approach began to emerge, radically new. . . . The missioners who remained began to learn instead of to teach, to serve instead of to lead."[42]

A veteran missionary with thirty years of work in Nicaragua says:

> Unless a person wants to "put on the mind of Christ," he'd do better not to enter Latin American work. . . . Christ came as one of the oppressed with a message of life for the oppressors. We, the church today, tend to come as the oppressors to the oppressed, telling them *we* have a message of life—and they say, "Oh, yeah? Show us!"[43]

Another American missionary who worked in Peru uses a christological perspective based on the well-known passage Matthew 25:31-46 to describe the experience of those who come to "recognize the face of Christ in the faces of the Latin American woman, campesino, or laborer." This is a recognition that grows out of the concrete, day-to-day experience of those who have pitched their tents among the poor, what Gustavo Gutiérrez calls "a material and spiritual nearness to the poor." It does not refer to those who occasionally visit the world of the poor as would a county agricultural extension worker, but to those who dwell among the poor.[44]

There is no doubt that missionary vision and action in Latin America during the twentieth century was challenged to come to terms with the social realities of tremendous disparities, unjust structures, and cultural factors that were shocking to a Christian conscience. How did missionary action affect these social realities? In the next chapters we explore briefly the relationship between mission and social transformation in the missionary work of both Protestants and Catholics in Latin America.

But there is also another question to be pursued. As already noted, Latin America today is receiving proportionately more missionaries, both Catholic and Protestant, than any other region in the world. Another feature surprising a careful observer is that today there are Protestant movements like COMIBAM[45] and Catholic movements like COMLA[46] devoted to placing Latin American resources into Christian mission elsewhere in the world. Should this region still be regarded as a "missionary field" toward which European and North American churches devote human, technical and financial resources as part of Christian mission? We have already seen why this question has been debated for widely varying reasons for over a century. The question is being raised differently today, however. With its five centuries of history marked by a Christian presence, should not Latin America instead be regarded as a "base of missionary action" from which missionaries are sent elsewhere in the world? Answers to this question will benefit from a basic understanding of the missionary history of Latin America.

4

Lessons from Missionary History

For a century and a half Latin America has been the scene of a dramatic polemical encounter between Catholics and Protestants. Although the atmosphere of this encounter has undeniably been warlike and destructive at times, it has also served as a stimulus to self-criticism and the renewal of the churches for mission. In thinking of the future of Christian mission in the world and in Latin America's participation in it, it is absolutely necessary that we pause to reflect on the past at the beginning of the new century. By examining the facts of history from a missiological perspective, such reflection can illuminate the road to take in the future in order to fulfill Christian mission.

As we have seen in the preceding chapters, speaking of Christian mission in Latin America today inevitably means taking into account the five centuries of Iberian conquest and mission that are part of our history. Protestants still think Latin America needs to be evangelized, and Catholics speak of a new evangelization. Likewise, as has been noted, at the outset of the third millennium both Catholic and Protestant students of mission believe that Latin America should no longer be seen only as a "mission field" to which missionaries come from elsewhere, but also as a "missionary base" from which evangelizers go out to other places. Latin American Christians must make their contribution to world mission.

LESSONS OF HISTORY

In view of the renewed sense of missionary responsibility that Catholics and Protestants in Latin America today seem to share, it is well to review the meaning and lessons of the history of both Catholic and Protestant missionary work, using a comparative approach to obtain a historical perspective. Rather than entering into a comparison of the *message and theology* that has been usually used in speaking of Catholics and Protestants, here I propose to pay attention to *methodology and missionary style*. In this regard, from the standpoint of theology we are in debt to Protestant scholars like Emilio Antonio Núñez and José Míguez Bonino, who for years have carefully followed developments in worldwide and Latin American Catholicism in the twentieth century and have explored the risks and opportunities that these developments offer us as Protestants. In Bogotá at the time of CLADE I (1969), Núñez alerted us:

> Vatican II has laid down a deep dividing line between the "preconciliar church" and the "postconciliar church." The Roman church is unquestionably being rejuvenated, putting aside its medieval garments, and getting in tune with the modern age.[1]

In a short but valuable work on Protestant identity, Núñez updated his observations on the effect of Vatican II, noting that in our continent Catholics have begun to imitate the evangelizing and pastoral methods of Protestants. In that connection he draws our attention to two important facts. First, he says, our identity does not depend on the dispute between Protestants and Catholics, because "being a Protestant [*evangélico*] means much more than being in contention with the Catholic Church. Many people are anti-Catholic without being Protestants."[2] Second, Núñez holds that "our Protestant identity does not consist only in our working methods or strategies."[3] For this Central American scholar and pastor, Protestant identity depends on the doctrinal convictions of Protestant Christians. He sums up convictions such as "the word of God at the center of the life of the Christian person and of the Christian church,"[4] and he reminds us that this truth is not something invented by the sixteenth-century reformers but something that they tried to recover.

After a number of years of research into the history of Latin American Protestantism, I have come to the conviction that the current situation of Catholics and Protestants in Latin America is not explained solely or fundamentally by doctrinal differences but also by different missionary practices. I think that when we look at the churches in the light of the process of their historic origins in our continent we can find better keys for understanding what Catholics and Protestants are today in Latin America, and the way in which they can participate in the Christian missionary task in the new century. We must try to follow an important rule in all dialogue, which consists in comparing the best of one with the best of another and not with the worst; likewise in comparing theory with theory and practice with practice.[5]

I have been engaged in a comparative study of missionary methodologies because of the consequence that they have for future missionary strategy. It is not my intention to try to condemn one focus and praise the other. Comparing missionary methodologies helps us understand better the ecclesiologies from which they are derived and the ecclesiastical structures to which they give rise. These different approaches reflect different ways of posing the nature of the church and the relationships between the church and the world. These are fundamental questions of theology that have consequences for social ethics, missionary or evangelizing methodology, and inter-church relations. How Catholics and Protestants visualize their own future in Latin America, their role in society, and their mutual relationships is connected to these fundamental issues.

BEYOND THE "BLACK LEGEND"

Any Latin American who is well informed about history can recall shameful pages on the role played by many Roman Catholic religious in the conquest of the Americas. As a Peruvian, I am well aware of the deceitful way the Spanish captured Atahualpa, the last Inca emperor, in Cajamarca. The Spanish monk Vicente Valverde played a sad role in this episode.[6] Perhaps no example better illustrates the blatant utilization of religion as ideology of conquest and the instrumental role played by the Roman Catholic Church. Justo L. González says that "the conquest of Peru is one of the darkest pages in the history of the colonization of the Americas" and that the church bears a good deal of the responsibility, "particularly in its representative Valverde."[7]

Nevertheless, if we only consider events like this, it is a "black legend" rather than history that we are accepting. We Protestants need to reexamine the facile way in which we have used this anti-Catholic and anti-Iberian black legend. The more we study the history of the sixteenth-century missions the better we see how this legend was shaped and learn to distinguish it from the facts. On this point the Protestant historian John B. Kessler makes this valuable observation:

> It is very easy to criticize the colonial church for the superficiality of its evangelization and for its defects, but it would be unjust to pass over the sincere believers who struggled against the abuses.[8]

Taking his own advice, in the Spanish version of his excellent book on the evangelization of Peru, before telling the story of evangelization from the evangelical side, Kessler offers a critical and honest summary of Catholic missionary work in the sixteenth century and the situation of the colonial church.

Within evangelical circles there is a need for more accurate knowledge of the complex history of the Iberian missionary wave that accompanied the sixteenth-century conquest, with its lights and shadows. More recent Catholic historians have done good critical work, for example, in some of the CEHILA volumes. A work that reflects the more recent missiological approach is expressively titled *Gracia y Desgracia de la Evangelización de América*.[9] Even though some villains like Valverde appear in the pages of this story, there are also figures whom we could describe as evangelical because of their desire to serve God by following biblical teachings in the way they carried out mission. There are people such as Toribio de Mogrovejo, a true pastor of the people, who struggled against the injustices of the plantation owners; or the Jesuit, José de Acosta, whose work *De Procuranda Indorum Salute* is marked with great evangelizing fervor and has lessons that are worthwhile even today.[10] The history of the implanting of Catholicism in Latin America has been enriched in recent years with many works whose chronicling and analyses contain rich lessons for missiology.[11]

METHODOLOGICAL COMPARISONS

There are comparative studies of the different Catholic and Protestant approaches to mission, and some have the advantage of not coming from a polemical spirit but rather from a historical and irenic spirit. We may mention, first, the work of Norman Horner, *Cross and Crucifix in Mission*,[12] which was the result of a research project carried out between 1956 and 1964. Horner had been a Presbyterian missionary for ten years (1939-49) in French-speaking Cameroon (West Africa), where he was able to observe Catholic missionary work close at hand. He then wrote his doctoral thesis in 1956, comparing Protestant and Catholic missions among the Bantus of Cameroon. Later at different times he traveled through Latin America, Asia, and the Middle East, pursuing his comparative study, culminating in his book. There is also comparative work in volumes three and five of the monumental history of the missions by Kenneth Scott Latourette[13] and in the histories of the missions by Stephen Neill[14] and Justo González.[15] Missionary work offers several aspects on which to do comparative research, such as the issue of the participation of lay people in missionary work or in that of the relationship between empire and mission. In this chapter I am going to limit myself to examining the issue of the purpose or objective of missionary action.

THE OBJECTIVE OF MISSION IN THE CATHOLIC TRADITION

A fundamental difference between Catholic and Protestant missionary methodology is their different approaches to conceiving the purpose of missionary activity. A statement by the Catholic historian Robert Ricard in the introduction to his classic book that describes the Catholic evangelization of Mexico in the sixteenth century offers us a very useful starting point. Ricard notes that

> more and more every day an idea is spreading among theologians who deal with mission issues that *the essential aim of mission among non-believers is not the conversion of individuals, but rather the establishment of the visible church*, with all the organs and institutions entailed in such visible expression of the church.[16]

This sharp statement by Ricard to some extent represents pre–Vatican II theology, and today it is questioned by some Catholic specialists.[17] However, Ricard expresses well the prevailing tendency in Catholic missionary practice. For him, this notion "falls perfectly within the logical line of Catholic teaching," for which the vision of the church has a strong sacramental accent. When this vision is formulated with precision it cannot but surprise, if not anger, a Protestant observer. Ricard recognizes that it is God's grace that converts a human being, but he reaches the following conclusion:

If it is the church that normally spreads divine grace through its sacraments because it is intermediary between God and his creature, the primary task of the missionary would logically consist in making the normal means of conversion available to non-believers.[18]

In recording the history of evangelization, Ricard places the church first and he looks at missionaries, "no doubt as converters, but even more as founders of the church."[19]

Missionary activity is preceded by clear ecclesiological definition in which the institutional and sacramental note predominates. This fits a Catholic tradition that, as specialists rightly point out, was continued at Vatican II. Before defining its theology and pastoral work of missionary action in the document *Ad Gentes*, the council fathers defined their ecclesiology in *Lumen Gentium*. Missionary methodology draws nourishment from the ecclesiological vision. Even so, it could be said a basic weakness of Catholic methodology is to be found here: Catholic mission in Latin America succeeded in setting up the institution but it failed to convert people.

The Protestant critique expressed by the pioneers of missiological reflection clearly pointed out the failure of this methodology. This failure was clearly defined in the writings of the generation of Protestant pioneers like Rycroft[20] and Mackay. Ecumenical thinkers, such as Báez-Camargo[21] and José Míguez Bonino, whom we have already mentioned, saw this and delved deeper into it.[22] However, in the 1970s Catholic self-criticism began to recognize this fact, precisely because at that time the social crisis of the continent shook up the nominalism of the Catholic faith of Latin Americans.

It is very important to keep in mind that the renewal of Catholic theology in Latin America has a missiological starting point. Liberation theologians, like Juan Luis Segundo and Gustavo Gutiérrez, at the outset of their careers, motivated by a strong pastoral concern, pointed to the weaknesses of Latin American Catholicism. For both of these authors, it is clear that the liberation positions that they reached did not initially arise from a politicized vision of Christian faith but out of a concern over what the church's mission today ought to be and how it ought to be carried out. As they observed the reality of Latin American Catholicism at that moment, they criticized what they saw as a "huge machine for making Christians," but one that had not obtained the true conversion of individuals to the transforming gospel. Segundo wrote:

> If Christianity can only survive social change in Latin America insofar as it becomes a personal, heroic, and internally shaped life in each person, pastoral activity ought to take on a *formally new* task. New in terms of the Constantinian era in which we have lived up till now; but also the oldest and most traditional: the task of *evangelizing*.[23]

Gutiérrez, moreover, performed a historic analysis of this missionary method, locating it within what he called "pastoral care of Christendom," a pastoral approach corresponding to the Constantinian era, which had already entered into crisis in Europe during the sixteenth century, but which only entered into crisis in Latin America during the period of independence from Spain and Portugal. For Gutiérrez the "Christendom mentality" was accentuated in Latin America because sixteenth-century Spain and Portugal did not experience the crisis of Christendom that shook the rest of the European continent. Spain became defender of the faith and persecutor of heresies. Speaking of Spain, Gutiérrez said:

> Its aspiration to extend the middle ages finds a suitable field in this continent because there are no strong social groups able to stand up to it. The fundamental task undertaken is baptizing: the whole continent is baptized. But Christianity does not sink deep roots in Latin America.[24]

He also criticized the fact that Christendom-type pastoral work was still continuing well into the twentieth century, and in opposition to it he proposed a prophetic pastoral work. His critique goes to the heart of the matter when he says of Christendom-style pastoral work:

> In terms of access to faith, in this pastoral option conversion (conversion of the heart, interior conversion) and belonging to the visible church, which takes place through baptism, are regarded as the same thing. One who is baptized is regarded as a believer, even if he or she is not so in practice. . . . Evangelization is ignored in favor of immediate sacramentalization.[25]

Gutiérrez also has a basic critique of sacramentalism when he analyzes the fact that Christian life was made equivalent to sacramental practice: "Matters go so far that the sacrament is regarded as salvation insurance, and the person's subsequent conduct does not matter much."[26]

The statements by Segundo and Gutiérrez were based on their knowledge of the history of Catholicism in the continent. Today we have much more information on Catholic mission in the sixteenth century that confirms these critical observations. The sociological interpretation of the crisis of this weakly rooted Catholicism vis-à-vis the modernization crisis we owe to a key work by Ivan Vallier. His analysis demonstrated quite precisely that the lack of depth of the profession of faith of Catholics explained how it was impossible for the institutional church to respond to the processes of modernization and why it sought to utilize political manipulation for social control. Vallier says:

> Because of the special historical and institutional conditions that prevailed from the time of the conquest in the sixteenth century up to the independence period, the Church had not consistently pursued policies aimed toward building religious solidarity or the deepening of lay spirituality.[27]

Vallier had pointed out that no thorough evangelization had taken place and that the church had been hastily "scattered" rather than "planted." Hence, because it could not count on enthusiastic loyalty from the population, when moments of crisis came, the institutional church defended itself with political means. That is, the church as institution had been set up in colonial society, but people had not been converted to Christianity to the point where their commitment led them to live out their faith in their daily behavior. Thus,

> the more the Church became politicized and tied to short-run adaptive strategies, the more the religious and spiritual interests of the rank and file weakened. The Church became a major political actor on behalf of the forces that promised to protect it as an institution, rather than a differentiated religious system with roots in the spiritual life of autonomous membership groups.[28]

THE OBJECTIVE OF MISSION IN THE PROTESTANT TRADITION

How is the question of the purpose or objective of mission posed in Protestant circles? It should be recalled that the Protestant missionary movement only got under way in the mid-eighteenth century, that is, two centuries after Catholic mission was flourishing. It came to see the purpose of mission in terms very different from those of the Catholic vision. Historians like Latourette, Neill, and Justo González agree that Protestant mission sprang out of the Pietist revival and was shaped by it. We ought to recall that Pietism above all else sought personal experience of faith for each believer as opposed simply to confessing a common creed collectively. This was a revival or spiritual awakening, and, as González notes, Pietism contained a protest against the older Protestant orthodoxy. Some of the Pietist leaders were academically trained theologians, but they were convinced that practical Christian life was worth more than theological formulas.

> This Christian life was generally understood in individualistic terms, and hence what was highlighted was the Christian's individual experience and obedience as an individual to the divine commandments.[29]

This Pietistic root found at the origin and driving impulse of the Protestant missionary movement determined the style and the way mission was carried out. The purpose of mission became more and more understood as the conversion of individual persons to the Gospel of Jesus Christ. This was very much the experience in Latin America and continues to be so, in contrast with the Catholic experience. González points out that in the twentieth century this tendency was accentuated. Núñez has emphasized this aspect in the practice and style of missionaries of the independent missions or faith missions, as they are called in English. He points out that from 1900 to 1949 those missionaries were "pre-millenarian in eschatology, Pietist in their vision of Christianity, and separatist in their basic attitude toward other ecclesiastical bodies and toward society in general."[30] Núñez finds in these traits the reason that the missionary generation was unable to take up the tasks demanded by the social context of poverty and injustice characteristic of Latin America.

It could be said that the specific features of Pietism in the Protestant missionary movement were sharpened in Latin America because of the tendency to stand out against the Christendom pastoral practice of the Roman Catholic Church. The positive side of the influence of Pietism was its renewing power within the dormant Protestant churches in Europe and North America and its ability to generate missionary energy in many ordinary Christians. The churches that arose from this effort were made up of people with a high degree of loyalty and a sense of belonging to the Lord, who was drawing them to a disciplined and self-sacrificing life in a hostile environment. This helped them to live as a minority whose high standard of personal behavior had possibilities for social transformation.

The negative side lies in the problem resulting from the excessive individualism of this conception and this missionary methodology; the emerging local churches and communities do not achieve institutional cohesion and do not have the sense of what it means to be the church as a body with continuity. Caudillo-style[31] leadership easily causes divisions, generational differences are not contained, and no pluralism of opinion is allowed even for secondary matters. The missions cannot avoid a spirit of commercial competition, heightened by glorification of numerical growth as the sole criterion of missionary action. That hinders cooperation among Protestants for mission, and despite numerical growth and the many churches that spring up, they cannot find a common voice to give witness in the face of the social and political problems of each nation. This lack of clear ecclesiology also leads to the sectarian attitude by which some churches tend to regard themselves as the only true church.[32]

The dangers of this missionary practice were recognized early on by Kenneth Strachan, who headed the Latin American Mission and shaped the missionary methodology known as In-Depth Evangelism. Strachan was one of the first missiologists who analyzed the strong Protestant missionary movement to Latin America that flourished after World War II.[33] As is known, during this post-war period the missionary enthusiasm and activity of the traditional or historical Protestant churches that until then had been predominant in Latin America began to wane. At the same time the zeal and activity of conservative and fundamentalist sectors increased, as they organized independent missions and sent strong missionary contingents to Latin America. "For better or worse," said Strachan, "the non-historic groups constitute a major factor in the determination of Latin America's Protestant future."[34]

Strachan believed that God might be using these groups or missions to pour new life into ecclesiastical bodies that had lost their strength and vitality. But the opposite was also possible; that is, these groups could reach the point of being instrumental in sidetracking the Evangelical church down sterile bypaths of doctrinal extremes and religious oddities and tragically remove it from effective contact with the main stream of Latin American life. And it can so intensify and magnify its divisions as to make it hopelessly unable to resist and overcome the anti-Christian pressures that are building up in the world today.[35]

This observation turned out to be prophetically true. On the one hand, evangelical advance has been based on individual conversion. And yet on the other hand the lack of a sense of church—the ecclesiological vacuum—has produced institutional weakness, a sectarianism that hinders cooperation for mission, and inability to forge alternatives in the realm of social ethics. For the last thirty years Protestant missiology has been making an effort to respond to this situation.[36]

SOME CONCLUSIONS

In this chapter I have limited myself to suggesting a line for research and reflection on an important issue for the future of mission *in* and *from* Latin America. Let us now draw some conclusions that are only tentative, until they can be deepened through historical and missiological work. First, there is a very important theological and pastoral work to be done in correcting the excesses of Protestant individualism. This has been the direction taken by the search for a model of holistic mission by the founding generation of the Latin American Theological Fraternity. A holistic approach recognizes the need for a personal experience of God's saving grace, but at the same time it recovers the biblical vision of the human being as a social being whose transformation takes place primarily in the context of a community that is in itself an expression of God's reign and a proclamation of the new creation.

The church is where the personal and community dimensions of salvation are first experienced. Hence, there cannot be an adequate evangelization without an adequate ecclesiology. An adequate ecclesiology likewise frees us from the sectarian temptation that hinders cooperation for mission among Protestants themselves. The excessive influence of para-ecclesiastical models of evangelization has been at the expense of the development of an integral mission in Latin America. At the same time, there is a need to review the understanding of the biblical vision of the relationship between church and world. In pointing toward one of the theological roots of this search, Núñez said very appositely:

> The exaggerated Christian-world dualism that in many places has led the Latin American evangelical church to hastily retreat from the social scene, may be ascetic and even Manichean, but it is not Christian. Nor is secularism that tries to make the church worldly and sacralize what is worldly.[37]

Certainly the theological task continues to be one of correction in pastoral work, and it is to be hoped that the Latin American missionaries of the future will develop a methodology that will not be a servile imitation of that of their Anglo-Saxon teachers.

Second, it may be asked how far Protestant growth in Latin America is explained by failures of Catholic pastoral work and missionary methodology, rather than because converts find more truth and superiority in Protestant teaching. Catholic missiologists recognize the challenge that Protestant growth represents for them. That is the case with José Luis Perez Guadalupe, a Catholic student of Protestantism in Peru, who worked for the Peruvian Bishops' Conference. He says that the Catholic church does not deal well with the issue of "sects" if it restricts itself to giving talks or short courses on the teaching of those sects, because the reasons why Catholics go over to Protestant churches are not doctrinal:

> We think no Catholic has changed to another group or church for doctrinal reasons, the reasons are experiential: no person who has left the Catholic church to join a religious movement (whether Christian or not) has taken the trouble to study and analyze the doctrines of each group or church, and after that chosen rationally which is the best and which group to join. In fact, many people first join these groups for a series of reasons, primarily experiential, and later on they learn just what this group thinks.[38]

We may reject the absolute tone of this statement. Nevertheless, my own pastoral experience and my observation and study partly confirm it. Here I offer two observations for consideration. First, where priests and lay Catholics have begun to imitate the pastoral and missionary methods of evangelicals, Protestant churches do not grow as fast as they do where Catholics are absent or not at work. Second, the older Protestant churches are experiencing a problem similar to that of Catholics. New charismatic-type movements and new independent churches are growing throughout Latin America at the expense of the more traditional Protestant churches. They draw in many Protestants disappointed with their churches for reasons of a pastoral nature, weariness with routine liturgy and preaching, and lack of relevance to practical everyday issues, and sometimes because of the moral failures of traditional Protestant leaders.

When Latin American Protestants ponder their participation in Christian mission in the coming decades, they need not only to participate in the mission of their churches on the local level but to become familiar with the history of the missions. In the next chapters we explore some forms of missionary action in face of social change in Latin America.

5

The Social Impact of Mission

Christian mission is where the reign of God breaks into history. That is how Jesus, the missionary par excellence, lived and understood it. That's why at different stages and in different contexts mission has been affected by the social processes surrounding it, and missionary action has in turn given rise to new social processes. When the missionaries of the first generation reached the city of Thessalonica, some Jews went to tell the authorities: "These men who have turned the whole world upside down, have also come here!" Since then, century by century, the pace of the advance of the gospel of Jesus Christ through Christian mission seems to have gathered speed in the midst of social change, and it has in turn been followed by a series of transformations. That is how it has been since the very beginning.

Jesus did not understand his own mission and work apart from the divine initiative that is at work in the world. What we see in the travels of Jesus over the dusty roads of Palestine is God acting in the world in a unique and visible way. The word of God enters human history, becomes history, and leaves its mark on history. Looking back from a twenty-century perspective, we can grasp the impact of the presence of Jesus in the world. It is a transforming, healing, challenging, upsetting, prophetic presence that calls for radical change and delivers it. It is a presence registered by the witnesses in specific actions of approaching the poor, healing the sick, teaching the ignorant, and of kindness to children, openness to the outcast, forgiveness to the repentant, criticism of the powerful and corrupt—culminating in self-surrender for our salvation, and all of it in the power of the Spirit.

EMPIRE AND MISSION:
AMBIGUITIES OF MISSIONARY ACTION

In our time, when our thinking takes as its starting point the historicity and impact of the presence of Jesus in the world, we must ask ourselves a question, even though it is difficult: Can the same be said of Christian mission in history as is said of Jesus? The missionaries of Jesus are also history; they are human beings whose action takes place in space and time, in the midst of other human beings. Many of them have made history, and so some peoples and nations can speak of their own history in terms of a "before" and "after" the coming of the gospel. Tragically there are some missionary situations where it cannot be said that the "after" has been better than the "before," when one can honestly have doubts about where the missionary presence has brought lasting and deep good.

Here we find ourselves facing the sharp question of the relationship between empire and mission. In the New Testament, Christian mission starts from the Jewish world in a distant province of the empire and advances toward the large Greco-Roman cities until it reaches Rome, then the capital of the world. Humanly speaking, the power that moves to mission is basically the spiritual power of the life and convictions of the missionaries who take advantage of all the roads and opportunities that the *Pax Romana* offers them for bringing the message of Jesus Christ. The empire provides the stage, but the great actor in the drama is the Holy Spirit, who moves women and men who have no prestige, economic power, or military strength. Nevertheless, as the Book of Acts documents, the missionary presence and transforming power of the gospel have their impact on society.

The application of social analysis for understanding the New Testament accounts and the apostolic correspondence enables us to better understand this impact on the social structures of the imperial cities.[1] It is at the point of entry of the gospel into Europe, the city of Philippi, where, as a result of Paul's missionary action, a rich merchant places her fortune at the service of Christian mission, a slave is freed from the exploitation of his masters, and a hardened jailer humanizes the conditions of prison life a little.[2] The same is true further on in Ephesus, where preaching against idolatry encounters acceptance in a significant sector of the population, to the point where the guild of image sculptors stirs up a sizeable disturbance to get rid of the troublesome but effective presence of the missionaries.[3]

CONSTANTINIAN CHURCH AND MISSION

Three centuries later, however, when the emperor Constantine embraces the Christian faith, the process of expansion and missionary penetration of the empire has peaked, and mission begins to take place within a new paradigm in which the union between church and imperial power gradually takes hold. From then on Christian mission will be increasingly associated one way or another with the culture that is being created in Europe, and with the presence and military action of kingdoms, principalities, and dominions that emerge. The Roman Empire declines, but the church becomes the guardian of Roman culture, and when it evangelizes the barbarians, their culture is merged with Latin culture. Europe is the result of that merger.[4] A new problem unknown to Saint Paul is presented to the monastic missionary movement that comes into being, partly as a protest against the paganization of the church. The monks cross new borders evangelizing but also civilizing.

Within the paradigm of the feudal world, in which the crusades against Islam play an important role, Christian mission begins to be associated with military action. This union reaches its high point in the Iberian missionary enterprise, which has been preceded by the war against the Arabs to reconquer the peninsula,[5] culminating in 1492, the same year in which Columbus reaches the Americas. At this point the European evangelizers see themselves also as "civilizers," and indeed the missionaries begin to think that the task of civilizing has to come before evangelization. A Franciscan historian of the Catholic missions introduces one of his works with this remark:

> The aim of this work is to analyze the process of civilization of the Indians by the American evangelizers. By civilization of the American Indians we understand . . . their insertion into a way of life as similar as possible to that of the people to which those who were involved in this process belonged and whom we will call civilizers.[6]

This is the source of the dilemmas raised for many in evaluating the Catholic mission that accompanied the Iberian conquest of the Americas. Alongside the conquerors came the missionaries who announced the message of Christ and established the Catholic church. Did this improve the lot of the Indians who were living here? Many accepted the faith and it took root, even to the point of merging with the existing native religions. The Indians also had to accept the position of victims of a feudal economic order whose servants they were.[7] The history of the Americas has been marked by the contradictions and abuses of this order that was imposed, despite the efforts of some missionaries to combat injustice or mitigate it.

THE PROTESTANT MISSIONS

Protestant missions began to flourish in the eighteenth century and reached formidable strength in the nineteenth and twentieth centuries. By then the medieval feudal paradigm had been replaced by the paradigm of modernity, characterized by individualism, faith in reason, the importance of the written text, emphasis on mass education, the rationalization of social life, the capitalist system of production and market, and the ideal of democracy. Within this modern paradigm the Protestant missions would be characterized by certain notes proper to modernity, to which the Protestant Reformation in fact contributed in both Europe and North America. The historian Stephen Neill[8] reminds us that starting with their origin among the Moravians of Central Europe, Protestant missions followed a model characterized by five distinguishing principles: (1) *Church and school go together.* Christians must be able to read the word of God, and hence children must be sent to school. If Christians are going to be able to read the word of God, (2) *the Bible must available to them in their own language.* Preaching of the gospel must be based on (3) *an accurate knowledge of the mind of the people.* (4) *The goal of mission must be definite and personal conversion.* At as early a date as possible, there must be a (5) *native church with its own national pastors.* These principles explain the type of Protestantism that has arisen in Asia, Africa, Oceania, and Latin America as the result of Protestant missionary work in the past two centuries. The arrival of Protestant missionaries in Asia and Africa in the nineteenth century coincided with the arrival of the British Empire and the other European empires. Many Asians and Africans who reflect on the past are critical of this alliance between empire and mission. It should be pointed out, however, that mission under the paradigm of modernity had greater possibilities of being a transforming force than medieval mission so that the colonized peoples would achieve their own liberation and struggle for a more just social order. It was in the mission schools where the natives learned to read the Bible in their own language, enhancing their culture, and where native leaders were trained for the native churches; in mission schools they learned ways of relating horizontally that were conducive to democracy. These missionary schools also provided training to political leaders who were to lead their peoples to freedom from the European imperial yoke.

There is a basis for venturing the opinion that these distinctive notes of the Protestant missions had a social effect closer to the values of the reign of God than those of mission carried out under the feudal paradigm. This opinion today must be subjected to the critique of an anti-imperialist reading of history. Even so, many facts of history indicate the amount of service of Christian missionaries, their devotion to the poor and needy, and the creativity of the projects emerging from this vocation. From a Protestant perspective, James S. Dennis compiled a three-volume work entitled *Christian Missions and Social Progress.*[9] A Catholic equivalent for Latin America is the classic book by the Argentinean Vicente D. Sierra, *El sentido misional de la conquista de América.*[10] Nevertheless, it should be noted that these two studies start with the assumption that the imperial advance and colonialism (European and North American in one case, and Spanish in the other) were morally legitimate enterprises as a framework for missionary action. Missiologists today cannot admit that presupposition without qualifications.

Protestant Mission and Social Transformation in Latin America

The history of Protestant missions in Latin America offers many examples of the relationship between the proclamation of the gospel, forms of service to the poor, and instances of social transformation. Several volumes could be filled with the simple accounts of the many and varied experiences of which the missionaries themselves or believers of subsequent generations have left written testimony. More recently some historians, sociologists, and anthropologists have overcome the narrowness of Marxist ideology or hostile Catholicism and have devoted themselves to recording and interpreting the facts. Our method is to group the many cases by categories or general models and to illustrate each model with representative examples.

A good number of examples of the social impact of missionary action can be grouped under three categories that correspond to the intention of the missionaries as a result of their missiological conceptions, or to the unexpected consequence of their missionary action that unleashed socially significant activities and processes. The categories we have in mind are missionary presence among the outcast, missionary involvement in the secular world, and the creation of alternative societies.

Presence among the Outcast

The Lausanne movement led to a growing awareness of the importance of missionary presence in the midst of those to whom the gospel is being brought. This costly, patient, self-sacrificing presence in solidarity is required for a mission shaped by Jesus. The vision was rediscovered by John Stott, who drew the attention of scholars to the text of the Great Commission in the gospel of John: "As the Father has sent me, so I also send you."[11] The words of Jesus give us not only the missionary imperative to go but also the challenging model of how to go: being a presence as Jesus was. Only a presence that is respectful and ready for sacrifice helps the missionary, for example, learn a people's language in order to communicate the gospel message to them, translate the Bible into their language, and train and disciple a first generation of local leaders for the churches that arise.

It is not only Bible reading but also rereadings of history that have prompted missionary presence among the poor in our time. Viv Grigg, a New Zealand missionary who inculturated himself in Tatalon, one of the poorest neighborhoods of Manila, has told how he was inspired by the story of Toyohiko Kagawa. In his reading Grigg discovered this Japanese Christian who had plunged into the poor in Shinkawa, the notorious Tokyo slum, in 1909 in order to bring them into contact with the love of Christ. He eventually came to be known as a labor leader, poet, and noteworthy Christian novelist.[12] Going back even further in time, Grigg discovered Francis of Assisi, the missionary who had decided to be wed to Sister Poverty.[13] Kagawa and Francis continue to be the inspiration for many Latin American Protestants involved in holistic mission.

In this connection it should be remembered that some sixteenth-century Catholic missionaries inculturated themselves among the indigenous populations of what is now Latin America; they plunged into them, studied their languages and beliefs, and wrote extensively about them. Out of the encounter of the Christian message and the indigenous population arose forms of syncretistic Christianity that are deeply rooted in the consciousness of these peoples. Nevertheless, the economic and social forms adopted by Spanish colonial society placed the Indians in a state of servitude. Furthermore, the shortage of clergy and conflict of the church with the emancipation movements in many instances led to a gradual weakening of the Catholic missionary presence.

By the nineteenth century considerable portions of the indigenous population were living under sad conditions of marginalization and exploitation. The

Protestant missionary effort was directed at them, in some instances because the very fact that they were abandoned by the government and the Catholic church afforded Protestant missionaries greater freedom. In other instances, the missionaries had a special calling to work in these marginal areas.[14] In various Latin American countries Protestant missions made significant progress among marginalized sectors, such as indigenous populations or ethnic minorities in the countryside and the city. The religious monopoly wielded by the predominant Catholic church often closed off other paths.

In many instances the initial intention of this presence among the marginal was to respond to the conditions of poverty and abandonment in which these people were living. From the outset it was a Christian mission with a social content. In other instances, although the initial intention was primarily evange-listic, it soon acquired a social dimension due to the pressure of the many needs, which aroused a latent Christian sensitivity.

A case from southern Peru illustrates what happened in many countries. During the nineteenth century Quechua- and Aymara-speaking indigenous people were among the most marginalized and exploited. Many historians agree that an im-portant attitudinal change took place in the country in the first two decades of the twentieth century, when intellectuals and then politicians became aware of the situation of the native peoples. However, even before a pro-indigenous movement arose, Protestant missionaries in the Cuzco area had gone to live among the Quechuas. Luis E. Valcárcel, a widely known pioneer of the study of indigenous peoples and cultures acknowledged the presence in 1896 and 1897 of British evangelical missionaries who created an experimental farm on the Urco hacienda; from the farm they developed new crops, agricultural techniques and processing, and offered the services of a clinic.[15] Also the Seventh-day Adventists spread among the Aymara-speaking people and offered health care and education in particular. In response to the criticism of the Marxist José Carlos Mariátegui that these were "assaults of imperialism," Valcárcel responds:

> I want to insist without the slightest polemic intent, that given the sad situation of Indians in Cuzco, the tender hand of the Adventist believer was the drop of water that refreshed the poor person's thirsty lips.[16]

The American missionary Frederick Stahl (1874-1950) and his wife, Ana, played a remarkable role throughout southern Peru. They came to Bolivia in 1909, paying their own way, and they went to live near Plateria in the depart-ment of Puno in 1911 and remained there until 1921. For health reasons they then went to work along the rivers in the Amazon on a steamboat named *Auxiliadora,* which was a floating sanatorium. The Stahls had been trained as nurses at the Adventist sanatorium in Battle Creek, Michigan, and Ana was also a teacher. A book published by Stahl in 1920 reflects a clear social and spiritual sensitivity and a firsthand knowledge of the terrible living conditions in the area.[17] José Antonio Encinas, a Puno educator who was not a Protestant and who eventually became Minister of Education, said in 1932:

Stahl goes around the district of Chucuito inch by inch. There is not a shack or hut where he has not brought the generosity of his spirit. He is a modern type of missionary whose conduct stands in contrast to the diabolic fury of the Spanish friars, who in the conquest tortured the spirit of the Indians, destroying their idols, ridiculing their gods, and profaning their grandparents' tomb.[18]

Encinas continues with his comparison of missionary methodology, and he attributes the apathy and anguish of Indians to the traditional use of the fear of hell as an instrument of religious control. By contrast, he notes:

Before placing the bible in the hands of illiterates, Stahl inculcates in them a sense of personality, self-confidence, and cherishing of life; he sought them as comrades rather than proselytes. He first cared for their health. Before that no one had gone around the miserable huts of the Indians relieving their pains a little.[19]

Adventist work in education also expanded remarkably from the first school in Plateria in 1913. By 1916 Plateria had 187 students and there were seven more schools with a total of 200 students. In 1918 there were twenty-six schools with 1,500 students, and by 1924, eighty schools had been built with a total of 4,150 students. These schools were set up at the request of Aymara communities, and in response to growing demand, the mission developed a plan to avoid paternalism and achieve a commitment to self-sufficiency from the people themselves. When a community requested a school, the people were challenged to provide the building and guarantee a minimum of eighty students so as to be able to cover pay for a teacher and other basic expenses.[20]

All this led Valcárcel to say that the presence of Protestant and Adventist missionaries over several decades had had a decisive role in the emergence of a new rebellious and defiant spirit, one creating alternatives: a true "storm over the Andes."[21]

Involvement in the Secular

More than once in the Book of Acts, the apostle Paul is seen having a discussion with Roman authorities or their delegates about matters connected to the intentions of the missionaries, the legality of their actions, and the social consequences of those acts. Paul is presented as a citizen aware of his rights and obligations and capable of defending his right to exercise them.[22] The author of the account in Acts is also familiar with the legislation and social structures of the empire. This tension between the strictly evangelizing aim of missionaries and the disrupting of the secular realm that their action entails will be a distinctive feature of missionary action century after century. In many cases missionaries are forced by circumstances, and they opt to systematically undertake actions likely to change the secular order.

The historian Norman Goodall offers several examples of such impacts in mission history of the last two centuries. Starting in the nineteenth century, Christian missions in the Pacific islands contributed to a restructuring of community life. When the native kings in some of the islands were converted to Christianity, they asked the evangelizers to help reorganize their nations on Christian principles. Methodist missionaries and those of the London Missionary Society helped create codes and laws drawn from Christian principles. Those who had only intended to evangelize natives found themselves drawing up laws that to this day remain enshrined in the constitutions of these islands as independent nations.[23]

Near Lake Titicaca in Bolivia is the Huatajata hacienda, a place where Canadian Baptist missionaries carried out an agrarian reform experiment in 1941, eleven years before a revolutionary government took the same radical measure on a national scale.[24] The story began in 1911, when an Italian who had been converted to the gospel at Peniel Hall in Los Angeles, California, traveled to Bolivia intending to invest thirty thousand dollars in some work of "educating the Indians and making them Christians." In his will he left his inheritance to a group of Protestants, entrusting the project to them. The Peniel Society, which was set up in 1912, bought the Huatajata hacienda, on which 250 indigenous peasants were living. This was a project for the evangelization, education, and agricultural development of the Aymara peasant population. The Baptists took over the project in 1920, and to their surprise they discovered that the peasants living in Huatajata were regarded as part of the property and that the people who had taken over management of the ranch had become the owners of these peasants.

This kind of feudal servitude was very common at that period in the history of Bolivia and the other Andean countries. By 1929 the annual conference of the Baptist missionaries recognized that works of service motivated by compassion were not enough and did not bring peasants to the gospel. Missionary Norman Dabbs commented: "It finally dawned on the missionaries that their position as landowners and serf-masters was overriding every benevolent attempt to uplift the people."[25] The need for profound changes of a structural kind at the ranch was raised, and the conclusion was reached that "the peonage system . . . which undermines the religious work in the region" had to be brought to an end.

At that time, however, there was no legislation or provision for peasants to become owners of the lands that the mission wanted to divide and distribute. Nonetheless, in 1941 the missionaries tried distributing land with land titles to the peasant families who lived there. Norman Dabbs, who wrote an account of the event, noted that when the land titles were handed over, the missionaries felt as though a great weight had been lifted from them. When the Revolutionary Nationalist Movement came into power in 1952, one of the radical steps that it took was the Agrarian Reform, a measure that was to change the country's social structure. Huatajata had become a precursor movement, and the gospel practice of love and justice had managed to step into the secular and transform it.

Protestant missionary work took a similar path in Mexico, where it has recently been the object of careful historical studies. Jean Pierre Bastian has studied the role played by religious dissidence in the 1872-1911 period as one of the leavening elements that led to the Mexican revolution.[26] Investigating the history of ideas and attitudes in these stormy years of the modernization of the nation, Bastian draws out the details of Protestant participation in the country's intellectual and political life. He sums it up thus:

> We have found these Protestant school teachers, journalists, and lawyers in all the free-thought societies, in the liberal clubs of 1901, in the anti-reelection movement in 1910 and finally in the armed struggle and revolutionary political struggle of the summer of 1911.[27]

The Mexican historian Rubén Ruiz Guerra has studied a somewhat broader period, 1873-1930.[28] Focusing his attention on Methodism, he has carefully studied the ideas of the Methodists, their preaching, their educational work, and their dialectical relationship to the country's political forces. Although the American Methodists had attended the university and came from churches that were part of the United States middle class, in Mexico they encountered great need and receptivity among the poor, to whom they devoted increasing attention. Starting with charitable works, they gradually became aware of the structural challenge that they were facing. Ruiz Guerra writes:

> Contact with a poverty that could not be concealed, however, caused the attitude of the Methodists toward it to change. It was very common at first to think that the poor were poor simply because intemperance and ignorance reduced them to it. Hence resolving the problem of poverty was a matter of offering to those who were suffering the means to get ahead: education and a high standard of morality.[29]

Missionary experience itself and contact with the changing theological currents among United States Methodists led to the conviction that new paths had to be taken. In 1916 the "Social Creed" approved by the Methodist General Council of the United States in 1908 became known in Mexico. It contained a political agenda: equal rights for all human beings, abolition of child labor, and regulation of women's labor. Nevertheless, starting much earlier, the missionaries had sought alliances with Liberal politicians and, despite some subsequent misgivings, that alliance persisted:

> This identification between Liberalism and Protestantism was practically unshakable. The social groups from which the Methodist leaders came assured that such was the case. . . . Let us recall, for example, that in order

to open up new fields of work the local Liberals were always sought out and asked to give their support to an itinerant preacher.[30]

Indeed, just as in other Latin American countries, the virtues of a Christian nature that Protestant mission produced and encouraged coincided with the ideas of politicians interested in leading their country along the path of modernization. This was what facilitated the kinds of alliances at particular times in which Protestants participated when they decided to move from simply aiding the poor to changing society.[31] We have here another example of how Christian mission went from a presence among the poor to involvement with the secular. In a tone of sociological objectivity, Bastian writes:

> The Protestant societies were no doubt the vehicle of this literate minority that was emerging from rural areas in transition and that sought to represent the people in an overall design that sought to extend to the entire society the guidelines and principles prepared throughout the Porfirio Diaz regime in the heart of these Protestant societies, just as in the other free-thought societies.[32]

Creation of Alternative Societies

The third way in which missionary action takes on a social dimension is the creation of an alternative society. Indeed, since the New Testament age the church can be seen as a new community that emerges by contrast with the surrounding society. The company of disciples whom Jesus calls the "little band" understands itself as a movement of renewal and fidelity intended to be "salt and light" to the world in which its members live. The Pauline epistles offer us theological definitions like "people of God," "new Israel," "household of God," which describe the newness of this community that is emerging from the Jewish world and taking root in the Greco-Roman culture of the large cities in the Mediterranean world. The epistles and Acts also offer material that reflects the alternative practices of this community with regard to money and its use, power, sex, stance toward government officials, and different kinds of social solidarity.[33]

Leaders of the predominant churches in a country often pejoratively use the category of "sect" to describe dissident minorities. Catholics do this in Latin America and Spain, as do the Orthodox in Russia and Greece, and Lutherans in Sweden. Sociology uses the term *sect* to describe the existence of a minority religious community as an alternative social environment, and it recognizes the social dynamism of behavior that it calls *sectarian*. It is interesting to observe that what historians and sociologists say about this aspect of the life of the early church is similar to what sociologists are saying today about the evangelical minorities and their social impact in Latin America. Observers of the life of these communities from a sociological and missiological perspective concur that there are factors of social transformation determined by the alternative way of life that create a new sense of identity and help promote ethical change.[34]

In this sense, we have already seen that there are types of mission that have given rise to communities that are very vital spiritually that often do not have an accompanying social agenda. Thus, for example, Pentecostal-type churches have multiplied remarkably among the urban masses of Brazil, Chile, and various other Latin American countries. Even though these groups do not have a social creed or agenda, they have undeniably had a socially transforming effect on the marginal populations among which they have grown. One of the first scholars who studied the question was the Brazilian Emilio Willems, who in the 1960s studied the impact of Pentecostal churches in Brazil and Chile. Since then his observations have been tested and studied in greater detail by other researchers.

According to Willems, grassroots Pentecostal churches in the period he studied were part of a historic process that included foreign immigration and secularization and that affected the social structures and values of the societies of Brazil and Chile. This grassroots or popular form of Protestantism became a factor that in turn contributed to social change, because the orientation of values—which can be described as the "Protestant ethic"—enabled the converts to function better in the new situation created by industrialization, urbanization, internal migration, and the opening of new frontiers.[35]

Willems devoted special attention to analyzing Pentecostal congregations institutionally, and he highlighted the participatory nature of their liturgy and their congregational life, which do not depend on the people's education level. He made special mention of the importance of the *tomada de Espirito* or "seizure by the Spirit," which "puts a seal of divine approval on the individual, who can now be elected or appointed to any office by the congregation."[36]

This seizure or anointing became a kind of legitimation in Pentecostal churches and helped integrate people pushed from the countryside to the city. Thousands of people from the poorest social layers could form part of an organized group in which they enjoyed the experience of entering a community, making their contribution, and receiving affirmation, consolation, and a sense of belonging.

The experience of the seizure also had a leveling effect because in order to participate actively in the community, one no longer needed the symbols of money or education, which were the prevailing forms of legitimation in the surrounding society. Participation in the liturgical life of the community included the gift of prophecy, and thus illiterate, simple people could offer a message that was heard and accepted by the entire community. This stood in contrast to the Catholic experience, where teaching was entirely in the hands of the ordained clergy, and even to that of the historic Protestant communities, where lay people with leadership positions were selected on the basis of factors like education and speaking ability. In some cases what began as liturgical participation also became part of community decision-making. Willems concludes that "the principle of unrestricted social mobility, embodied by the pentecostal sects, is obviously at variance with the limited opportunities for upward mobility within the general society."[37] In itself this proved to be an excellent training ground for participating in secular society when later a democratization process was under way.

As in the case of other Protestant churches, Pentecostalism specifically prohibited new converts from using alcohol and tobacco. But what was especially important in the Pentecostal experience was that these prohibitions went along with a strong emphasis on an emotional conversion moment, an anointing with the power of God, which in some cases was the point of breaking away from old habits. Thus, the ascetic way of life that was part of conversion went hand in hand with a celebratory kind of adoration and community life, which made those who had gone through that experience very firm. This new style of life helped improve the situation of believers in terms of food and housing. Savings were thus generated, which, when used for small businesses, allowed for upward mobility in society. "The economic importance of pentecostal asceticism lies in the fact that it frees a portion of personal income for acquiring things that symbolize a higher standard of living."[38]

Recovering a sense of personal dignity, belonging to a community where spiritual and human talents flourish, experiencing personal transformation with ethical consequences that reshape family and home life, practicing the joyful asceticism that makes saving and capitalization possible—all this helps people emerge from oppressive poverty and break away from the surrounding fatalism. This is the basis for a process of social transformation generated by the new faith in Christ.

Something similar has been shown in the rural area by studies of the effects of missionary work on some indigenous communities, which because of their size and location are like small laboratories in which the transforming effect of faith in Jesus Christ can be seen. A noteworthy case that has been studied very carefully by a non-Protestant anthropologist is that of the Quechua-speaking peasant population of the province of Chimborazo in the Colta region of Ecuador.[39] The Gospel Missionary Union in 1953 went into a missionary field that other Protestants had abandoned. In 1956 they began night classes in basic literacy for women, and in 1957 they opened a school with teaching in both Quechua and Spanish. They set up a hospital in 1950, and for the first time the peasants received medical attention from people who spoke their own language. Then in 1961 evangelical radio broadcasting in Quechua and Spanish began.

The stable presence of missionaries in Quechua lands for over twenty-five years speaking the people's language bore fruit. The author of the study comments, "Because the Indians of the highlands easily mistrusted foreigners, this stability of staff was very advantageous for the success of this mission."[40] By 1966, 330 people had been baptized in the churches founded by this mission, but by 1982 over 8,000 people had been baptized, which means a community of approximately 24,000 people affected by the gospel. This was a significant enough number to begin an anthropological investigation on the effect of this religious conversion.

Careful study of these churches leads Blanca Muratorio to conclusions worth pondering. Ethical behavior has changed: "The moral precepts emphasize discipline, abstaining from tobacco, alcohol, extra-marital sexual relations, and all the 'excesses' considered sinful."[41] There has been an "ethical redefinition" and recovery of a sense of dignity, which can be seen, for example, starting with appreciation for having the Bible in their own language. This shows others that Quechuas can read and that whites and Spanish-speakers do not have a monopoly on information and education:

Through bible reading, representation of biblical dramas and religious films, the Quechuas are beginning to understand other cultures and to understand themselves as incorporated into a shared humanity as equals.[42]

In short, according to this writer:

It can thus be concluded that among Protestant peasants, a new self-identity, pride in their own language, a sense of belonging to a shared humanity, and a desire to be educated make up an integral part of a new ethnic identity as the direct result of their recent conversion to Protestantism.[43]

Not everything is positive in the study, because Muratorio is critical of the conservative political posture or the individualism of these new converts, but that does not prevent her from recognizing the transforming effect of this kind of holistic mission.

In the kinds of evangelization and mission that have given rise to these movements one can see the ability to sow a spiritual seed that flowers in the emergence of indigenous communities. These communities are rooted in a local reality, and missionaries are able to mobilize potential leaders who will lead their people out of poverty and marginalization. One does not see the paternalism that has sometimes characterized the social aid of the more traditional churches, which see the poor as helpless people who can only live on the compassion of those who are richer or more powerful. Such paternalism generates dependence and even social resentment. Some Protestant denominations still continue to subsidize institutions and maintain paternalistic bureaucracies after a century. They fail to draw on the undeniable potential present in every human being touched by the gospel, sometimes because they themselves have lost faith in the transforming power of the gospel. By contrast, the spiritual transformation in the grassroots churches has brought about a true movement of social betterment that helps people to live their lives more fully, in keeping with the Creator's intention.

A glance at the history of the relationship between Christian mission and social transformation is an exercise that prompts admiration and gratitude for the beautiful pages that one finds. It is also an exercise in which we must moderate our optimism with the realism that comes from a biblical vision. While resisting any triumphalistic or apologetic aim of demonstrating the moral superiority of evangelicals, it is nevertheless important to recognize the value of the facts themselves, which have been regarded as a response to human needs and a path of social solidarity and of the emergence of the poor as social actors. Some of the cases mentioned here did not have a happy ending or political success. Nevertheless, they expressed an authentic desire not to stay uninvolved but to see behind the needs a call to obedience from Christ.

Some of these cases point to the *promise* of the Protestant missionary experience. Nevertheless, a critical examination of the result of some of these experiences over the long run shows the *precariousness* of young Latin American Protestantism, even of the kind that we define as "popular." This dialectic between promise and precariousness constitutes an important missiological lesson for the future. Our framework of interpretation is not economic determinism or utopian socialism. It has to be a theological framework. We have to understand the facts of mission in the light of the reign of God, the model of Jesus Christ, the reality that, as Paul said, missionaries are bearers of "a treasure in clay vessels," and Christian hope. From this framework will come criteria for appreciating the past, prophetically critiquing the present, and seeking effectiveness in the Lord's service.

6

From Mission to Liberation

"The Roman Catholic Church in South America needs the Protestant missionary movement. There is good in that Church in South America. There are good men and women in it. In spite of the falsehoods and vicious elements in it, there is truth also. That the good in it may triumph over the evil there is need of external stimulus and purification."[1] For our current missiological sensitivity these words from Robert Speer, written in 1913, sound triumphalistic and even condescending, but they turned out to be prophetic. They were part of a book written to promote Protestant missionary work in Latin America and to explain the validity of that kind of missionary work in countries that were claimed by the Roman Catholic Church. The description of the moral and spiritual condition of the Latin American countries was critical, with dramatic and somber tones. However, coming from mainline Protestantism, Speer combined his evangelical missionary enthusiasm with an ecumenical sensitivity about the Catholic church. He was aware that other missionary organizations sending missionaries to Latin America were far more radical in their criticism of the Catholic church.

What would appear as description tainted by Protestant bias at the beginning of the twentieth century was later repeated by Catholic theologians and missiologists, in a self-critical manner, sometimes with equally dramatic and somber tones. During the Inter-American Catholic Action Week held in Chimbote, Peru, in 1953, after a careful and detailed study of the religious situation country by country, delegates concluded that in Latin America "the vast majority of Catholics are *solo de nombre*; that is, nominal Catholics. . . . Though baptized and believing in the Catholic faith, those nominal Catholics do not practice their religion or allow it to influence their daily lives in any appreciable degree."[2]

In the four decades between the year 1913, when Speer wrote, and the year 1953, when the Chimbote gathering reached similar critical conclusions, there was a period of intense Protestant missionary activity from mainline denominations as well as some independent faith missions. As a result, there was steady growth of Latin American Protestant communities. Like other missiologists, Speer was of the opinion that the Protestant presence was going to be an incentive for

Catholic renewal. He also said, "The Protestant churches will not absorb the Roman Catholic Church. They will in a measure purify it. . . . The presence of Protestant missions alone will lead the Church into a self cleansing and intro-duce the forces, or support whatever inner forces there may already be, which may correct and vivify it."[3] John A. Mackay expressed the same opinion, which he believed was shared "by many thoughtful Catholics." He also quoted a French Catholic abbot who had expressed in Mexico that "the best thing that could happen in the spiritual life of the Continent would be an increasingly strong Protestant movement; that would oblige the Church to put her house in order, and get ready to fulfill her mission."[4]

It is a fact recognized by most observers and participants today that during the second part of the twentieth century the religious situation that Speer and Mackay described changed notably. A new vitality was fermenting in Latin American Catholicism, and some of the renewal movements within it now reached many parts of the world, beyond Catholic circles. This is evident as we look at the historical overviews of that period, which is better understood when we take into account the interaction of developments in both Catholic and Prot-estant camps. German historian Hans Jürgen Prien's one-volume history of Christianity in Latin America is a remarkable interpretative effort; unfortunately, it is available only in Spanish and German.[5] Prien is both a historian and a missionary, and he has provided a factual account of what happened in the criti-cal decades between 1950 and 1980, a period of intense social and political change. He describes this period in his last chapter under the heading "Crisis of the Missionary Identity of the Church." Crisis here is not to be understood in a negative, pessimistic fashion, but rather as an "agonic" time, to use a famous metaphor from Miguel de Unamuno, a time of agony, of struggle that is an indication of life. Liberation theologies, Base Ecclesial Communities, a lively christological exploration, conscientization, new ways of studying scripture at popular levels are all movements and ideas that have found acceptance around the world. They are perceived by many as the contribution of a revitalized Ca-tholicism to the church universal.

This chapter examines the period of missionary activity in Latin America that comes right after the Second World War. Undoubtedly the fact that mis-sionaries should be sent to a territory that had been evangelized centuries ago and had come to be considered a mission field again poses an array of theologi-cal and missiological questions. I am interested in finding out the catalytic role played by Protestant growth and then by Catholic missionary activity in the renewal of the Catholic church. This could be a case study of the revitalization of an old form of Christendom through the renewal of missionary patterns. The missionary source of transformations within the Catholic church has not been adequately studied. In fact, I suspect that the emphasis of liberation theologies and Base Ecclesial Communities on their "Latin Americanness" has tended to obscure the role of the foreign missionary presence. Can a foreign missionary action be a source of revitalization and transformation for a church? It is an important missiological question because Protestantism, in its ecumenical or evangelical forms, is also experiencing a crisis of missionary identity. A careful review of facts with its consequent reflection may be of some assistance for the future. In fact, many Latin American Protestants in the 1960s and 1970s were asking critical questions about the role of foreign missionaries coming to Latin America in that post–World War II period.

POSTWAR MISSIONARY EFFORTS IN LATIN AMERICA

Immediately after World War II there was an intensification of missionary activity from North America to the rest of the world. The first five years (1945-50) were a time of crisis for the missionary movement in Asia. The growth of Maoism in China and the eventual Communist takeover of that land resulted in the expulsion of foreign missionary personnel. Hundreds of Catholic and Protestant missionaries who were displaced from Asian territories were sent to Latin America. Among Protestants this period saw the explosion of missionary interest expressed in a great variety of independent or "non-historic" missionary organizations.[6] That development coincided later on with a decline of missionary interest and activity from some of the older mainline denominational and "historic" missions that had been active in the initial establishment and growth of Protestantism in the continent. Historians are still recording the facts and evaluating them.[7] On the Catholic side, European and North American missionary involvement in Latin America experienced a process of growth, partially because of developments in China.[8] This growth was followed by a period of serious crisis and intense evaluation.[9] However, its impact could not be denied.

In this brief review of some of the most interesting facets of a missionary process I bring my own perspective as a Latin American evangelical, and I have to acknowledge that I am still in the process of becoming acquainted with the nature and history of North American Catholicism, which is definitely different from Latin American Catholicism. The contrast between these two forms of Catholicism was perceived and emphasized by Catholic missionaries. In a book on missionary education published in 1958, Father William Coleman pointed to these differences as he offered a description of Latin American Catholicism.[10] He clearly states that the differences are to be understood within the universality of Catholicism, but he also offers a very convincing description of the historical reasons that explain the critical situation of the 1950s. A more recent book on missionary education by Mary McGlone deals with Christianity in the Americas and the relationship between North American and Latin American Catholics pointing to the different historical developments and offering valuable information about the most recent history.[11]

My own commentary is that the critical perspective that Coleman and other Catholic writers offered came precisely from their missiological stance. It is the outside perspective that allows the critical approach that sometimes is not possible from within. We have to remember that Catholicism had a missionary stance in the United States. Catholics had learned to live in a society that had no established church but had a Protestant majority and deep-seated attitudes of anti-Jewish and anti-Catholic nativism. In contrast with Latin America, Catholics had not been an established church in the United States but rather a growing religious minority. In fact, they had experienced amazing growth, mainly through immigration. At the time of independence in 1776, there were approximately twenty thousand Catholics in a population of three and a half million (0.6%). By 1860 there were three million Catholics in a population of 31 million (almost 10 percent); by 1920, twenty million of over 100 million people (20 percent); and by 1960 forty million out of 180 million (22 percent). This percentage has been maintained up to the present. (It is interesting to note that approximately 30 percent of United States Catholics today are Latinos.) Franklin Littell reminds us that at the time of independence "the new nation was a heathen nation—one of the most needy mission fields in the world. And for the major part of the nineteenth century, Protestant and Catholic missionary societies in Europe were sending to it missionaries, tracts and money to save the New World from relapse into utter irreligion."[12] The theological contribution of North American Catholics to the concept of religious freedom in Vatican II as well as the missionary contribution to Latin America can only be understood within the frame of their unique historical experience in the United States.

An important milestone of Catholic history during the twentieth century in Latin America was the formation and development of the CELAM (Consejo Episcopal Latinoamericano), the Latin American Bishops' Council. Before the formation of CELAM, there had not been any organization for permanent consultation and cooperation among the bishops of the different countries. There was no common vision or consensus about a pastoral strategy. In reference to the case of the church in Peru, Klaiber says that "until the creation of CELAM only the militants of Catholic Action and a handful of bishops and priests had any vital contact with other parts of Latin America."[13] By contrast, since 1916 the missionary boards of historic Protestant denominations had held consultative conferences known as "congresses" in Panama (1916), Montevideo (1924), and Havana (1929) with a growing indigenous initiative and leadership from Latin American churches, and they seemed to have a common missionary strategy. After World War II, Latin American Protestant churches started a new cycle of consultations that were not initiated by mission agencies. The first Latin American Evangelical Conference (CELA) was held in Buenos Aires (1949), the second in Lima (1961), and the third in Buenos Aires (1969). Missionary Protestantism had not started from one church center, nor was it monitored by any central agency. However, in Latin America itself during the first half of the twentieth century the different missionary agencies moved slowly but steadily to a certain degree of coordination and consultation. There were also "comity" agreements dividing countries into areas of work for different denominations in order to avoid duplication.

This growing and organized Protestant presence was one of the factors that stirred up among Catholics a growing awareness of the need for coordination of their resources and activities in the vast Latin American region. Initiatives from the Vatican were followed by the Latin American bishops, and financial help was provided by Catholics from Europe and North America. Though most Latin American records are strangely silent about North American participation in the process,[14] Costello reminds us that a champion of the idea of CELAM, one who played a significant role in its development, was Monsignor Luigi Ligutti, an Italian-American who became an enthusiastic prime mover and "developed a triangle between Latin America, North America, and Rome."[15] The four assemblies of CELAM were institutional expressions of decisive moments that mark the evolution of the Catholic church in the post–World War II period: Rio de Janeiro (1955); Medellín (1968); Puebla (1979); and Santo Domingo (1992).

From a missiological perspective I am specially interested in developments between the first and second assemblies, that is between Rio de Janeiro in 1955 and Medellín in 1968. The assembly in Rio de Janeiro (July 25-August 4) was actually a constitutive assembly that was organized in conjunction with the International Eucharistic Congress in the city that at that time was the capital of Brazil.[16] Some movements preceded CELAM, such as the Catholic Action mentioned by Klaiber. As has been pointed out, a Catholic Action congress in Lima in 1953 was a key stage in the process of taking an inventory of the Latin American situation, the challenges it posed to the Roman Catholic Church, and the resources that the church had with which to respond. We have already quoted the valuable summary of these findings that William J. Coleman offered for the English-speaking reader. This kind of inventory was one of the aims of CELAM from its start in 1955.

The content of the first CELAM assembly in Rio de Janeiro has been almost forgotten. It did not have the repercussions that Medellín and Puebla were to have not only on church circles but on the general social and political life of Latin America. A chronicler of the event concludes that "the fruit of so much work does not sound encouraging or relevant today."[17] Important from the viewpoint of this study was this concern, which CELAM expressed strongly: the growth of Protestantism was a danger that Catholicism had to take very seriously, as was the growing influence of Marxism among the masses, and the social unrest that fostered it. Like secularization, communism was a serious concern for many Christians in the West in those days of the Cold War and ideological polarization. The shortage of clergy was another problem mentioned, and the final document offered a proposal that proved to be crucial as time went on: a request for foreign priests. "The conference considers that this solution could be facilitated if the superiors move to Latin America the personnel that has been displaced in the territories that have come under communist dominion. With this there would be more personnel to help in rejecting the influence of Protestant pastors who having been displaced from the already mentioned territories are being sent in alarming numbers to Latin America."[18] This proposal was the beginning of a process of self-awareness that would increase as a result of missionary action.

As we pointed out in chapter 3, six years after the Rio assembly, in a historic speech at the University of Notre Dame (August 17, 1961), Monsignor Agostino Casaroli, delegate from the pope, voiced the same concern and asked for missionaries. He requested a sacrificial answer from the North American Catholic church, presenting a dramatic demand that one-tenth of all human resources in terms of personnel, men and women, be sent as missionaries to Latin America in order to help Catholics there face a crisis that had reached alarming proportions. He quoted Pope Pius XII, who had referred in a speech to the menaces that Catholics confronted: "the inroads of Protestant sects; the secularization of the whole way of life; Marxism, the influence of which is felt in the universities and is very active, even dominant in almost all labor organizations; and finally a disquieting practice of spiritism."[19] He also requested specifically that missionaries be engaged in educational work "in a special manner in order to combat the perilous propaganda spread by such schools directed by Protestant sects."[20]

Mary McGlone summarizes the response to the speech at Notre Dame: "The crowd immediately applauded Msgr. Casaroli, but more than that, the U.S. response to the call would come in the form of personnel and funds. In the next thirty-five years thousands of priests, religious, and laity would serve in Latin America, and the church in the United States would collect more than $72 million to support the endeavors of the Latin American Church."[21] American response to the call brought a significant increase in the number of missionaries sent to Latin America, from 489 in 1940 to 1,767 in 1958 and 4,589 at the peak in 1968.[22] Canadian response was also generous, from 1,000 missionaries in 1960 to 2,000 in 1971.[23] Europeans also responded to the call of the pope. A new wave of French, German, and Belgian priests went to Latin America in a missionary pilgrimage that would make some of them famous around the world in missiological, historical, and sociological circles: José Comblin, François Houtart, Ireneo Rosier, Hubert Lepargneur, Roger Aubry, Emile Pin, Eduardo Hoornaert. They were conversant with the theological trends and pastoral movements that had been developing in Europe during the war and after it. Through a growing body of scholarship that is now available, we know that the presence and action of these missionaries started to have an impact in what had been a static situation, within which the church had adopted a defensive and almost defeatist attitude.[24]

An important aspect of that action was the immersion of several of these missionaries among the poorest segments of population in Latin America. With their characteristic pragmatism and activism the North Americans used the experience brought from their countries and responded to the dramatic demands of the conditions. Costello shows how the experience of some of these priests and nuns coming from communities that in their history had faced social struggles as immigrants in the United States provided organizing and defensive abilities in social work that were applied in their response to poverty in Latin America. They organized rural leagues, credit unions, neighborhood clubs, and they pioneered a style of pastoral ministry that was new to Latin America. On the other hand, the Europeans sharpened their tools of social analysis in order to understand the pastoral and theological dimension of the situation. The 1950s and the 1960s were years of experiments and of definite confrontation with the harsh realities of Latin America.

In the thirteen years between the Rio and Medellín CELAM assemblies, the presence of the missionaries contributed to unearthing some of the painful realities of Latin American Catholicism. The foreigners were also able to foster, catalyze, and encourage Latin American voices that were embarking on their own in the process of self-criticism and reform that was so necessary. Describing it as a "great missionary movement to Latin America," Father Jorge Alvarez Calderón from Peru recalls those days:

> First urged by Pope Pius XII, but more energetically fostered by Pope John XXIII, the movement gathered strength at the end of the sixties when large numbers of missionaries from the United States, Canada and Europe answered Pope John's call to "reevangelize" our largely Catholic continent. For perhaps the first time in our history, the clerical church came into direct contact with the poor and the working classes.[25]

Not everybody was enthusiastic about this missionary effort from Europe and North America. A process of critical evaluation developed, and the most articulate and radical voice was that of Monsignor Ivan Illich, an American priest who since 1961 had been training Catholic missionaries for Latin America. Illich's concern, as expressed in a now famous article written in 1967, was that unless radical changes in ideology and method were applied to the missionary effort, its true final result would be the postponement of the radical reforms that the Catholic church in Latin America desperately needed. He referred specifically to the fact that "men and money sent with missionary motivation carry a foreign Christian image, a foreign pastoral approach and a foreign political message." The long-term effect would be to convert the Latin American church into a satellite of a North Atlantic project. "The Latin American church flowers anew by returning to what the conquest stamped her: a colonial plant that blooms because of foreign cultivation."[26] Prien shows that what would appear as extremism in Illich was a critical vision that had been expressed by missionaries themselves in efforts at self-evaluation.[27]

This strong criticism had its effect, especially on some sending agencies. In the case of North Americans, missionary experience itself had become a source of serious questioning. A report presented in Rome in 1969 by Bishop Eduardo Pironio, the secretary of CELAM, reveals that missionary activity of foreign priests had been the subject of debate among the bishops. The report registers the criticisms and then lists the positive values of the foreign assistance as well as its negative aspects. It is really an excellent missiological piece of advice. The final balance is positive, concluding that any serious and objective evaluation "should not paralyze the assistance nor cloud the essential sense of missionary urgency."[28]

MEDELLÍN, A TIME OF RENEWAL

When the time came for the second assembly of CELAM, held in Medellín in 1968, we do not see a defensive church, one frightened by Marxists and

Protestants. Awakened in part by Vatican II, but also in the process of assimilating the missionary experience of those thirteen years, in Medellín there was a clear and articulate call for repentance and change. Significant in that meeting was the presence of a new generation of Latin American theologians. They had gone to the European sources of theological and pastoral renewal to give shape to their reflection about the Latin American reality. For instance, Gustavo Gutiérrez and Juan Luis Segundo, two of the most articulate liberation theologians, studied in Europe in the late fifties and came back to work and reflect. The bishops in Medellín moved from *immersion* among the poor, pioneered by the missionaries, to an *option* for the poor, that is, a proposal to identify with the cause of the poor. This was nothing less than a political and social realignment for a church that had occupied such an influential position in the history of Latin America.

A recent historical study by Jesuit historian Jeffrey Klaiber about the process of democratization in Latin America interprets positively the process of change in the Catholic church and its effect on society at large. He says that "against all predictions to the contrary, including those of Max Weber himself, the Catholic church changed: it ceased to be a bulwark of the established order and turned into a force for social change."[29] The documents of the bishops' conference in Medellín represent a notable reformulation of the mission of the church, which involved a new reading of the Latin American situation and of many biblical texts, reflection about some of the missionary experiences that North Americans and Europeans had gone through, and approval of bold new pastoral practices. In every aspect of this reformulation we see, at least partly, developments that were creative ways of responding to what had been detected in the analysis and observation of Protestant growth.

This new way of conceiving and accomplishing the mission of the church went through severe trials in the years after Medellín. How far could the reformulation go? How ready was the church to transform its structures in radical ways? There is no consensus among observers and participants about the degree to which the third assembly of CELAM in Puebla in 1979 represents a return to pre-Medellín positions. From a very conservative perspective, Monsignor López Trujillo, president of CELAM at the time the Puebla conference was being organized, admitted that in Puebla the agenda was to make corrections to what were perceived as the excesses of Medellín.[30] From a liberationist perspective, historian Enrique Dussel offers an interpretation that says the same after the event.[31] However, one fact is clear: Within the deteriorated economic, social, and political circumstances of Latin America, missionary work had changed its nature. Many foreign missionaries, as well as Latin American priests and nuns, suffered harassments, expulsion, torture, and even death. Missionary work became a dangerous activity even for North Americans, whose passports in other circumstances would have guaranteed their protection. Under military and repressive regimes even some bishops were killed in the movement of political reaction prompted by the new way of conceiving and acting the Christian mission. In many cases it has been demonstrated that missionaries who suffered were not politically active or engaged in subversion.

It cannot be said that all the renewal and ferment that took place in those decades went in the same direction, or that every aspect of it was the result of missionary action. However, it seems that there is a clear relationship. We will examine three areas of missionary life and action to see this process of change.

A NEW UNDERSTANDING OF THE BEING OF THE CHURCH

One of the effects of the Protestant presence in the Latin American countries was to question the quality of the Christianity represented by the Roman Catholic Church. Some of the more radical Protestant missionaries denied that the kind of institution that had fostered the conditions of inequality and exploitation characteristic of life in Latin America could be considered a Christian church. Others pointed to the need for deep and serious reforms. This initially produced a negative reaction and a defensive attitude among Catholics that in some cases has persisted until the present. But it is evident also that beginning in the 1950s we see the rise of a new attitude, with a clear disposition to become self-critical. Foreign missionary action connected to this reform-minded sector. Thus Maryknoll missionaries publicized in English the results of the Congress of Catholic Action in Chimbote, Peru (1953). This was a clear effort at self-analysis, and it did not spare words that sounded like an echo of what Protestants had been saying for decades.[32]

Application of social analysis within the frame of a more progressive theology reflected the real dimensions of the crisis. Under the leadership of François Houtart, Director of the Center for Socio-Religious Research of Brussels between 1958 and 1961, the social and ecclesiastical situation of Latin America was studied carefully through the project Feres-Friburgo. Several sociological tools were applied in order to understand the facts, country by country. Research teams were formed in fifteen countries, and more than twenty volumes were published in Spain. Though the teams were formed mainly by European and Latin American priests and social scientists, an enthusiastic sponsor was the American monsignor Luigi Ligutti, and the research was financed by North American funds of the Homeland Foundation. Part of the same project was an effort to analyze in depth the real dimensions of the Protestant growth, through which some of the most evident defects of the Catholic life and ministry had become visible. Spanish Jesuit Prudencio Damboriena, consultant for the Vatican, published a two-volume study of Protestantism in Latin America. Well researched and planned, the book has a valuable statistical base and careful studies about Protestant missionary methodologies but is very critical of Protestant missionary work.[33]

Ireneo Rosier, a Carmelite from Belgium who had studied the crisis of Catholicism in Europe along the lines of de-Christianization, conducted a study in Chile that had a chapter on Protestantism. The description of the Protestant advance was really a way of analyzing Catholic failures. Some things that were essential and fundamental were called into question:

What attracts people in Protestantism is the person of Christ and his doctrine. . . . The beauty of the Christian life in small communities, the greater
depth in one's life and the concern for saving one's soul explain the influence of Protestantism among the people. . . . Protestantism has opened a
direct way to Christ, while in Catholicism it is as if the authentic face of
Christ would be veiled by civilization and the complications of so many
centuries.[34]

This process of self-criticism acquired more sophistication in the pastoral analysis
of Juan Luis Segundo and Gustavo Gutiérrez. Again, basic things are called into
question, not out of a spirit of iconoclastic criticism but out of pastoral and
missionary concern. The pastoral and missionary intention of these theologians
has been forgotten and obscured by the persistent reference to what in their
theology seems to be a call for political and social action on the part of the
church. But some of the things that they have been saying have to do with the
basic question of what it means to be a Christian today in Latin America, and
consequently what the mission of the church is in those lands, and how it is
going to accomplish that mission. Before the publication of his best-known book
about the new theologies, *Theology of Liberation,* Gutiérrez had written a short
but valuable booklet about the pastoral situation in the continent.[35] The spirit of
that booklet is summarized in a paragraph of another publication from 1969:

The Latin American Church is in crisis. . . . The scope and seriousness of
the situation is of enormous proportions. Long gone is the era when the
Church could handle questions and problems by appealing to her doctrines and distinctions. Today it is the Church herself that is being called
into question by many Christians who experience in their daily lives the
terrible distance that separates the Church from her roots in the gospel and
her lack of harmony with the real world of Latin America. She is also being
called into question by many people who are far away from her—many
more than our traditional pastoral outlook is willing to admit—who see her
as an obstructive force in the effort to construct a more just society.[36]

We are aware, of course, that there were clear differences in the attitude, outlook, and theological perspective from which Protestant thinkers quoted earlier,
Ireneo Rosier, and Gustavo Gutiérrez wrote. The missionary proposal that could
be derived from each of these three visions would be different. But all of them
point toward a new understanding of the mission of the church, which one way
or another has touched the very being of the Catholic church in Latin America.
Gutiérrez has summarized it well, "What is demanded by Medellín is to change
the focus of the church—the center of its life and work—and to be present,
really present, in the world of the poor—to commit the church to living in the
world of the poor."[37] By being among the poor the church would learn how to
see the world with the eyes of the poor. Theologians thus are invited to do
theology from the perspective of the poor, to adopt as their own the vision of

those who are oppressed in society. It is a call to adopt the vision from the underside of history and to read God's word from that perspective.[38]

A NEW UNDERSTANDING OF THE MESSAGE OF THE CHURCH

The proclamation of Jesus Christ as Savior and Lord and the challenge to follow him in obedience to his call were central in the message of Protestant missionaries to Latin America. This Christocentric nature of their gospel was interpreted in relation to the cultural and spiritual reality of the continent in *The Other Spanish Christ,* a classic book by John A. Mackay. For this famous theologian, "a common need presses upon the Spanish and Anglo-Saxon worlds: to 'know' Christ, to 'know' Him for life and thought, to know Him in God and God in Him."[39] Observers would agree with the remarks we quoted from Rosier about the popular Protestantism he studied in Chile, that it "has opened a direct way to Christ." A Christocentric thrust became evident in the Catholicism of the final decades of the twentieth century. It was possible to detect it in manifestations as varied as the Christologies of Jon Sobrino and Juan Luis Segundo, the evangelistic methods of the Catholic charismatics,[40] and the popular poetry paraphrasing scripture.[41] What is especially significant for an evangelical observer is the new role that scripture has in these pastoral and theological efforts.

When Protestantism started to spread through Latin America, the Bible was central in its missionary action. Up to that time the Bible had been practically unknown by the people. In many instances the agents of the British and American Bible Societies distributed the Bible, which had an impact long before there were Protestant churches and missions dedicated to planting churches. As Methodist bishop Sante U. Barbieri wrote, the Bible was "a silent pioneer of evangelism" and had a key role in "opening furrows in virgin soil and of preparing the way for the work of the Spirit and the testimony of the converted witness."[42] This was a pillar of the Protestant missiology, which considered Bible translation and distribution as the beginning of missionary activity that would allow for the communication of the faith and the development of indigenous churches. The practice corresponded to convictions about the authority of scripture, the testimony of the Spirit, the accessibility of Christian truth to the individual through the word, and the need for cultivating piety through Bible reading.[43]

To understand the impact of the use of the Bible on the life of Catholics, we learn a lot from personal testimonies. An eloquent example is the anecdote provided by Father Jorge Mejia, one of the most eminent Roman Catholic Bible scholars of the continent. He tells us that when he was a child of ten he found a Bible in his family library and gave himself to its reading, "secretly, of course." Then he proceeds:

But I was soon found out and severely reprimanded, if I remember well for two reasons: first, because I had exposed myself to the occasion of reading certain rude stories, improper for children; secondly, because the bible I had found was a Protestant version. This, I think, was very typical of Catholic mentality among Latin American educated classes thirty or even twenty years ago, before the Bible renewal got under way. On one hand there was a certain diffidence about the Bible. It should not be read freely, lest some innocent reader come upon shocking language or descriptions. On the other hand, most available editions in Spanish were of Protestant origin.[44]

This anecdote is representative of the fact that it was the Protestant initiative, and the observation of how Protestantism was able to put the Bible in the hands of the people, that partly brought about the biblical renewal, within Catholicism in Latin America. This renewal of course, also had sources in Europe in movements that found adequate expression in Vatican II. By 1967, explaining the effect of conciliar decrees in relation to scripture, Walter Abbott, S.J., pointed out that the Bible would be the chief source of theology and that the training of priests from then onward "should be built around a Bible-centered theology rather than polemically oriented theology." This did not mean an abandonment of Catholic tradition, but more precisely, this:

> What has been swept away is the polemical focus developed during four centuries of controversy with Protestantism. A primary focus on the positive teaching of the Scripture means revision of seminary textbooks, catechisms and all other religious literature. Not all parts of the vast Roman Catholic Church move at the same speed, but the process has begun that should result in the restoration of the proper role of the Bible.[45]

By comparison with what existed before, we could say that Bible renewal in Latin American Catholicism moved with speed. Mejia attributes a breakthrough to the presence of Monsignor John Straubinger, a German missionary priest and Bible scholar who came to Argentina in 1938. His translation of the Bible was appreciated by evangelicals, who found the notes of this Bible expressing some of the perceptions that would only become widely known after Vatican II. Mejia also points out the important role played by priests who went to study in France during the postwar period and were influenced by the French Bible-centered pastoral renewal. Love for the Bible was also characteristic in other missionary priests who came from Europe.

This flourishing of biblical studies and especially the entrance of biblical categories in theological work could only cause joy among Protestants. Evangelical theologian Emilio Núñez spoke clearly about it in the 1969 Congress of Evangelism in Bogotá. He acknowledged that it was undeniable "that the Roman Catholic church is undertaking an unprecedented effort for the translation, publication, distribution and use of the Bible." However, as a representative of a more conservative sector of Protestantism, Núñez went on to add: "From all changes in post-conciliar catholicism no one is more promising of a better future for the life of thousands of Catholics than this new attitude towards Sacred Scripture."[46] The Catholic rediscovery of the Bible opened for Protestants a set of key questions in relation to hermeneutics, contextualization, missionary strategy, and ecumenism. In a field very dear to their tradition, they found themselves before an unexpected interlocutor that was posing especially the dramatic question of the relevance of God's written Word to the contemporary needs of a changing society. The most challenging aspect of this interaction was that Catholics who had come to see the world with the eyes of the poor started also to read and understand the Bible through the eyes of the poor. In his evaluation of liberation theology René Padilla acknowledges the magnitude of the challenge. Criticizing that theology for its Marxist leanings, its selective use of scripture, its concessions to sociology, or its espousing of socialism does not answer the key question. Padilla writes:

> I will not use these arguments too quickly, however, lest I fail to face the challenge not only of liberation theology but also, and primarily, of the poor with whom liberation theology has sided. The question for me is not, How do I *respond* to liberation theology, so as to show its flaws and incongruities? But rather, How do I articulate my faith in the same context of poverty, repression and hopelessness out of which liberation theology has emerged?[47]

The existence of specialized missionary orders in the Catholic church provided avenues for implementation of new convictions about the importance of scripture. Orders such as the Daughters of St. Paul and the Divine Word Missionaries have provided the infrastructure and personnel for publishing and distributing Bible commentaries studies and expositions at a rate and quality that Protestants find hard to match. The United Bible Societies continue to be an interdenominational and now inter-confessional effort with which most Latin American Protestants and many Catholics cooperate for translation, publication, distribution, and use of scripture.[48] But in relation to Bible scholarship and study material, Protestants are now behind in terms of volume and quality of publications. At the same time, there seems to be substance in the allegation that the new wave of North American missionaries coming from evangelical Protestantism in recent years seems to be weak in the area of biblical training and conviction.

A NEW MISSIONARY METHOD: PASTORAL RENEWAL

In the process of self-analysis in face of the growth of Protestantism, Rosier pointed out the way in which Christian life was experienced in the small communities as a decisive aspect of its attraction for the masses. He also made extensive use of the pastoral observations of the Jesuit Ignacio Vergara, who had made a study of Protestantism in Chile in 1956. Vergara was especially intrigued by the strong sense of personal missionary responsibility that the Pentecostal groups were able to instill in their followers.

> Another very important system of their methodology is the spread of small groups all over the country. These local groups have many advantages:

they increase the responsibility of the followers, they facilitate constant religious practice, and instruction is adapted to the various categories of persons and small groups. The meetings are very close to the homes of people, and they are held at an hour that enables workers to attend. The personal contact between leaders and followers is easier when the area which is reached is small. The leader is one of them, a person who lives their own problems, knows all of them personally, and belongs to the same social class. . . . All this helps develop a brotherly community. In it the followers and the new who arrive find a familiar atmosphere, a sincere welcome, help in difficult moments, and mutual union.[49]

Point by point this description coincides with descriptions of the Base Ecclesial Communities, a pastoral innovation that was hailed as "Latin America's most important recent contribution to the Roman Catholic Church's pastoral practice worldwide."[50] In the second chapter of his book *Ecclesiogenesis*, Leonardo Boff recounts that in the Brazilian northeast Dom Agnelo Rossi initiated in 1956 a movement of popular catechists that was to become very influential in the pastoral strategy that the Brazilian bishops developed in the early sixties. According to Boff, the spark that moved Dom Agnelo was the complaint of an old woman who remarked that in her town in Natal the three Protestant churches were lighted and filled with people while the Catholic church was closed and in darkness because the people could not find a priest. Other writers confirm Boff's anecdote:

The bishops concerned over a chronic lack of priests, the inroads of Evangelical Protestants and the growth of left movements, joined with pastoral agents to design an Emergency Plan in 1962. Included was a section urging bishops to "identify natural communities and work on the basis of their life situation," and to give lay Christians in these communities "a more decisive role."[51]

We are confronted here not only with a question of methodology but also with a deeper question for Catholic ecclesiology, namely, the structure of the church and its ability to be really missionary, which is not a problem of Catholics only. The criticism of the massive non-personal church becomes eventually a criticism of the clericalism involved in a pastoral approach in which there is no room for the action of lay people. It is precisely what some of the most perceptive critics of missionary presence had pointed out. The danger for the church in Latin America was to depend too much on foreign missionary help, to the point that it would avoid dealing with the structural problem behind the chronic lack of clergy. This had been one of the besetting problems of the Roman Catholic Church throughout its history in Latin America. Jesuit theologian Juan Luis Segundo thought that this was one of the marks that made the church look "exhausted and depleted." He sets the problem within a context in which several related factors appear:

> In existence for four centuries now, it does not have enough priests of its own to carry out its functions; it must import them from abroad in such great numbers that they make up half of the priestly population. It lacks missionaries to send to its marginal inhabitants in rural regions and primitive wastes. It lacks pastoral agents of all sorts to do the work of fashioning truly liberative communities. It lacks the economic support it needs from its own faithful in order to satisfy its most urgent needs; here, once again, it must import financial aid from abroad.[52]

Many missiologists who have dealt with this issue point to the sources of the problem in the practices of the colonial church. For instance, it is clear now from historical research that the Spanish church during the colonial centuries was reluctant to allow those born in the colonies to become members of the hierarchy in the ten archdioceses and thirty-eight dioceses in Spanish America.[53]

It was precisely about this point that Illich made his radical argument; in spite of good and generous intentions, Catholic missionary work in the Latin American mission field was prolonging dependence. Worse, it was stifling the possibilities of reform that were the only hope of change for the church. From a missiological perspective it is interesting to pay attention to the elements that should be included in that reform, according to Illich.

> This foreign transfusion—and the hope for more—gave ecclesiastical pusillanimity a new lease on life, another chance to make the archaic and colonial system work. If North America and Europe send enough priests to fill the vacant parishes, there is no need to consider laymen—unpaid for part-time work—to fulfill most evangelical tasks, no need to re-examine the structure of the parish, the function of the priests, the Sunday obligation and clerical sermon; no need for exploring the use of the married diaconate, new forms of celebration of the Word and Eucharist and intimate familial celebrations of conversion to the Gospel in the milieu of the home. The promise of more clergy is like a bewitching siren.[54]

Undoubtedly there is here a lesson and a warning sign for evangelical missionaries and missiologists who still see Latin America as a mission field. It may be helpful to recall the definite contrast between the Catholic and the evangelical policies in regard to this point. On the one hand—as historian Kenneth Scott Latourette points out—from their beginning Protestant missions came at a period in which a "distinctive feature of the expansion of Christianity . . . was the extent to which Christian missions became an enterprise of the rank and file of the membership of the churches."[55] The missionary societies of Protestant origin were able to mobilize lay support and lay involvement in the missionary enterprise. On the other hand, in the evangelical type of Protestantism that fostered the missionary movement and nurtured it there was an effective and consistent practice of the Protestant principle of the priesthood of all believers. The role of an ordained clergy or a select group of people bound by special and very demanding vows did not occupy in Protestant missions the key place it had among Catholics.

The rise of a native leadership was also facilitated by another key factor, pointed out in Stephen Neill's statement, that "the first principle of Protestant missions has been that Christians should have the Bible in their hands in their own language at the earliest possible date."[56] In the case of Latin America the distribution of scripture in many cases preceded the presence of the missionaries and prepared the way for them. The reading of scripture as a requirement of entrance and continuity in the church, as well as the popular forms of Bible instruction developed as part of congregational life, gave to lay people the possibility of leadership in the local congregations and participation in mission. This was not possible at the same pace for Catholicism, in which the centrality of the eucharist in the life of the church demands the presence of clergy.

Thus we arrive at the central difference between the structure of the type of popular Protestantism that has developed more, and the Catholic structure. For this writer, both the missionary experience and the strength of the biblical argument are on the side of Boff, who points to the difference between a church that is born out of the people and one that is imposed from above. The matters of control and authority are clearly linked here to the concept of the ministry. The volunteerism and missionary zeal of Pentecostals and other independent evangelical groups are a source of renewal and a driving force in the appearance of thousands of new congregations spread over the continent. It constitutes in the contemporary Latin American setting a vivid expression of what Luther meant by the priesthood of all believers. The great question it poses to the more developed and institutionalized forms of Protestantism concerns the loss of their initial vigor, either because of an adolescent clericalism or because of the loss of missionary concern.

CONCLUSION

The simple words of Jesus "You will know them by their fruits" (Mt. 7:16) may be applied to evaluate and put to the test four decades of missionary action, both Catholic and Protestant, in Latin America. Foreign missionary work in Latin America during the postwar period has had a renewing effect on the spiritual life of the continent. Some elements of the Protestant missionary experience have served both as a challenge and as a model to Catholic mission. Catholic renewal has taken those elements further into a creative movement from which Protestant missions could learn a lot. Contemporary Protestant theologians from Latin America, both evangelical and ecumenical, are also embarked on a fresh understanding of their traditions and their biblical basis in order to respond to the challenges of this moment of history. Latin America continues to be a missionary challenge and an enigma. The lessons of the past four decades are invaluable as Latin American Christians become a missionary force for the twenty-first century.

PART THREE

MISSIOLOGICAL PERSPECTIVES ON POPULAR PROTESTANTISM

7

Popular Protestantism: A Missiological Perspective

In June 1910 the major figures of the great Protestant missionary enterprise that had flourished in the nineteenth century gathered in Edinburgh, Scotland. It was a high-level meeting that brought together missionary strategists, theologians, and leaders of the large Protestant denominations. With a great sense of urgency the aim of the gathering was to try to "complete the evangelization of the world in our generation," but they left Latin America out of their field of missionary action because they considered it to be a Christian continent. As has been noted, church historians believe that Edinburgh was a decisive moment in the history of the missions. It was also the start of the ecumenical movement that would culminate in the creation in 1948 of the World Council of Churches, an organization that gathered together some of the oldest and most revered churches in Protestantism.

Also in 1910 two poor Swedish immigrants to the United States left Chicago for Belem do Pará in Brazil. During a Pentecostal type of ecstasy they had received a vision and concluded that God was calling them to be missionaries in that far-off place. Their labor gave rise to the first congregation of the Assemblies of God in Brazil, the largest single denomination in Latin America today.

The participants in these two events moved in very different worlds, but we cannot understand the missionary history of the twentieth century without understanding the movements that these two events represent, especially in Latin America. A half century would pass before these two movements would meet, acknowledge one another, and accept one another as part of the Christian missionary impulse. In 1961 two Chilean Pentecostal churches were admitted as members in the World Council of Churches. This development was a surprise to many people who until then had not recognized Pentecostal denominations as Protestant. Just three years previously, in an ecumenical document on evangelism, an Argentinean theologian referred to Pentecostals as a "sect."[1] Actually until mid-century one frequently heard Pentecostals referred to as a sect among denominations such as Lutherans, Baptists, Methodists, and Presbyterians. Yet this movement had been incredibly successful in carrying out the Christian missionary task.

In 1966 the famous evangelist Billy Graham brought evangelical churches and missionary organizations together in a World Conference on Evangelization in Berlin. He was able to gather a significant number of evangelical missionary leaders from the entire world. That was the global public platform in which the evangelical sector of Protestantism first accepted Pentecostals as fellow believers in the task of world evangelization. Those of us who were present at that event in Berlin will never forget our surprise during the part of the program that was devoted to hearing reports about the advance of evangelization in the world.[2] Country after country and continent after continent, from places as different as South Africa, Chile, Korea, and Yugoslavia, the reports indicated a remarkable expansion of Pentecostal churches. In many places there were more Pentecostals than all other Protestants put together. Many evangelicals had not even noticed the Pentecostal presence in their countries, but at Berlin they became aware of it. The most recent biography of Billy Graham[3] describes in detail the doubts and conflicts that the evangelist and his organization faced before deciding to invite well-known Pentecostal preachers to take part in that Berlin Congress. Thus it was only well into the sixth decade of the twentieth century that ecumenical Protestants and evangelicals granted Pentecostals their Protestant "citizenship papers."

There has still not been enough reflection on the meaning of the Pentecostal movement for Christian mission in the twenty-first century. Because of its remarkable numerical growth, sociological studies of the movement are on the rise. In Latin America academics like Jean Pierre Bastian tend to refuse to identify Pentecostals as Protestants, and they present them as "a collection of new non-Catholic religious movements."[4] It is not surprising that some Pentecostals also question their relationship with Protestantism, and claim to have their own unique identity. In this chapter I try to consider Pentecostalism from the standpoint of Christian mission. I attempt to place it within the broader framework of the overall growth of Christianity and of the forms that Protestantism has taken as it becomes contextualized in different cultures.

THE PENTECOSTAL FACT

Following the classification proposed by David Barrett, with my own modification, three waves can be distinguished in the Pentecostal movement of the twentieth century. The first wave is *classic Pentecostalism;* the second wave is also known as the *Charismatic movement;* and the third may be defined as *neocharismatic.*[5] Here we will pay more attention to the first wave because its presence and work are still decisive for Latin America from a missiological perspective.

The first wave is connected to the "speaking in tongues" by Agnes Oxham that occurred during a divine healing service in Topeka, Kansas, on the eve of the New Year, 1901; it is also linked to the figure of Charles Parham. Shortly afterward, another group sprang up on Azusa Street in Los Angeles with a black preacher named William Seymour. The distinctive feature of this movement is "speaking in tongues" as a proof that the person has received an anointing or special blessing from the Holy Spirit. Speaking in tongues is understood to be a special renewed form of the Pentecost experience described in chapter 2 of the Book of Acts. The presence and power of the Holy Spirit are central in both the practice and self-image of the movement's pioneers.[6]

Work is still being done on a history of the classic Pentecostal movement, and there are different interpretations of its origins and connections. Now, a century after its beginnings, we can note certain currents and tendencies that scholars classify and describe.[7] At the outset, however, it was like a leaven that affected many churches and different denominations, without clear limits or boundaries. From the beginning of this movement a tremendous interest in missions was evident in its protagonists. Indeed, some of the first Pentecostals believed that the gift of tongues would enable them to carry out missions elsewhere in the world without having to learn another language.[8]

Led by missionary zeal to other places in the world, the movement spread rapidly. An illustrative example is the already mentioned case of the Assemblies of God in Brazil, which is now the largest denomination of its type in the world.[9] The two Swedish Baptists who founded the movement were the pastor, Gunnar Vingren, and the laborer, Daniel Berg, who had emigrated to Chicago in search of work. There they had a Pentecostal experience in a Baptist setting that led them to decide to travel as missionaries to Belem in the state of Pará in Brazil in late 1910. These enthusiastic missionaries were surprisingly creative. They did not have money and were a simple pastor and workman, whose churches with a great deal of hardship had provided funds for a one-way passage to Brazil. Berg, who was a metalworker, found a job that enabled the two of them to live; it was Vingren who was the gifted evangelist. They first went to a Baptist church in Belem, but in the end this church rejected the gift of tongues and overly enthusiastic worship of the newcomers. The two missionaries set up an independent church that grew and spread and became the Assemblies of God in Brazil.

A GRASSROOTS KIND OF PROTESTANTISM

This wave can be said to be a *popular kind of Protestantism* that then evolved to the point where denominations like the Assemblies of God, Pentecostal Church of God, or Foursquare Gospel Church were set up. Spontaneous outbreaks of this kind also occurred in Latin America; an illustrative example is the Pentecostal Methodist Church in Chile. In this instance the revival began with Willis Hoover, a Methodist missionary doctor who had a Pentecostal experience in 1902.[10] His church in Valparaíso, Chile, grew remarkably, and there were charismatic and healing experiences. Methodism was a somewhat middle-class church, with its liturgy and well-developed church order, and it did not show any openness to this explosion of spirituality. Thus Hoover and his followers left the Methodist Church and formed the Pentecostal Methodist Church, now the largest in Chile. The Methodists themselves have remained a relatively small church.

These examples illustrate the realm of "marginality" from which the Pentecostal movement sprang. It is the emergence of a missionary and evangelizing leaven, a movement *from below*, that takes on unexpected dimensions and is then projected back onto the older and more established churches, as has occurred at other moments in Christian history. Its roots and a process of theological and methodological continuity can nevertheless be uncovered. The historian Donald Dayton has located the theological roots of the Pentecostal moment specifically in the late-nineteenth-century holiness movements,[11] from which came denominations such as the Church of the Nazarene, the Pilgrim Holiness Church, and the Free Methodists, all of them sharing a common root in the teachings of John Wesley about a Christian life. Wesley is the source of the ideas that in addition to conversion there must be a second experience of grace, that discipline of life seeks sanctification, and that the fullness of the Holy Spirit can bring that about. Thus far, we have been speaking about what we may call classic Pentecostalism.

Somewhat different is the second wave, also known as the *Charismatic movement,* which spread in the 1960s within older Protestant denominations, such as the Lutherans, Anglicans, Presbyterians, Methodists, and in some places within Catholicism. Representatives of this wave are figures such as Larry Christensen (Lutheran), Michael Harper (Anglican), Juan Carlos Ortiz (initially from the Assemblies of God in Argentina), and the Catholic cardinal Joseph Suenens. Glossolalia and divine healing were part of this movement, *but sociologically it did not bear the marks of poor grassroots people as did the first wave.* Because it generally did not set up separate denominations, it retained the sociological features of the denominations within which it emerged.

Two observations underscored by Bastian may be made here.[12] First, there is the decisive role played in this movement by the Full Gospel Businessmen's Association, started by the wealthy Armenian-American dairy farmer Demos Shakarian. Following the practice of business culture and of Rotary Clubs, this association holds meetings to evangelize business people and merchants in luxury hotels (thus shunning identification with any particular church). Although it began within the Assemblies of God, this movement has had a strong impact on the Catholic Charismatic movement.[13] Second, there is the existence of an organized and growing Charismatic movement within Catholicism. Since the 1970s Catholic charismatics from the United States have played an important role in promoting their movement in Latin America. According to Bastian's interpretation, the Catholic church was able to control and to a certain degree neutralize the liberation theology movement in Latin America, but it is finding much harder to deal with the continuous growth of Pentecostal churches that attract nominal Catholics.

Paradoxically Catholic Pentecostalism seeks to offer a bulwark against the radical Catholicism of base-communities and appears to be the best means for combating the sects. In fact, the Church is resorting to two means to contain the Pentecostal advance: a revival of the popular devotions, and encouragement of the Catholic Charismatic Renewal.[14]

The third wave may be defined as *neo-charismatic*. It is represented by the new churches without a clear denominational tradition that some call "post-denominational." These churches have appeared in recent years in the United States around charismatic figures who generally do not pay attention to theological issues, and whose worship, preaching, and marketing methodologies are taken from the subculture of the so-called televangelists. They emphasize prosperity, and they have been exported from the United States to other countries, such as the Verbo church in Guatemala, which became famous because military president Efrain Rios Montt was a member. In South America similar churches have arisen spontaneously, some of them as outbreaks from Charismatic Catholics, such as Agua Viva (Living Water) in Peru, Ecclesia in Bolivia, or Ondas de Amor y Paz (Waves of Love and Peace) in Argentina.

To understand the current missionary situation, we must comprehend the missionary significance of the Pentecostal movement. In my reference to this movement as a type of "popular Protestantism" *I am writing primarily of the first wave, namely, classic Pentecostalism.*[15] The second wave has served as a ferment of renewal in various denominations. It is still very early to know what direction the third wave will take.

My own observation and ongoing contact with Pentecostal churches in the Americas leads me to accept the conclusions of the systematic work of scholars like Walter Hollenweger[16] in their description of this kind of church. Certain features of this Pentecostal movement respond to the realities proper to our contemporary circumstances. For example, it has grown in large urban concentrations, primarily among the poorer classes. Its worship, organization, evangelization methods, and preaching style *are very suited to its grassroots or popular setting.* The worship style is spontaneous and does not adhere to a written order. It is also participatory, inasmuch as anyone can pray aloud, prophesy, or praise the Lord. To be participant one need not have an education or even be able to read.

In these churches preaching is narrative in style rather than a presentation of arguments or a carefully reasoned exposition. A good Pentecostal preacher knows how to tell stories and in this sense is closer to the oral culture from which the Bible arose than the literate culture of the Protestant middle class. In the style of the most successful preachers a few key points are repeated, and one need not be able to read to follow them. Preaching seeks to make it easy to memorize without reference to the written text, and often the preacher and the audience have memorized portions of the Bible. Long before other denominations in Latin America, Pentecostals contextualized their music by using guitars and tambourines rather than the classic harmonium or organ of English-speaking Protestant missionaries.

Consequently the Pentecostal churches are a kind of Protestantism that draws in poor people. It is also a kind of Protestantism to which the poor have made their own contribution. That is why the name *popular Protestantism* is apt. It should also be noted that there are some Protestant churches of a grassroots type that do not necessarily have the Pentecostal emphasis on speaking in tongues but are close to the style of the people in other ways. Pentecostal scholars who interpret Pentecostalism from within highlight the importance of a certain autonomy within its popular character, one that comes from a conflictive breakaway in its origins. Juan Sepúlveda, for instance, interprets the conflict as two-directional. First, as "a conflict between a religiosity centered in the objectivity of dogma and a religiosity which gave priority to the subjective experience of God." Second, and socially more significant, as "a conflict between a religion mediated by specialists of a cultured class (a specialized clergy) and by an enlightened culture; and a religion in which the poor people have direct access to God, and in which the relationship with the sacred can be communicated legitimately in the language of the culture itself, and in popular language."[17] This would be equivalent to a "socialization or popularization of the magisterium," but because of its root in a religious experience, it locates the ability of Pentecostalism not so much in external social factors nor in theology, but in the specifically religious structure of Pentecostalism. Bernardo Campos has developed the concept of "Pentecostality" to indicate what defines the movement. He says that

> In theological terms, *the Pentecostal* in Latin America, like anywhere else in the world, is a religious experience of the divine. As a religious experience it represents a *ritualized extension of the originating Pentecostal event* (Acts 2:1-13) whose claim and need is to express the essence of Christianity—namely, "the foundational Pentecostality"—in the intensity of a spirituality that repeats early Christian life, which serves as a founding myth.[18]

THE SOCIOLOGICAL FACTORS

In any religious movement we encounter three aspects that must be examined in order to understand it: *beliefs* or doctrines, *rituals* or forms of expression of religious feeling; and *institutions*, that is, how it is organized to exist as a community and to spread its faith. All of this is connected to an *ethics*, that is, a system of values and norms of behavior. Evangelicals generally focus a great deal on beliefs and doctrines and on the individual aspects of the corresponding ethics, but they tend to ignore other factors. Anthropologists and sociologists, on the other hand, are very attentive to rituals and to the institution, to the customs and way of life of people. These external data, which can be measured statistically, are the basis for sociological conclusions.

The very rapid growth of popular Protestantism in the second half of the twentieth century has drawn the attention of sociologists, precisely because their numerical weight tends to make Pentecostals socially and politically important. Indeed, the first interpretive studies of Protestantism in Latin America, such as those of Emilio Willems[19] and Christian Lalive D'Epinay,[20] were not focused on the Protestantism of the missions and so-called historic denominations that had been working in Latin America since the nineteenth century. These denominations generally tried to "win over the elites for Christ," and their agenda was one of educational and cultural modernization. But they did not have a great numerical impact. It was popular Protestantism that succeeded in attracting the masses and hence the sociologists. As they studied the growth of grassroots churches in Latin America, the attitude of sociologists—whether they were Marxists, Catholics, or had no specific ideology—changed from scorn to interest. Sociology tends to explain growth almost entirely by external factors proper to the social environment of our era of transition, without appreciating the internal, spiritual drive proper to a movement that has a particular belief. Some Catholic interpreters of popular Protestantism tend to do the same, as do some Protestant interpreters when they approach popular Catholicism.[21]

One factor that is examined, for example, is the effects of urbanization; it is noted that in the huge urban concentrations in Latin America people who have left their small rural community find themselves lost and disoriented, bereft of their customary reference points. Migrants in a large city can lose their sense of self, and that sensation of anonymity and of lack of belonging to a community can easily lead to alcoholism, drugs, or violence. Sociologists observe that the grassroots churches give people who are experiencing such feelings an experience of personal dignity. When they go into the churches, they are welcomed with an embrace or a handshake. They can participate in giving praise, raising their arms, praying, and shouting without having to study theology. From a missiological standpoint we can say that in this environment of freedom and participation they hear the gospel presented in an accessible way and attain an experience of the divine, of the power of God that the preacher is talking about. These experiences have a transforming effect on such people.

The sociologists have also noted that the older and more established churches, very often despite their good intentions and even a social agenda, have not achieved a great deal in terms of transforming people. Sometimes they carry out their social activity in a very paternalistic way and create dependency. By contrast, the churches that have no social agenda and that move about on this grassroots level have a socially transforming effect on their members. Precisely because of the new sense of dignity and belonging, they help people reorganize their lives. What we evangelicals call conversion and sanctification, a sociologist sees as reorganizing and redirecting one's life. What the sociologist may describe, but does not always explain, the missiologist can explain by paying attention to the internal as well as the external factors, namely, spiritual dynamism, faith in the transforming power of the Holy Spirit, and the ability to develop contextual methodologies.

Some other aspects are even more enigmatic for the academics. For example, sociologists cannot understand how people in these popular churches contribute to building their own churches and carrying out their projects despite their poverty. Catholic scholars are intrigued by this, and sometimes it plainly bothers them, because in Latin America the members of the Catholic church do not contribute much money. Much of the church's operation comes from government money, income from property held by the church since colonial times, and generous aid from churches in Europe and North America.

If people's loyalty is measured by what they contribute to their churches, these poor people in grassroots churches give proportionately much more than believers in other churches. Certain sociologists tend to explain it with conspiracy theories, claiming that the CIA or rich donors from North America send money so that people will convert to these churches. The more honest Catholic scholars recognize that it cannot be explained by external factors. Even Protestant observers sometimes find this all an enigma.

The missiological approach, as already noted, poses the question of how Christian faith has been transmitted over the centuries, and it starts from the premise that in the very structure of faith in Christ there is an exigency to pass on that faith, a missionary imperative. Its questions are aimed at finding better methodologies that are consistent with belief and effective in carrying out the mission. But missiology can take advantage of what the social sciences have to say. When taken in conjunction with theological understanding, these sciences can offer keys for self-criticism, correction, and continuity of mission.

CHRISTIANITY'S GREAT SHIFT SOUTHWARD

We have tried to pay attention to missiologists such as Andrew Walls, Walbert Bühlman, and Walter Hollenweger, who propose that the Pentecostal movement must be understood as part of a broader movement, of what may be called "the great shift of Christianity to the South." Popular Protestantism has grown in the South, that is in Africa, parts of Asia, and Latin America. Likewise, in the early years of this new century we find that Christianity has lost strength in Europe and North America and is now a religion of the southern peoples. Christianity used to be regarded as a western religion or one proper to the white man. That is no longer the case. Andrew Walls reminds us that

at the beginning of the [twentieth] century, some 83% of those who professed the Christian faith lived in Europe and North America. Now, some 60% (probably) live in Africa, Asia, Latin America, or the Pacific Islands, and that proportion is rising every year. The center of gravity of the Christian church has moved sharply southwards. The representative Christianity of the twenty-first century seems set to be that of Africa, Asia and Latin America, and the Pacific region. These areas look destined to be the launch pad for the mission of the church in the twenty-first century.[22]

Hence the numerical strength of Christianity has turned upside down, but Walls and Hollenweger continually remind us in missiological publications that students of mission have not yet fully realized what this change means. Hollenweger offers an interesting explanation:

Political history is written by the victors. Mission history is written by the missionaries. It is unavoidable that such a history is biased and ignores the story from the "underside," the story of those who have been evangelized. Furthermore, the priorities and the categories of interpretation are those of the "sending" culture. The theological status of the pre-Christian context is usually underrated.[23]

I could add that Protestant scholars, including Pentecostals in Latin America, have tended to underrate the pre-conversion context of the members of their churches.

A simple but helpful interpretative key comes from David Barrett in the first edition of the *World Christian Encyclopedia,* which he edited. Based on the detailed statistical tables he had compiled, Barrett reminded us that since 1950 the growth of the church in the Third World was the result of two developments: first, the missionary expansion of existing western denominations, and second, what he calls "a massive proliferation of Non-White indigenous denominations."[24] This non-white, non-western character of what we could call popular Christianity is a key to describe it and define it. However, in Latin America it acquires a particular identity because culturally Latin America is a hybrid, with western culture a substantive ingredient. In the great cities the defining question is more social than cultural. We find that even as we compare members of traditional denominations and grassroots churches in Latin American countries. Hence, we must recognize that the majority Christianity of today is not that of the theology or pastoral care textbooks taught in seminaries and theological institutions, usually translated from English. Christianity today is different from that conceived by missionaries in the early twentieth century. Twenty-first-century Christianity will be of another color and of another kind; it will be more like popular Protestantism. (I must insist that the term *popular* means "of the people" and has no connotation of disdain or superiority.)

Several of these factors were considered by Mike Berg and Paul Pretiz in a very informative book subtitled "Grassroots Christianity Latin American Style."[25] They gathered a great amount of information about a variety of movements, focusing their study on grassroots churches which they define as "those churches whose origin cannot be immediately traced to an intentional foreign missionary action or which have broken sufficiently from established groups to display a distinctly local flavor."[26] Paying special attention to numerical growth and to indigeneity, they have disregarded Barrett's typology and have created their own, which is rather imprecise, but they do provide important clues for missiological observation and reflection about what we call popular Protestantism. Berg and Pretiz ask important missiological questions, ones that I find explosive in Latin America: "Can the Gospel take root in the soul of a people so deeply that it becomes a folk religion? Can such grassroots Christianity entirely displace an old folk religion? What shape will the Church take in such a situation?"[27]

In terms of mission, Africa presents us with a challenge that is exceedingly interesting and has much to teach. David Barrett did a study in which he proved that when in an African community the whole Bible was translated into the people's language two things happened: there were schisms and divisions, and remarkable numerical growth. Barrett's study is aptly titled *Schism and Renewal* and is concerned particularly with the situation of Protestantism.[28] As long as the Bible was not available in the people's language, the missionary was the sole spokesperson for the truth, for God's will, for theology, and for everything else. When the whole Bible became available in the language of ordinary people, they began to say that they no longer needed this filter provided by the missionary: Now we can read God's word directly, because God speaks our language. The natives have begun to read the word *with their own eyes.*

Thus the people in these new African churches begin to do things in their own way. Many missionaries or missiologists who have been trained in the western world have the impression that in the way they do things the natives are out of control or wrong. They even go so far as to deny that such churches are genuine Christian churches. They observe churches with wandering charismatic prophets, pilgrims who go with their staff from town to town; prayer of praise that uses dancing and drums; and various kinds of exorcism as a normal part of church life. These churches that read the Bible with their own eyes have the viewpoint of their own culture. Their faith is centered on Jesus Christ, but they live and express it in the terms of their own geography and history. They normally live within the tension between the universal dimension of their faith, which connects them with Christians of all times and places, and the particular dimension by which they are rooted in their own culture.

In some cases these churches find in the Bible keys for understanding things that the missionary had left behind. I recall a case from my own experience. Once I was in the Peruvian jungle during a meeting of bilingual teachers sponsored by the Summer Institute of Linguistics, and a teacher from a native community joyfully told me that they now had the Gospel of Mark translated into their language. He told me that in the Gospel of Mark he had found many verses about demons and spirits. I told him it was true. He then said something like this: "Our linguist has told us that all this about spirits and demons was for the first century, not for today." Then he looked me firmly in the eyes and told me emphatically, "But we know that there really are demons and spirits: they're around here." I was impressed by the acceptance and respect with which this brother spoke to me of the linguist who had translated the Bible into his language, and at the same time I admired the freedom with which this indigenous teacher made his own reading of the word based on his own experience and connecting the text with what he had lived.

In the case of Latin American popular Protestantism, missiologists interested in evangelization and numerical church growth were the first ones to pay attention to the missiological lessons that could be drawn from Pentecostal growth. A statistical study of church growth conducted throughout Latin America by three researchers of the Church Growth school gathered data and offered missiological reflections. One important fact was that mainline and conservative foreign missions working in these countries were far less successful than Pentecostals in attracting people. Pentecostal foreign presence in the missionary force was very small by comparison, but its work seemed more fruitful.[29] Peter Wagner focused on numerical indicators and his pragmatic analysis stayed on the surface for want of theological connecting points and sociological sensitivity.[30] Kenneth Strachan applied some of his observations to the development of an evangelistic methodology that was influential among Protestants in the 1960s and 1970s.[31]

However, what I find most significant for missiology is the way in which some Catholic missiologists have come to the point where they can formulate a more precise understanding of popular Protestantism, starting from questions on their ability to attract the masses and moving then to the service of Christian mission. We must devote attention to them in the next chapter.

8

Popular Protestantism and Catholic Missiology

Missionary expansion of Protestantism in Latin America has affected the Roman Catholic Church in various ways. One effect of the dynamic presence of an alternative religious force has been an exodus of nominal Catholics to the ranks of Protestant churches. Yet another effect has been the unleashing of a process of self-criticism that reached even official levels and helped strengthen Catholicism in the region. A typical case was Peru where, according to Jesuit historian Jeffrey Klaiber, in the early twentieth century Protestantism and liberalism emerged as challenges influencing the church: "The urgent need to deal with the modern world, albeit timidly and in a limited way, and reach agreement with the modernizing groups in Peruvian society, was largely a reaction to these threats."[1]

In more recent years the rapid growth of popular Protestantism has heightened the concerns of the hierarchies in the region. One of the best-informed Catholic scholars in this regard is the Belgian Passionist priest Franz Damen, who was executive secretary of the Department of Ecumenism of the Bolivian Bishops Conference. Damen noted the fact that "according to statistics in Latin America, every hour on average 400 Catholics join Protestant sects, who now represent an eighth, i.e., 12.5 percent of the population of the continent."[2] Damen also studied the reactions of hierarchies to this phenomenon by pointing out that, in numerical terms, this exodus of Catholics to Protestantism has already surpassed what happened in Europe in the sixteenth century. It is nevertheless noteworthy that it was Catholic specialists in missionary research like Damen who took the time to do a realistic, missiological, and pastoral analysis. The Protestant studies that overemphasized sociological analysis criticized the popular churches because they did not serve the cause of left-wing political militancy, the so-called popular struggles in the 1960s and 1970s. They failed to notice its missiological nature.

SECT: THE CONSTRUCTION OF AN IMAGE

In considering some reactions by Catholic missiology, we must note again that in official Catholic terminology the term used most often for grassroots or popular Protestantism is *sects*. Catholic missiological literature in Latin America plainly shows that for the hierarchies, and for their missiologists, it is the popular forms of Protestantism that are most disturbing and arouse the greatest anxiety. This is reflected in a book meant to encourage mission by missiologist Roger Aubry, who, in a chapter entitled "Sects and Evangelization,"[3] drew attention to the growth of "sects":

> We are not speaking here about the traditional Protestant churches with which we maintain ecumenical relations, sharing the same yearnings for evangelization, justice, and peace. We are talking about the so-called *sects*, most of which have come from up north during this century, particularly in recent decades. Among them we center our attention on the pentecostal-type sects or those with pentecostal leanings in their worship expressions and in their doctrinal structure.[4]

Among the sects that Aubry mentions as problematic due to their rapid growth are the Assemblies of God, the Church of the Nazarene, the Church of Christ, the Church of God, and the churches that emphasize healing. Citing data from the publication *Pro Mundi Vita*, Aubry noted that these sects are growing vigorously and "represent almost 80 percent of non-Catholic confessions; for example, they constitute 73 percent in Nicaragua, 83 percent in Costa Rica, 84 percent in Guatemala."[5] Utilizing official data from Catholic bishops' conferences, Aubry pointed to the contrast in the case in Chile where Pentecostals are 14 percent of the population, whereas the remaining Protestants are not even 1 percent, and he notes that in Brazil Pentecostals "constitute 70 percent of Protestantism." In his typology Aubry obviously makes a distinction between two groups: *those that are growing*, which he calls sects and characterizes as Pentecostals, and the rest, which he calls Protestant churches.

This same attitude is reflected in a handbook intended to offer guidance on the sects, in which an Argentinean Catholic expert says that

> for years ecumenical relations have preferred to establish another name less charged with negative connotations to designate the "sects," thereby recognizing they also have some positive elements that deserve the church's consideration. Today the preferred expression is "free religious movements" even though their proselytizing activity is always viewed as "sectarian."[6]

Inasmuch as the book studies Baptists, Adventists, and Pentecostals, along with Jehovah's Witnesses and Mormons, it is obvious that the same terminology that we have been noting is being followed. Without making the necessary theological distinctions, it is obvious that those forms of Protestantism that evangelize and are growing numerically are presented as sectarian, and that is how they are distinguished from the rest.

One might expect that this Protestant growth would come to be understood from a missiological perspective inasmuch as Latin American societies are becoming increasingly pluralistic, but the vocabulary of official documents from Catholic bishops displays a hostile stance that has been hardening. A degree of evolution in how the different types of Protestantism in Latin America are described can be detected. The documents of the assemblies of CELAM, the Latin American Bishops' Conference, are a good index to measure this evolution. At their 1955 meeting in Rio de Janeiro, the bishops made no distinction but simply noted "the serious problem posed by Protestantism and the various non-Catholic movements that have been introduced into Latin American nations, threatening their traditional Catholic culture."[7]

Thirteen years later at Medellín (1968) the bishops did not use the terms *Protestantism* or *sect* but insisted on different types of ecumenical cooperation with the "various Christian confessions and communions."[8] Eleven years later at Puebla (1979) a distinction was made between "churches," with which ecumenism is practiced and that participate with Catholics in bilateral or multilateral councils, and, on the other side, "the 'free religious movements' (popularly 'sects')."[9] About them, the document says "we cannot fail to notice that these groups indulge in marked forms of proselytism, biblical fundamentalism, and strict literalism with respect to their own doctrines."[10] At Santo Domingo (1992) the pope had harsh words for sects. Speaking to the Latin American bishops, he said,

> Like the Good Shepherd, you are to feed the flock entrusted to you and defend it from rapacious wolves. A source of division and discord in your ecclesial communities are—as you well know—the sects and "pseudo-spiritual" movements mentioned in the *Puebla Conclusions*, whose aggressiveness and expansion must be faced.[11]

Further on the pope invoked the conspiracy theory to explain the "advance of the sects":

> Moreover, we should not underestimate a particular strategy aimed at weakening the bonds that unite Latin American countries and so to undermine the kinds of strength provided by unity. To that end, significant amounts of money are offered to subsidize proselytizing campaigns that try to shatter such Catholic unity.[12]

WHAT CAN CATHOLICS LEARN?

The previously mentioned work of Franz Damen takes a different tack and is in the line of what we may call a "Catholic missionary approach," in contrast to what would be a "police approach," which condemns these churches and seeks to disparage them because they can no longer be suppressed by force as in the past. The "missionary approach" had been used by some Catholic scholars in Chile, such as the Jesuit Ignacio Vergara and the Carmelite Ireneo Rosier, who approached Protestantism, including the Pentecostal movement, with scholarly honesty and critical sympathy.[13] Rather than trying to halt this advance by using state power and social coercion, the Catholic church ought to investigate its own pastoral and missionary faults and even ask "What can we learn from these movements?" José Comblin, a missionary in Brazil, has been more recently one of the most eloquent voices expressing this view:

> Do the pentecostal churches has something to teach us? It is customary in the Catholic world to look down our noses at pentecostals, calling them "alienated" or "inferior." Meanwhile they are growing overwhelmingly and at an ever-increasing rate. Pentecostals can be found in every village in northeastern Brazil, even in the remotest areas. There are even cities in which the majority of the population is evangelical. Their chapels and communities multiply and their rate of growth far surpasses that of the Base Ecclesial Communities. It is as overwhelming as a tidal wave that nothing can stop.[14]

Comblin focuses his study specifically on Pentecostals, relying on what they say about themselves, on the systematic approach of social scientists, and on firsthand observation by Catholics.

The question of firsthand observation of Pentecostals by Catholics has missiological significance. I have found Catholics who write about Pentecostals and define policies about them but have never been to a Pentecostal church and have never talked to a Pentecostal pastor. They remind me of Pentecostal converts from popular Catholicism who have never read a Catholic Bible commentary and are unaware of changes in the Catholic church, yet they preach and teach about Catholicism. After a fact-finding trip of immersion among Catholics and Protestants in the cities of São Paulo and Caracas, Phillip Berryman reflects on this ignorance about Pentecostalism among Catholics who hold positions of responsibility. He interviewed an auxiliary bishop in Rio de Janeiro at the time the press was referring to impressive numerical growth of evangelicals, and he also talked to a widely known liberation theologian about the issue. He found both defensive and uninformed. Berryman reflects:

> A conservative bishop and a major liberation theologian had both questioned the reality of evangelical advance and emphasized the strengths of the Catholic church in very similar terms. Virtually none of my Catholic interviewees had devoted any attention to examine evangelical churches firsthand.[15]

Berryman's book is valuable precisely because it is the result of on-site observation, extended interviews with Catholics and Protestants of different tendencies, as well as use of research from social scientists in the two countries he visited. His book is a substantive source for missiological reflection.

FIVE MISSIOLOGICAL LESSONS

We have noted in a previous chapter the endeavor of self-criticism that went along with the rise of some strains of liberation theologies, a self-criticism that was partly the result of the Protestant advance and of Vatican II.[16] In assessing this growth of popular Protestantism from a missiological and pluralistic perspective, Catholic scholars indicate key points in Catholic missionary strategy that ought to be reconsidered. I will take up five of them.[17]

First, Damen refutes conspiracy theories that explain the Pentecostal movement as part of an intentional cultural penetration from the United States that is financed with political purposes. We might at this point recall the words of the pope in Santo Domingo quoted above. From firsthand observation and acquaintance with the movement Damen concludes that "it still seems impossible to prove that there is a strategic connection between U.S. expansionist policy toward Latin America and the spread of religious sects in the continent."[18]

His observations and studies have enabled him to verify three facts that are very important and must be taken into account: first, that the sects are primarily a religious rather than a political phenomenon; second, that a growing number of sects are not North American but Latin American in origin; and third, that many of them quickly take root in the country and become independent. Damen thinks that the defensive stance of the hierarchies must be criticized. He thinks that such a stance leads to false interpretations that do not seriously study the reality of Protestant advance, and that Catholic leaders are deceiving themselves when they do not recognize the truth of their own pastoral and theological failures. In his conclusion he calls for self-criticism and realism:

> I think that the avalanche image reflects not so much the reality of the sects as the state of soul and mind of the Catholic church in Latin America. Ever since the conquest, it has been used to wielding hegemony in the religious field, and it has still not reached the point of accepting and assuming religious pluralism as a reality. The image of an avalanche is useful insofar as it helps it avoid dealing with the complex reality of the sects.[19]

Second, these Catholic missiologists highlight and admire the ability of the popular churches to *mobilize all their members in the task of evangelization.* Thus, for example, Roger Aubry describes what he calls "active participation in the life and mission of the church." Using traditional language, he admires the fact that "all converts are active members who have to promote the life of the sect and work toward the conversion of those who are not yet converted."[20] Aubry recognizes that this evangelizing effort is "very generous," but he criticizes the fact that sometimes "it seems more proselytizing than evangelizing." To him it seems that evangelization ought to take place in an atmosphere of respect and freedom, but that some methods do not take that into account. His conclusion has a note of self-criticism: "We must confess that on our side, despite the serious efforts that are being made, few lay people are actively and creatively involved in the pastoral activity of their parish or their church."[21]

Here Aubry is in agreement with Damen, who also describes the evangelical missionary drive as a distinctive note of the popular churches:

> With their systematic and enthusiastic proselytizing, the pentecostal and millenarian sects present themselves as deeply missionary communities of faith where the task of evangelization does not become the responsibility of a specialized group of people, for it is the *mission* of each member of the community.[22]

Damen is struck by the fact that the Pentecostal groups that are growing most rapidly are also those that in proportion to their size have the fewest foreign missionaries. This leads him to the self-critical observation:

> They thereby expose a weakness of the established churches, i.e., their relative inactivity in mission today, the tremendous difficulty that they find in developing a missionary spirituality of the communities of faith, and their seeming inability to initiate lay missionary programs.[23]

It is Comblin who poses most clearly a key missiological question. He considers that this missionary outreach may be the most decisive factor of Pentecostal life and adds: "Pentecostals do not do this out of a sense of obligation but because of an inner compulsion.Their testimony wells up inside of them and they can do no less than speak in season and out of season." Then he poses these questions:

> All of these people were once Catholic. When they were Catholics they remained inert and passive, timid and withdrawn. They did not dare to speak in public. What happened to them? Did Jesus change them, as they say? Are they indeed inspired by the Holy Spirit?[24]

Third, from the missiological standpoint it is noteworthy that some of these scholars have come to the point of recognizing that the evangelizing effort of the popular Protestant churches provides *some people their first experience of Christian faith*. Thus, for example, before the meeting of Latin American bishops at Puebla (1979) the CELAM Missions Department circulated a working document called *Missionary Panorama* that described the "new missionary situations" in Latin America. The *Panorama* recognized that "most Latin Americans generally describe themselves as 'Roman, Catholic, and Apostolic,' even though their ecclesial adhesion is often based more on a customs-based attachment to the church than on deep faith convictions."

This document also considered the way in which certain social processes such as migration reveal the weakness of the bond between the masses and the Catholic church, or simply—we would say—the total absence of a personal and saving faith in Jesus Christ. The missiologist John Gorski observes that in facing these new situations, "if a typically missionary dynamic is not sufficiently present in the general pastoral work of the Catholic church, it is characteristic of the activity of the sects." The existence of this missionary drive explains how

> the Protestant and other sects are profitably penetrating these urban and rural milieux. They offer many people their first concrete and challenging experience of the Word of God, of community and ecclesial mutual aid, and of moral transformation. These sects often harvest the fruits of latent religious feelings and of a missionary drive that is absent from Catholic pastoral activity.[25]

A *fourth characteristic* of these churches that Catholic missiology highlights is *their truly grassroots or popular character.* The methodology, liturgy, and style of these churches very much reveal that their members and leaders come from the people. In this sense they are truly contextual, even though they have never spun out theories about contextualization. The Spanish Jesuit José Luis Idígoras, who was a missionary in Peru for several decades, highlighted this aspect with greater precision in a study of "the popular character of the Protestant sects." Idígoras held that in North America Protestants were "people of popular religion. Let us consider the many pentecostal congregations that are obviously uninterested in anything speculative and directly seek charisms that can be seen and felt and are effective in the community."[26]

He then discussed the growth of this type of popular Protestantism in Latin America and even the emergence of variations of a local nature that have been appearing:

> Their founders are not theologians or men of the hierarchy. They are Christians of the poor classes whose theology is rudimentary, who are endowed with heavenly visions, and preachers who wander through plazas and streets. They speak of their spiritual experience and draw in people of their own milieu who in turn become spontaneous preachers without grandiose theologies. It is the people's world of living experience that prevails over the world of science and power.[27]

Idígoras contrasts this popular nature of Pentecostal pastors with the elitism of Catholic priests. He criticizes the secularizing training that priests receive and goes so far as to say: "And that is why it is not surprising that among the priests in our countries some are hostile to popular religion or promote secularized systems, such as integrating historical materialism into theology."[28]

By contrast, he tells us:

> The reality of Protestant pastors is generally quite different. They come from the ordinary people as much as Catholics. But they live closer to the people and their training tends to be less philosophical and more

theological. It is fundamentally based on reading and interpreting the Bible, without much use of exegetical methods. That way they more easily retain the popular mentality with which they began their training. And so their preaching is closer to the religious feeling of the people.[29]

Finally, in fifth place, these churches are observed to create *an atmosphere of community* and family for the poor in the city. In this regard Angel Salvatierra, a priest and scholar for the Ecuadorian Catholic bishops, offers another example of pastoral and missiological self-criticism. He points out that while facing the disproportionate population growth in Latin America, Catholicism finds itself with its priest shortage and its pastoral practice limited by "excessive concentration of responsibilities on priests." Here he observes that these methods are in contrast with the evangelizing and missionary practice of the evangelical popular churches.

> The sects try to respond with their own methods to the religious demand of the poor and outcast, who find in them a space of community and brotherly-sisterly life, a place where they can celebrate faith by giving the senses and emotions free rein, a community that makes them discover their evangelizing mission and even enables them to take an active religious role based on the Word of God, a religious vision of existence in tune with the sense of dependence on the sacred experienced by the people, and a family-like help in dealing with material needs.[30]

The factors noted by Salvatierra are said to be "those that offer a primary explanation of the growing penetration of the sects" and can only be perceived by a judgment that takes the dimension of the sacred seriously. In this he coincides with Comblin who also underlines "fraternal community" and "personal worth" as realities provided by these popular churches. He emphasizes the personal care and the contrast with the Catholic experience. Based on his own pastoral experience in the Brazilian northeast, he says:

> What one immediately notices in any of the Pentecostal churches is the warm personal concern. At a time when the Catholic church—alleging a paucity of priests—has reduced to almost nothing its personal attention for the vast majority of Catholics, Pentecostal caring provides a very attractive alternative for many people.[31]

It seems that this is the point at which the analyses of popular Protestantism made by social scientists, historians, and theologians of a liberationist bent who are highly politicized have most fallen short. A convergence has recently been taking place between studies from Protestant sources and approaches by Catholic missiologists, that is, specialists who bring to the study concerns informed by the theology and history of the missions, and by the life of the churches in a broader sense than the strictly political. These authors seem more open to accepting the situation of religious pluralism in Latin America, and hence they approach popular Protestantism with a less hostile attitude.[32]

The recognition of these qualities of popular Protestantism does not mean that these Catholic authors have put aside their own convictions about the church of Rome. Each of the works cited also sharply criticizes Pentecostals. However, these assessments represent a step forward in comprehending the differences and similarities between Protestants and Catholics when one thinks of Christian mission in the twenty-first century. The fundamental question is thus whether Catholicism can see popular Protestantism as God's work in the world, as a fruit of the action of the Holy Spirit. These same questions are posed to many Protestants in the older denominations, who also feel challenged, if not threatened, by the growth of popular Protestantism.

CHANGES IN CATHOLICISM

Missiological approaches have had their effect in the more recent changes that have taken place within the Roman Catholic Church. Perhaps the most precise indicator has been the recent synod of bishops of the Americas, held from November 16 to December 12, 1997, in Rome. It brought together around three hundred bishops and cardinals. Latin American bishops met with those of the United States and Canada, thereby pointing to a strategy intended to achieve greater official coordination between these regions. Emphasis was placed on what is known as the new evangelization; "the church in the past had stressed sociological solutions to poverty whereas now the emphasis should be on conversion."[33] The new regional structure will mean in practice, for example, greater financial aid from North to South and coordination of efforts on Hispanics in the United States, who have been becoming Protestants at a rate that concerns Catholics.

The document *Ecclesia in America* is the text of the post-synodal Apostolic Exhortation that the pope presented in Mexico on January 22, 1999. In it one finds an official summary of the pastoral and social agenda of the church of Rome for the coming years. The document deals in one paragraph with Protestants, and what it says about them is revealing. As we saw earlier, Rome always distinguishes between the Protestant churches that participate in the ecumenical dialogue led from Geneva by the World Council of Churches and the more dynamic and evangelizing Pentecostal churches, which it calls sects. *Ecclesia in America* states: "The proselytizing activity of the sects and new religious groups in many parts of America is a grave hindrance to the work of evangelization." It then mentions the ecumenical attitudes that Catholics ought to have, but it leaves no room for doubt about Catholic exclusivism: "These attitudes, however, must not be such that they weaken the firm conviction that only in the Catholic Church is found the fullness of the means of salvation established by Jesus Christ."[34]

There is also a self-critical effort that has two significant aspects. One refers to pastoral methodologies and proposes that in view of the Protestant advance the church should undertake "a thorough study, to be carried out in each nation and at the international level, to ascertain why many Catholics leave the Church."

> Pastoral policies will have to be revised, so that each particular Church can offer the faithful more personalized religious care, strengthen the structures of communion and mission, make the most of the evangelizing possibilities of a purified popular religiosity, and thus give new life to every Catholic's faith in Jesus Christ.[35]

The second point of self-criticism has to do with a change of emphasis from the social to the spiritual. The document notes the observations of some of the participants in the synod to the effect that

> it is necessary to ask whether a pastoral strategy directed almost exclusively to meeting people's material needs has not in the end left their hunger for God unsatisfied, making them vulnerable to anything which claims to be of spiritual benefit.[36]

As we pointed out earlier in this chapter, several Catholic scholars of Latin American Protestantism had been drawing attention to this question, referring particularly to the popular Protestant churches where what people find primarily is not money or social services but "an experience of God." The document reaches the conclusion that

> a Church which fervently lives the spiritual and contemplative dimension, and which gives herself generously to the service of charity, will be an ever more eloquent witness to God for men and women searching for meaning in their lives.[37]

What the synod document points out is something that any attentive observer may now notice in Latin America: Catholic priests and lay people are imitating many of the pastoral and evangelization methods that have been created and used by Protestants, especially by the popular churches. Thus, for example, many Catholic television programs have the same structure as Protestant programs, the popular hymns from the 1970s and 1980s have been incorporated into Catholic songbooks, and Bible study in small groups and meetings in homes with time for testimony, biblical meditation, and prayer are now being used. In some cases the methods have been modified and adapted, but in other cases it has become hard to distinguish what is Catholic from what is Protestant.

This Catholic awakening constitutes a challenge to the identity of Protestants and to their creativity. They force us to think about many aspects of the practical life of the churches. Today, for example, Catholic bookstores have more abundant and varied material on Bible study, group dynamics, work with young people and adolescents, use of art for Christian education, videos on

Christian and biblical themes, either produced originally in Spanish or translated, than Protestant bookstores.

Even so, beyond questions of method, the changes in Catholicism force us to define what are the distinguishing features of our Protestant faith. We ought to ask, If there is a church that successfully imitates evangelical methods, how are we different from it? Why do we continue to exist as different churches? That poses for us the theological problem of the foundations of Protestant faith expressed in the various "faces of Protestantism," to use Míguez Bonino's phrase. As we try to show in the next chapter, theological and identity issues are important, and Protestants have to use the missiological means provided to them by understanding their own history and theology. Although a postmodern stance toward faith relegates theological issues to the background, they are indispensable for understanding the missionary reality posed by popular Protestantism.

9

Missiological Reflection on Belief, Experience, Structure

The notes of popular Protestantism that Catholic missiologists have been highlighting are not really the characteristics of the classic Protestantism that arose in the sixteenth century. In all honesty, we cannot say that the Lutheran or Calvinist churches were characterized by mobilizing all the faithful for mission, by having members and pastors from among the lower levels of society, or by their evangelizing zeal. Although many Latin American Protestants, including many Pentecostals, see Luther and Calvin as patriarchal figures in their spiritual history, the immediate predecessors of Latin American Protestantism were actually the Pietists, Moravians, and eighteenth-century Methodists, who were precursors of the great Protestant missionary movement that was to flourish in the nineteenth century. It is important to keep in mind that in these movements there are clear portents of the Pentecostal movement that has flourished in the twentieth century.[1]

Thus in trying to imagine Christian mission in the twenty-first century, it is well to pose questions such as: What can Latin American Protestants learn from their forebears in the faith? Likewise, what can they learn from this popular Protestantism, which has grown by leaps and bounds? If one observes the beliefs and way of life of Latin American Protestants, the relationship with the Pietists, Moravians, and Methodists—our parents in the faith—is more evident than the relationship that we might have with Luther and Calvin—our grandparents in the faith. Nevertheless, we generally invoke our grandparents in the faith more than our parents. Reexamining our inheritance may turn out to be important when we look toward the future and consider the specific missionary challenge posed to us at the beginning of the twenty-first century: Latin American participation in Christian mission on a global scale. This examination of history clarifies a question that is important for mission: the relationship between *belief* about the content of faith, *experience* of faith, and *structure* for spreading the faith, as it has been given in the various forms of Protestantism.

This is precisely the point that must be highlighted because both the great Protestant missionary movement of the eighteenth and nineteenth centuries and the missionary drive of Latin American evangelicals and Pentecostals in the twentieth century *are directly related to the concept and practice of the priesthood of all believers.* This concept was formulated first by Luther, and if we read him in context, it entailed a rejection of two evils prevailing in the Christendom that he was seeking to reform: sacramentalism and clericalism. In other words, the exclusive power claimed by the institutional church for administering divine grace through external practices despite the corrupt moral condition into which that very institution had fallen, and the monopoly of clergy on the tasks proper to the life of the church, in which the faithful ended up being mere spectators.[2]

Luther, however, failed to create new structures that would facilitate the participation of all believers as priests of God in mutual ministry. A century after Luther the Lutheran churches themselves had fallen into sacramentalism and clericalism. Pietism and the revivals in Europe were movements of spiritual renewal that succeeded in creating new and contextual structures and practices that facilitated the priesthood of all believers. This fundamental concept of Protestant faith cannot be separated from a vision of the work of the Holy Spirit in the world and of the gifts that the Spirit gives to all believers, beliefs that are fundamental to the practice and theology of mission. Thus it seems to me that I have to pose the following as a thesis worth investigating: The evangelical missionary vigor of the eighteenth and nineteenth centuries *came from the Holy Spirit and could be made manifest when structures were created that allowed for the exercise of the gifts of all believers and their participation in mission.*

Likewise, the missionary vigor of the Latin American popular Protestant churches in the twentieth century came from an impulse of the Holy Spirit, who finds churches ready to recognize that the Spirit gives gifts to all and to structure themselves so as to allow the impulse of the Spirit to be made manifest. The observations in this chapter will move in two directions: a careful consideration of the historic process that makes it possible to establish with some clarity the continuity between Pietism, the Wesleyan revival, and the Pentecostal movement, and the course of missiological thinking during the twentieth century and into the present, which has been rediscovering the importance of recognizing, understanding, and following the action of the Holy Spirit in Christian mission.

OUR CLOSEST PROTESTANT RELATIVES

It is precisely the approach to mission that forces us to reexamine what our Protestant legacy is and how it can provide us with keys for mission in the twenty-first century. As has already been said, we Latin American Protestants are much closer to the Pietists and revivalists of the eighteenth and nineteenth centuries than to the sixteenth-century reformers. To reflect on our participation in mission, we need to explore this part of our legacy more carefully. What we have received from Pietism, the Moravian movement, and the revivals can help us forge missionary models for the twenty-first century.

More than once I have referred to the precision with which the historian Justo L. González offers us a description of the origins of the modern missionary movement that unfolded during the eighteenth century as something new in the history of Protestantism. Interest in missions went hand in hand with "an *awakening of individual religiosity.*" One note that González highlights is that

the leaders of this new awakening *were protesting against the rigidity of the older Protestant orthodoxy*, and although they themselves were for the most part properly trained theologians, they tended to *emphasize the importance of practical Christian life over theological formulas.*[3]

In addition to this pragmatism, the Pietists insisted on the personal experience of conversion in individual obedience to the divine commands. They did not have a sectarian spirit, because they remained within their own churches or denominations, in order to be, as it were, a leaven of renewal. As González states, "If sometimes that was not the outcome of such movements, it was not due so much to the schismatic spirit of their founders as to the rigidity of the churches within which they arose."[4]

The German Pietism of Spener and Francke, men of great knowledge and piety, had an influence on zealous promoters of mission like Count Zinzendorf, and then on Wesley in the British Isles and on the Great Awakening in North America. Protestant missionary expansion therefore brought along with it the marks of Pietism and the movements that followed it:

The Protestant missionaries of the nineteenth century tended to emphasize the necessity of an individual decision by converts much more than Catholic missionaries, or even the first Protestant missionaries had done.[5]

Kenneth Scott Latourette, another widely known historian of Christian missions, established the same historic connections when he presented the Carnahan conferences in Buenos Aires in 1956. After making a masterful presentation of contemporary Protestantism and of the challenges facing it at that time, Latourette stated that

the vital minorities of Protestants in Europe are largely from the Puritan-Pietist-evangelical tradition. That current is even more responsible for growth in numbers and influence outside Europe. This means that world Protestantism increasingly has a Puritan-Pietist-evangelical complexion.[6]

These three descriptive notes—Puritan, Pietist, and evangelical—which are the mark of missionary Protestantism, are connected to the theological notes proper to the Reformation of the sixteenth century that were developed more thoroughly by the type of churches that are known in England as free churches. In another missiological text Latourette says that "these represent the extreme wing of Protestantism and are those which have stressed most salvation by faith and the priesthood of all believers."[7] He also points out how in expanding through this missionary current during the nineteenth century, in practical life, the Protestant movement went on to accent those doctrines as well as the right and duty of individual judgment in religious decisions. He concludes, "And doing this brings them closer than ever in their witness to the heart of the gospel."[8]

The characteristics that I have emphasized in these descriptions are the ones that are most commonly associated with the majority of Latin American Protestants. Their extreme aspects, such as excessive individualism, have often been criticized with the use of terms like *pietistic,* always negatively. However, popular Protestantism in Latin America displays these Pietist notes of spiritual enthusiasm, personal conversion, and attention to the visible practice of faith more than to doctrinal formulations, and along with them goes missionary fervor. My claim here is that these popular Pentecostal-type churches that have grown notably in Latin America often embody the notes of the missionary drive of the Moravians and Pietists better than other Protestant churches that regard themselves as guardians of the Protestant legacy. I am referring to *the practice* of these grassroots churches rather than to their ability to repeat a formal theological discourse. I also thereby intend to say that the renewed and Pietist Protestantism that forged the eighteenth- and nineteenth-century missionary movement created structures that made it possible to embody the priesthood of all believers in practice better than the Lutheran and Calvinist churches of the sixteenth century. The popular Protestant movement in Latin America has likewise created structures that facilitate its mission.

If we take into account the observations of the Catholic missiologists that I considered in the previous chapter, we recognize the resemblance between what they describe and what González and Latourette are describing. However, I also think it important to state that today's grassroots churches are expressing these evangelical notes and this missionary drive *within conditions proper to the culture of poverty* in which they move. That is, the Pentecostal movement is a contextual and popular expression of the legacy of sixteenth-century Protestantism, an expression that has emerged within the world of poverty in North America and Europe, as well as in Latin America. In both instances, the Protestant legacy was mediated by the Pietist or revivalist experience. The term *popular Protestantism* fits because contextualization has taken place in a creative way in response to the particular features of the world of the poor.

Two clarifications must be made at this point. First, I will say again that here I am not talking about the neo-charismatic or post-denominational churches that have come on the scene in the last decade or so but rather about the grassroots popular churches, most of which are related to the Pentecostal movement. Second, I do not share the European-rooted view of interpreters such as Jean Pierre Bastian who refuse to recognize as Protestant the Pentecostal movement and popular Protestantism, simply because they do not bear the marks of the middle-class culture with which Protestantism tends to be identified in Europe and with which the older Protestant churches in Latin America are identified.

As we have seen, there are efforts to explain the transforming and missionary drive of the popular churches as a simple reflection of the social and economic conditions in which they emerge and spread. From a missiological standpoint, we can call this "sociologism" because there is no consideration of the possibility that these churches might have their own spiritual dynamic and a spiritual message that explains their expansionary and transforming power. Sociologism starts from the assumption that particular religious forms ought to fulfill a determined social role and evolve in a predictable manner, according to the hypothesis of the sociologist, for whom neither theological concepts nor a vision of the Christian churches in their historic continuity is of any importance.

By contrast, the starting point for the missiological view is a theological vision of the church and its mission in society. It cannot fail to see the role that the different forms of Christianity have played in the transmission of the Christian experience and the message of Christ over twenty centuries of history. Hence, it seems more appropriate to us to open our minds and our eyes to the possibility that the same Holy Spirit who caused the missionary vision to arise from among the poor refugees who made up the Pietist and Moravian people is today energizing the popular churches that are growing in response to the deep needs of the Latin American masses. I think that on this point the reflection of a theology of mission can help us to better capture the relationship among belief, experience, and mission structure.

THE HOLY SPIRIT AND THE MISSION OF THE CHURCH

In the second half of the twentieth century there was a growing conviction that it is the Holy Spirit who takes the initiative in carrying out Christian mission, not only because the Spirit drives the church's own missionary dynamism, but because the Spirit is in action in the world creating conditions and preparing the recipients of the message. No theologian has expressed this with more clarity than Emil Brunner in *The Misunderstanding of the Church,* which is a valuable contribution to our thinking on the church at this point. In this book, originally published in 1951, Brunner reminds us that in order to understand what the church is we must understand it in its *continuity* from its origins in Christ until the present. This poses a fundamental question, which Brunner believes has New Testament support, that is, "that it is not merely a question of the continuity of the word—the maintenance of the original doctrine—but also of the continuity of a life: that is life flowing from the Holy Ghost." Brunner presents an argument and at the same time challenges us to recognize that something is missing in the modern view:

> The fellowship of Jesus lives under the inspiration of the Holy Spirit; that is the secret of its life, of its communion, and of its power. To use a blunt modern word, the Spirit supplies the "dynamism" of the *Ecclesia.* . . . We ought to face the New Testament witness with sufficient candor to admit that in this "pneuma," which the *Ecclesia* was conscious of possessing,

there lie forces of an extra-rational nature, which are mostly lacking among us Christians of today.[9]

Brunner develops at some length his understanding of this "extra-rational" action of the Spirit and reminds us that

the Holy Ghost is God: but the *Ecclesia* in its experience of the Holy Spirit experienced God as the One whose impact on human life penetrates these depths of the soul, touches these hidden energies, mobilizes and harnesses them in the service of His holy will.[10]

The conclusion to which this theologian leads us further on is quite striking, if we keep in mind that he is a scholar with a deep vocation who wrote a great deal and followed a rigorous methodology. He claims that

theology is not the instrument best adapted to elucidate just *this* aspect of pneumatic manifestations. For theo-*logy* has to do with the Logos and therefore is only qualified to deal with matters which are in some way logical, not with the dynamic in its a-logical characteristics. Therefore the Holy Spirit has always been more or less the stepchild of theology and the dynamism of the Spirit a bugbear for theologians.[11]

In setting forth the way in which the community of Jesus originally spread, Brunner stresses equally the instrumentality of the word of God and the supernatural power of the Spirit. Conversion requires a specific word, but also a power that goes far beyond the word of the preacher. There is a kind of dialectical relationship between the word and the power: "Here the mighty energies of the Spirit are more important than any word, although these energies, insofar as they are those of the Holy Spirit, owe their origin to the Word of God." It is precisely the practice of mission that opens people to the action of the Spirit:

Present day evangelists and missionaries usually realize this fact far better than we theologians, who not only undervalue the dynamic power of the Holy Ghost, but often know simply nothing of it.[12]

Some Protestants enthusiastic for Christian mission in the early twentieth century had highlighted the role of the Holy Spirit as the driving power of mission. Arthur Tappan Pierson (1837-1911), a Presbyterian converted to the healing movement, who edited the well-known missionary magazine *Missionary Review of the World*, emphasized the role of the Holy Spirit in his books. It was he who coined the expression "the evangelization of the world in our generation," the slogan of the Edinburgh missionary conference previously mentioned. Adoniram Judson Gordon (1836-95) was a critic of the notion of Christian mission as a work of civilization, and in his writings he also highlighted the work of the Holy Spirit in mission. Albert Benjamin Simpson (1843-1919), another Presbyterian who was drawn into the healing movement, founded the Christian and Missionary Alliance. He highlighted the work of the Holy Spirit but rejected the idea that the experience of speaking in tongues was necessary for salvation.[13]

To these names we have to add that of Roland Allen, a former Anglican missionary in China whose missiological works were written in the second decade of the twentieth century but only began to find a readership in the 1960s. In *The Spontaneous Expansion of the Church*[14] and *Missionary Methods: St. Paul's or Ours?*[15] he compares the methods of the Anglican missions of his own time with those of the New Testament. Allen emphasizes the marked contrast between the spontaneity of the early church and the bureaucratic and tradition-bound slowness of some modern churches. He explains the difference on the basis both of inadequate structures and lack of faith in the mobilizing power of the Holy Spirit.

In the second half of the twentieth century Protestant missiology underwent a notable renewal, specifically with the contribution of missionaries and evangelists who, starting from self-criticism of their own missionary endeavor, explored the New Testament material with a sense of urgency and openness and rediscovered the reality of the Holy Spirit and the Spirit's role in mission. The topic deserves careful study, but for the moment we limit ourselves to mentioning a series of examples that illustrate the development of this missiological reflection.

In *Pentecost and Mission*[16] Harry Boer, a missionary who served with the Christian Reformed Church in Nigeria, argued that missionary work has paid a great deal of attention to the Great Commission but not enough to Pentecost. The starting point in the New Testament is not the imperative of the command of Jesus but the fullness of the Spirit in the church, which comes at Pentecost. He proposes that the theology of mission be revised and reminds us that

> much has been written about the work of the Holy Spirit in the salvation of men, but very little about His crucial significance for the missionary witness of the Church. The subject has not been wholly ignored but, while it deserved to be central in missionary reflection, it has been allowed to remain in the periphery.[17]

The most systematic work on the relationship among belief, experience, and mission structure is that of Howard Snyder, who for some years was a Free Methodist missionary in Brazil. At the 1974 congress on evangelization at Lausanne he made a seminal presentation on the church.[18] Starting with that work, Snyder began to explore what we can learn from the great revivals in terms of *how a vision of the Holy Spirit was reflected in ways of organizing for mission*. Snyder uses the figure of "new wine and old wineskins" to speak of the tension between spiritual experience and structure. When the new wine of the

Holy Spirit renews the church for mission, the old wineskins are unsuited—they no longer do the job.[19] Snyder studies this process through the centuries. He discovers that the genius of the revivals that have been the source of great missionary advances is the ability to create new wineskins for new situations.

This is especially clear in the case of John Wesley (1703-91), a great preacher whose spiritual life was rich and deep and was combined with a solid theological formation, and hence his message was powerful. Wesley was also a great organizer.[20] His perception of the pastoral needs resulting from increasingly crowded cities at the outset of the Industrial Revolution led him to reorganize the life of local congregations into small groups called classes and bands. This made it possible for the multitudes who followed him within the new industrial society then emerging in England to find a new way to pastor one another. This was a contextual application of the notion of the priesthood of all believers. Thus the concept rediscovered by Luther found structures that enabled it to be applied on a broad scale two centuries later. A Latin American interpreter of Methodism makes the point clearly and vigorously:

> With this important role granted by Methodism to lay believers, a forgotten and buried aspect of early Christianity was retrieved: namely, that it was primarily a lay movement, led by lay people; a movement without hierarchical barriers, with no clergy or priestly caste and no ecclesiastical bureaucracies.[21]

Before the Methodists though, it is well to recall, the Waldensians in the Middle Ages, the Anabaptists in the sixteenth century, and the Moravian Pietists who preceded Wesley practiced discipleship and shepherding in small groups.

In short, openness to the renewing action of the Spirit was an opening to a spiritual experience that revitalized faith and devotion to Jesus Christ, which was then manifested in a missionary and evangelizing impulse. Along with this drive came creativity in methods for announcing the gospel that were appropriate to the new social and cultural settings. Efforts were also made to create pastoral structures that would help new converts grow in their grasp of the faith and in the practice of the new life. As we have seen, the first transcultural missionary impulse from Protestantism was to emerge from these renewed communities.

A note common to the authors that we have considered is that they start from their missionary experiences and from serious reflection on them. When they reflect out of a theological—or more precisely, biblical—framework, they rediscover the central role of the Holy Spirit in mission. Starting from this discovery, they question the closed stances within irrelevant traditions, the ecclesial structures that prevent Christians from participating in mission, and the obsolete methods that prevent the missionary vocation from being fully realized. I want to emphasize that in all these authors that I have mentioned we find a missiological self-criticism of the missionary enterprise, and it comes from persons who are vitally committed to mission. This is not the classic anti-missionary attack that springs from a priori anti-imperialism or from mere academic sophistication. That is why it goes to the sources of the missionary impulse in the Holy Spirit and seeks historic models that can be contextualized for our age.

In Latin America, Allen's ideas were influential in the thinking of Argentinean missiologist Kenneth Strachan, who articulated the vision of In-Depth Evangelism in the 1960s. They were also influential in the missiological reflection of Melvin Hodges, a Pentecostal missionary whose work we will consider later as we study Pentecostal missiology. The In-Depth Evangelism movement and Strachan's thought were precisely the impetus needed to mobilize the entire church and the opening to the action and power of the Holy Spirit to bring that about. Strachan said:

> We cannot convince of sin, we cannot illuminate the darkness, we cannot convert, we cannot regenerate, we cannot build. Only the Spirit of God takes responsibility for such operations whether in the first century or the twentieth century.[22]

Making Strachan's thinking his own, Orlando Costas pointed out that mobilizing the church was a theological and practical necessity, but that it entailed

> a revolution in current missionary strategy. For if the modern church has failed in anything it is in its ecclesiastical professionalism, in the anti-biblical distinction that it has made between professional minister and lay person.[23]

LEARNING FROM THE POOR

At the outset of the twenty-first century we find that we have a vigorously Protestant missionary movement going out from Latin America and taking part in mission on a global scale. Statistics recently compiled indicate that around four thousand Latin American missionaries from some three hundred missionary organizations are in other continents.[24] How useful can the invocation of historic consciousness that we have proposed here be to them? This Latin American missionary vigor is seeking missiological direction and viable models. Can we learn from our forebears? Today Latin American Protestant missiologists have advanced in their understanding of this process and its consequences for Christian mission. That is what we see in the solid work of Valdir Steuernagel on historic models of missionary obedience. This Brazilian missiologist examines and interprets theologically several models of mission that have existed in history, starting from the time of Julian the Apostate, going by way of Francis of Assisi, and extending to the Moravian Brethren. He reminds us of the conversation between Jesus and Nicodemus in John 3, the analogy of the wind as symbol of the breath of the Holy Spirit, and then says:

Mission understood in pneumatological language is a single two-faceted act. It is first perceiving the breath of the Spirit and its direction, and then it is running toward where the Spirit is blowing.[25]

Thus we have here a double movement in the life of the church: first, looking toward what is happening and discerning there the action of the Spirit; and then, in an act of obedience, setting out toward where the Spirit is pointing. Steuernagel sees this as an act that is "always risky and ambiguous, for all human interpretation of God's will is limited, and all obedience is contaminated by history and the reality of our sin."[26]

Discerning the breath of the Spirit requires openness and sensitivity in order to recognize that behind some events that look new and unusual may be the strength and power of the Holy Spirit. The act of obedience demands creativity to forge new structures to serve as vehicles of obedient missionary action at each moment of history.

What, then, are some of the lessons on mission that we can learn from these close relatives of ours? I am going to limit myself to summarizing some points in Steuernagel's seminal work.[27] The missionary practice of the Moravians was the practice of a whole community, which through the experience of suffering and exile had attained internal cohesion and was highly motivated. It sent out a remarkable number of missionaries in comparison to its size. It was a practice that responded to the call of difficult places that demanded an incarnational and costly insertion. This practice was backed by a theology in which the Holy Spirit occupied a central place, but this theology sought expression in simple, comprehensible terms rather than in the classic categories of Greek thought. Count Zinzendorf, one of the guides of the Moravian community, spoke of the Trinity as a family, and making use of a careful study of the Bible's own vocabulary, he spoke of the Holy Spirit as a mother.

Although among the Moravians there was an emphasis on personal salvation, as in Pietism, there was also a strong sense of the community; the community's advice and decisions were taken into account and accepted by the missionaries. There was a firm trust in the preparatory presence of the Spirit in the world, and hence the missionaries did not see themselves as the main heroes or protagonists. The limited resources of the Herrnhut community from which the Moravian missionaries went out necessarily entailed a strategy of self-sustaining missionaries. Each group became responsible for its own survival in the country to which it was sent, and thus the missionaries were free of the control of the ecclesiastical and imperial structures of their age.

Each of these points bears rich lessons that are sometimes in sharp contrast to missionary practices today. Yet Steuernagel also proposes that we must look critically at the Moravian model. Pietist individualism did not allow for sufficient attention to the character of the communities that were to emerge from missionary activity; what was uppermost was the idea of the salvation of individuals. As has been said, the Protestant missionary movement that arose in the mid-eighteenth century, because of its Pietist roots, sought above all the personal experience of faith for every believer in contrast to group conversion or the simple confession of a common creed in a collective way.

The sixteenth-century Reformation has always been regarded as a return to the word of God, a process of purification of the church through a return to the Bible. This task did not end with that generation. The Reformation gave rise to the idea of an *Ecclesia reformata semper reformanda* (A church reformed and always reforming). Missionary Pietism and the Moravian experience were movements of a new reformation through a new openness to the word—not just the word, however, but also the Spirit. In the initial impulse of evangelical and Pentecostal growth among the poor of Latin America there was also a note of return to the sources. It may not always have been a return to the written and rational sources of the faith but certainly to the sources of spiritual vigor centered on the experience of Christ as experience of the power of his name. Even among the ranks of Pentecostals, voices have emerged today calling for a return to the sources of the Bible and self-criticism of a movement that is explosive but also ambiguous.[28]

Self-critical memory of the past, however, should not close our eyes to the vigorous reality of the present, even in the midst of its frailties. Hence I want to end with a challenge from José Comblin, who has written a remarkable book on the Holy Spirit.[29] He believes the dynamism of the Base Ecclesial Communities and Pentecostal churches demonstrates that the Holy Spirit is at work in them. He highlights the experience of the poor and uneducated, who in the heat of their enthusiasm take up the word and become its bearers:

> If these speeches were being made by educated people there would be nothing spiritual about them. They would be natural to people with intellectual training, natural to those whose positions of authority have made them at home with words. The spiritual element is that of radical conversion: the dumb speak. The experience of the Spirit is in taking up speech.[30]

Comblin points to the extraordinary effects that Bible reading produces among the poor, the sense of discovery of the laity who see themselves as actors on behalf of the word, of this word that they seized but that has also seized them. Therein lies the essence of mission:

> The effect of conquering speech is that Christians are becoming missionaries. Those who have discovered words feel impelled to make them public. Missionary vocations are spreading in the communities. The experience of speech reaches its highest point when receivers become transmitters.[31]

This description of what is happening today among the urban masses of North America is like an echo of the fervor that was present in the beginnings of the Protestant missionary movement.

At this point in the history of mission in Latin America the popular Protestant churches have a massive and historic presence that allows for a theological evaluation of the effect that they have had or they may have on Latin American society. We will explore first the Latin American missiological reflection of the evangelical churches and then what is developing from the Pentecostal side, the self-critical vision that is possible within a theological and missiological framework.

10

From Mission to Theology

Thus far we have sketched some facts of Christian mission that challenge us with various issues of a missiological nature. These lands have had a Christian presence for five centuries now, resulting from two great missionary waves, Catholic and Protestant. Today the Latin American world continues to be a laboratory in which movements and trends that will shape Christianity in this new century are acting as a leaven. In this laboratory we have seen the new and old ways of doing mission, the social impact of mission in the past, and the numerical explosion of popular Protestantism and its effects on Catholicism. Before we explore the missionary dynamism emerging from the Latin American churches for participation in global mission, it seems adequate at this point to sketch an outline of the systematic and critical reflection that has been accompanying missionary action; this may give us some keys for understanding Christian mission in this new century. As the emphasis of this book has been the more recent growth of evangelicals and Pentecostals, I am going to focus primarily on evangelical thinking, which is less known in the English-speaking world. The work of ecumenical missiologists such as Mortimer Arias and Emilio Castro has provided an account of the missiological work in Latin American circles related to the World Council of Churches.[1] Orlando Costas also has offered a valuable survey of the missiology from the older Latin American Protestant churches.[2] The missiological reflection from evangelical and Pentecostal churches is not so well known.

TOWARD AN EVANGELICAL THEOLOGY OF MISSION[3]

The missionary ground from which evangelical theology in Latin America has been emerging must be kept in mind. It is the lifeblood of churches that are relatively young and fast growing within the environment of a declining Christendom. This means that evangelical theologians find themselves on the margins of the cultural establishments of their countries but close to the center of the missionary action of their churches. Their interlocutor has been more frequently the evangelical activist with whom they sit in the pew or march on the streets on Sunday rather than the academician crossing the "t"s and dotting

111

the "i"s of the history of Western ideas. They are part of communities that still see the world as a territory to be evangelized for Christ, and the gospel as a transforming message that will bring forth a new spiritual, social, and political creation. For the time being they find themselves in Galilee, but they are committed to taking the transforming gospel to Judea, Samaria, and even unto the ends of the earth.

Approaching the task of doing theology from this missionary stance, we come to experience this beginning of a new century as a transitional moment, one of those periods in which theologizing can be at the same time painful and fertile. Not long ago, in 1992, remembrance of the fifth centennial of the Iberian conquest and christianization of the Americas brought back to the missiological debate the old question of the relationship between mission and empire, evangelization and civilization, gospel and culture, especially within the frame of transcultural mission. The question of how God acts in history, within the ambiguities of the rise and fall of empires, has been posed again with new relevancy. The urgency of the question is also determined by the need for a radical departure from the Constantinian pattern of a missionary enterprise that relied on military power, social coercion, economic conquest, and technological prowess. This demands a fresh look at the biblical pattern.

On the other hand, as we have seen already, around the world today there is a growing awareness that Europe and North America, the strongholds of Christianity at the beginning of the twentieth century, are rapidly becoming a pagan territory where the Christian presence must take again a missionary stance. In the northern world this involves for Christians the perplexing assignment of criticizing and distancing themselves from the culture that Christianity helped to create, learning to live as "resident aliens."[4] Latin America was the first part of the world where this kind of critical appraisal of Christendom took place. The Protestant missionary presence at the beginning of the twentieth century forced upon Catholicism the question of its nominalism, its institutionalism without spirit.[5] Only in the 1960s, with Vatican II and the rise of liberation theologies did Catholics develop a self-critical stance that questioned the cherished assumptions of Christendom in Latin America.[6]

Beginning in the 1960s a growing number of evangelical pastors, missionaries, and theological educators became involved in the search for answers to these questions within the Latin American context of social change and revolution. For this generation neither the ecumenical dialogue of Geneva nor the liberation theologies born in Roman Catholic soil offered adequate answers.[7] Ecumenical theology from Geneva was shaped by a mood and a stance that reflected the uncertainties and the fatigue of a declining Protestantism in Europe. Liberation theology from Catholic sources was heavily dependent on the assumption that Latin America was "a Christian continent." In such a predicament evangelical theologians became engaged in the development of a contextual theology that aimed to be "forged in the heat of Evangelical reality in Latin America, in faithfulness to the Word of God."[8] That theology was not to be "an adaptation of an existing theology of universal validity to a particular situation

. . . aided by benevolent missionary paternalism"; rather, its aim was to offer "a new open-ended reading of Scripture with a hermeneutic in which the biblical text and the historical situation become mutually engaged in a dialogue whose purpose is to place the Church under the Lordship of Jesus Christ in its particular context."[9]

Outside Latin America, evangelicals had been posing similar questions in different contexts. I have recently summarized the process and the way in which evangelism in North America, missionary activism from evangelicals, and the rise of new and vigorous churches in the Third World converged at the Lausanne Congress of Evangelism in 1974.[10] From that event came an important missiological document known as the Lausanne Covenant and a process known as the Lausanne movement.[11] The missiological reflection from evangelicals in Latin America contributed significant elements of reflection and action to the Lausanne movement. This movement made possible a new reading of scripture as a communal exercise involving the multicultural and international fellowship of believers around the planet. Latin Americans made a substantial contribution to the discussions about gospel and culture in the Lausanne-sponsored Willowbank consultation (1978), sharing the conviction that there was an urgent need to develop a fresh reading of the Bible as a dynamic interplay between the text and the interpreters.[12] This contribution was incorporated in the *Willowbank Report,* which sets an agenda for evangelical mission theology. Protestantism can only be enriched and revitalized by it, being ready to accept the consequences of this new dialogical situation:

> Today's readers cannot come to the text in a personal vacuum, and should not try to. Instead, they should come with an awareness of concerns stemming from their cultural background, personal situation, and responsibility to others. These concerns will influence the questions which are put to the Scriptures. What is received back, however, will not be answers only, but more questions. As we address Scripture, Scripture addresses us. We find that our culturally conditioned presuppositions are being challenged and our questions corrected. In fact, we are compelled to reformulate our previous questions and to ask fresh ones. So the living interaction proceeds.[13]

In this process Latin American evangelicals also found valuable parallels and coincidences with the questions being explored by evangelicals in other parts of the world;[14] with the insights of the Anabaptist tradition uncovered creatively by John Howard Yoder;[15] with the probing and questioning of Jacques Ellul into scripture, tradition, and sociology;[16] and with the post-imperial missiology of men such as John Stott, Michael Green, Andrew Walls, and Lesslie Newbigin.[17]

EVANGELICAL MISSIOLOGY AFTER LAUSANNE

In the more recent decades evangelical theologians in Latin America[18] entered in an active and fruitful dialogue at a global level, for which the main foci were the Lausanne movement, the Theological Commission of the World Evangelical Fellowship, and the International Fellowship of Evangelical Mission Theologians. In the case of Latin America most of the contributors to this dialogue have come from the Latin American Theological Fraternity, which was founded in 1970.[19] Within these circles, and in spite of the hostility of some conservative missiologists in the United States,[20] the concerns and the reflections rising from the life of evangelical churches in Latin America have entered the global dialogue. This has proved the validity of the conviction that

> we should seek with equal care to avoid theological imperialism or theological provincialism. A church's theology should be developed by the community of faith out of the Scripture in interaction with other theologies of the past and present, and with the local culture and its needs.[21]

Evangelical thinkers in Latin America have taken a two-pronged theological approach: On the one hand, a *critical task*, which has included an ongoing debate with the liberation theologies that dominated the theological scenario in the 1970s and 1980s. Such a critical task in some ways was a continuation of the debate with the Protestant predecessors of these theologies.[22] The most extensive and organic works embodying this critical approach come from Andrew Kirk,[23] Emilio A. Núñez,[24] and Samuel Escobar.[25] Several other contributions were gathered in a collective volume outlining an Anabaptist commentary about liberation theologies.[26] What is distinctive about the evangelical stance is its emphasis on the primacy of biblical authority in its theological method and its insistence on keeping evangelistic activity at the center of the mission of the church. However, its critical task has also developed a consistent clarification and debate against the theological assumptions—not always explicit—of the so-called Church Growth mission theory, with its overwhelming institutional and propagandistic weight.[27]

On the other hand, evangelical theologians have given themselves to the *constructive task* of developing a theology of mission that expresses the dynamic reality and the missionary thrust of their churches in Latin America. They have been working to provide a solid biblical basis for new patterns of evangelism and discipleship in continuity with their heritage of a Bible-centered form of presence and mission committed to spiritual and social transformation. They have worked on the assumption that if commitment to biblical authority is going to do more than simply pay lip service to it, a fresh exploration is required into the depths of the biblical text, with the questions raised by the Latin American context. Moreover, commitment to biblical authority should not limit itself to certain beliefs in the area of soteriology but also to fresh explorations into a biblically based social ethics.

An eloquent example of this twofold approach may be found in the dense pages of René Padilla's *Mission between the Times*.[28] In this important book and other writings Padilla offers a missiological reflection based on detailed exegesis of the biblical text. A different approach was taken by Orlando Costas, whose reflection was evangelical in its inspiration and emphasis but less polemical against liberation theologies and at the same time more pragmatic about Church Growth missiology. His book *Christ outside the Gate*[29] and his posthumous work *Liberating News*[30] show him at his best in the way of formulating a theology of contextual evangelization and mission. In both books Costas takes liberation themes but works with them incorporating the missionary thrust and the evangelistic passion of the evangelical perspective. Another important characteristic of Costas's work is his effort to take seriously the dialogue with missiology and ecclesiology from mainline and ecumenical theologians.[31] The themes and styles of these thinkers are more closely related to the way in which they practice their faith in daily ministry than to the demands of academic debate in the European or North American settings. In this respect they coincide with ecumenical missiologists who keep their theological work closely connected to the life of their churches, such as Emilio Castro and Mortimer Arias.

THE SEARCH FOR A MISSIOLOGICAL CHRISTOLOGY IN LATIN AMERICA

A brief historical reference is necessary in order to grasp the continuing relevance of some questions of old. Because Latin America was already a Christianized continent when the early Protestant missionaries came to it, Christology became the first privileged theme demanded by their missionary theology. The reason for this was, first, as Míguez Bonino has reminded us, that the evangelical heritage of the awakenings was very influential on the theological outlook of the Protestant missionary movement and Christology was a very important part of that heritage. Christology was informed by a soteriological emphasis. The center of the message of the missionaries was Jesus Christ as a personal savior. Míguez Bonino is of the opinion that this evangelical emphasis had a reductionist effect because important aspects of Christology were left aside. "Thus, theology is practically swallowed up in Christology, and this in soteriology, and even more, in a salvation which is characterized as an individual and subjective experience."[32] This criticism needs careful evaluation in the theological task of the future because the centrality of Christ in the evangelical message is a decisive and defining element. From a missiological perspective one could say that it has been the most valuable contribution of Protestantism to Latin America. It has made possible true evangelization, through which many people have come to meet Christ for the first time, and it has been also a challenge for the renewal of Catholicism in these lands.

The second reason for the development of Christology was that when Protestantism arrived, there were abundant visible symbols related to Christ in the public life of Latin America. Art, architecture, and the overwhelming presence of the Catholic church in public life were signs of the presence of Christ. Questioning the quality of that presence became part of evangelical theologizing, even as a form of legitimizing the Protestant missionary enterprise. Along these lines, the most lasting contribution—because of its contextual frame and evangelistic thrust—came from the Scottish Presbyterian John Alexander Mackay (1889-1983). After theological training and cultural immersion in the Spanish culture in Spain, he was a missionary for sixteen years (1916-32) in Latin America, later a mission executive, and then president of Princeton Theological Seminary.[33] A missiological exploration around the theme of Christ in Latin American culture was his central concern, which he developed in his classic work *The Other Spanish Christ*.[34]

What Mackay found striking in the Creole Christ of Latin America was what he described as his lack of humanity, the fact that he appeared almost exclusively in two dramatic roles: "the role of the infant in his mother's arms, and the role of a suffering and bleeding victim. It is a picture of a Christ who was born and died, but who never lived."[35] This Creole Christ was for Mackay a "southamericanized" version of the Christ of Spanish religion, in which he had become the center of a cult of death. Following the analysis of Miguel de Unamuno and other Spanish philosophers, Mackay observed that the dead Christ was seen only as an expiatory victim. Moreover,

> he is regarded as a purely supernatural being, whose humanity being only apparent, has little ethical bearing upon ours. This docetic Christ died as a victim of human hate, and in order to bestow immortality, that is to say a continuation of the present earthly, fleshly existence.[36]

Mackay's missiological agenda as an evangelist and a teacher to Latin American youth in the 1920s and 1930s was designed as an evangelical response to the kind of Christendom without Christ that he found in those lands. At the top of this agenda was Christology, and the way in which he outlined the task became decisive and influential even in our time. Mackay's books in Spanish are masterful works in their contextual presentation of the Jesus of the gospels.[37] They develop the agenda that is summarized in the following extended quotation. Responding to an interlocutor who would say that Christ as a child and a victim corresponded to the two central truths of Christianity, the incarnation and the atonement, Mackay wrote:

> Yes, but incarnation is only the prologue of a life, while atonement is its epilogue. The reality of the former is unfolded in life and guaranteed by living; the efficacy of the latter is derived from the quality of the life lived. The Divine child in His Mother's arms receives His full significance only when we see the man at work in the carpenter's shop, receive the Spirit in the Baptismal waters of Jordan, battle hungry and lonely with the tempter, preach the glad tidings of the Kingdom to the poor, heal the sick and raise the dead, call the heavy laden and children to His side, warn the rich and denounce hypocrites, prepare His disciples for life and Himself

for death, and then lay down His life not as a mere victim of hate or destiny but voluntarily and in dying ask His Father to forgive His slayers. In the same way the Crucified, in mortal anguish on the cross, is transfigured when we think that in life he had experienced the temptations of a strong man and overcame them. It was the man who died, the true, the second Man, the Lord from heaven as man, such a man as never has been nor shall be.[38]

Mackay added to these proposals his concern about the need to proclaim Jesus as the resurrected Lord, because in Latin America the vision of the risen Christ "has been no less dim than that of the historical Jesus."[39] Because the true Lordship of Christ had not been acknowledged in South American religion, "He remains to be known as Jesus, the Saviour from sin and the Lord of all life."[40] At this point Mackay also hammered on a theme that was distinctive of his theology: the difference between an attitude of distant admiration of Jesus, which he described as "the balcony," and one of committed discipleship, for which he used the metaphor of the "road." Because Jesus is Lord he is to be followed on the "road," which is the place where life is lived in the midst of tensions, where conflicts and concerns become the soil from which ideas are born. Thus discipleship after Jesus is the ground of true theology. "Truth as it relates to God is always existential in character, involving a consent of the will as well as an assent of understanding. Assent may be given on the Balcony, but consent is inseparable from the Road."[41] The praxis of obedience to Jesus Christ is then the way of access to the truth of God.

The theology of Mackay had a definite missionary and evangelistic thrust.[42] He developed an apologetical missionary approach that explored deep-seated points of contact between the gospel and the Latin American soul shaped by the Iberian culture. Well into the 1950s Mackay's agenda was being pursued by the first generation of Latin Americans who tried to articulate their evangelical faith in a contextual manner. Some of the first theological works originally written by Protestants in Spanish were journalistic, homiletic, and poetic in style, but they embodied a rich biblical Christology in an effort to communicate the gospel to large audiences that were ignorant of the main aspects of the life and teachings of Jesus. Thus, for instance, the Mexican Gonzalo Báez-Camargo developed a rich and elegant prose that made popular his column in *Excelsior,* the daily newspaper with the largest circulation in Mexico City. His articles about "The Hands of Christ," Jesus the carpenter as "The Proletarian of Nazareth," and the cleansing of the temple where Jesus was presented as "Our Lord of the Whip" were reproduced in hundreds of publications and collected in book form; they continue to show lasting value.[43]

The revival of Christology within Roman Catholicism came much later and the course of events was different.[44] It was partly Vatican II, with its emphasis on the use of scripture and a contextual liturgy in the vernacular, that brought a renewal in which the rediscovery of the Jesus of the gospels was an important component. It came at a time when there was a cultural movement of return to the Iberian and indigenous sources of Latin American identity and a new appreciation for folklore. The words of the Mass in Spanish to the tune of folkloric rhythms from Mexico, Chile, or Argentina were for many Catholics in Latin America the first intelligible contact with the christological core of the Christian liturgy. A paraphrase of the gospels versified with the metric of the gaucho popular poetry of Argentina became a best seller through which many young people understood for the first time the life of the incarnate Jesus as "one of us."[45] On the other hand, the presence of a new wave of North American and European Catholic missionaries, with a missionary style that emphasized "presence" rather than "conquest," pointed to the validity of the practice of Jesus as a missiological model. These facts brought into Catholicism a renewed christological search that followed the lines of Mackay's agenda, though it was not directly related to it. It is not our task in this chapter to consider this new form of Catholic Christology, but returning to the agitated days of the sixties and seventies, it is important to consider how also among evangelicals in Latin America the christological search was intensified in an ethical direction.[46]

FROM CHRISTOLOGY TO SOCIAL ETHICS

Justo L. González, now a well-known theologian and historian in the English-speaking world, originally came to North America from Cuba. In 1965 he wrote his short but very influential book *Revolución y Encarnación.*[47] It was a study of the Johannine material in the New Testament as a way of calling evangelicals to become aware of the kind of docetist Christology into which they had fallen, one that was proving sterile, especially in relation to social ethics. Coming out at the time in which social activism and revolutionary militancy had increased to critical levels in Latin America, González's book was an effort to develop a social ethics that would use a christological paradigm as a foundation. This book was followed in 1971 by *Jesucristo es el Señor*, in which González outlined with great clarity the development and the meaning of the doctrine of the Lordship of Jesus Christ.[48] Both books in a way summarized a contextual interpretation of Christology as a way to figure out the nature and mission of the church. Though both had a definite pastoral intention, which accounted for their clear, brief and straightforward style, they were based on the careful historical research of González's well-known works on the history of Christian thought.[49]

González refined some points of the argument during a colloquium about social ethics in which he concluded that there was almost general agreement "to reject the docetism of those who see no more task than that of saving souls for a future life . . . (and) to reject the ebionism of those who imagine that their action in society and in history is going to establish the Kingdom of God."[50] In one of his most recent books González has deepened the analysis of christological themes within the larger trinitarian thrust of his exposition. Working from the concerns of the Hispanic context in the United States in the

1990s, he has explored both the social context and the social connotations of the development of christological dogma. In his attack on gnosticism and docetism he writes:

> Docetism, while seeming to glorify Jesus, in truth deprived him of what in the New Testament is his greatest glory: his incarnation and suffering on the cross. In the last analysis, what docetism denied was not only the reality of the incarnation and the suffering of Jesus but the very nature of a God whose greatest victory is achieved through suffering and whose clearest revelation is in the cross.[51]

During the same period in which González first wrote, several members of the Latin American Theological Fraternity were engaged in evangelistic work, especially among students and professional people. It was an effort to communicate the basics of the Christian faith to people who had rejected any connection with churches and were sometimes in the process of adopting Marxism as a worldview. In the late 1950s and during the decade of the 1960s it became natural and necessary for these evangelists to follow also Mackay's christological agenda and to focus their public announcement of the gospel on campuses on the basic facts of Jesus' actions and teachings as presented in the gospels. These were unknown to the average student at that time. In some cases an apologetic note about the historicity of Jesus became necessary due to the debate with Marxist interlocutors in the academic and intellectual world.[52] The material developed in workshops and courses all over Latin America was summarized in Samuel Escobar's presentation at the First Latin American Congress of Evangelism (CLADE I) held in Bogotá, Colombia, in November 1969.[53]

This missiological proposal challenged evangelicals to recover a memory of the transformative dynamics that had been part of their presence as the seed of important social changes. It was a critical evaluation of fundamentalist trends in the North American missionary effort that preached a dichotomy between evangelism and social responsibility. It was also a call to realize that evangelism could not be carried on without a responsible awareness of the context of social turmoil and liberation struggles that marked Latin American life at that point. As Jesus had accomplished his mission by an incarnate presence in the middle of history, the church was called to take seriously the human and social reality of its presence in Latin American society. As Jesus had lived a life marked by his commitment to service to the point of going to the cross, the church was called to serve those in need in Latin America with a sacrificial spirit. As Jesus had been raised from the dead so that in his name there was power to change lives, the church was to announce the gospel and its transformative power by the action of the Holy Spirit. Thus being faithful to its Christocentric heritage but being also alert to the demands of the context, reading the signs of the times, evangelicals had to recover the socially transformative thrust of a biblical and holistic missionary style. The "Declaration of Bogotá" was an effort to summarize the tone of the Congress:

The process of evangelization takes place in a concrete social situation. Social structures exercise a powerful influence on the Church and on those who receive the Gospel. If this reality is not taken into consideration the Gospel is distorted and the Christian life impoverished. Consequently the time has come for us Evangelicals to assume our social responsibility, on the biblical foundation of our faith and following the example of the Lord Jesus Christ to the last consequences.[54]

One outcome of the Bogotá congress was the formation in 1970 of the Latin American Theological Fraternity. A central concern of the founders was the development of a contextual theology of evangelization. Their explorations converged with the work being developed by evangelical theologians in other parts of the world. They found great affinity with what John Stott had started to develop in his series of Bible studies at the World Congress of Evangelism in Berlin in October 1966, especially in his emphasis on the Great Commission as it is presented in the Gospel of John.[55] Evangelical work around this subject in Latin America became an important contribution to the Lausanne Congress in 1974 and to the Lausanne Covenant. The "Response to Lausanne," drafted by the Radical Discipleship group, incorporated aspects of the ongoing christological reflection that could not be incorporated into the covenant.[56] The most recent work of evangelicals from Latin America in the area of Christology has to be understood within the frame of this historical development.

An important self-critical note of those years came from the bitter awareness that the same docetism that Mackay had criticized among Roman Catholics had soon started to develop also among evangelicals. This development could be traced back to the negative effect of post–World War II independent missionary efforts from North America that were heavily influenced by Dispensationalism, the mentality of the Cold War with its suspicion about social change, and the delayed effects of the liberal-fundamentalist debates.[57] On the basis of missionary experience, theological dialogue and research in texts, René Padilla came to the conclusion that the problem was not limited to Latin America. Actually, evangelicalism around the world had become affected by docetism:

> Despite its theoretical acknowledgment of Christ's full humanity, evangelical Christianity in Latin America, as in the rest of the world, is deeply affected by docetism. It affirms Christ's transforming power in relation to the individual, but is totally unable to relate the Gospel to social ethics and social life. In our case Mackay's challenge remains unmet.[58]

A MISSIOLOGICAL CHRISTOLOGY

As it has already been stated, by the logic of the Christendom that characterizes Latin America, Catholics and Protestants alike entered the christological debate as soon as they tried to think through their faith or figure out their identity and mission. In the introduction to a book that collected some of the Latin American christological writings of that period, Míguez Bonino outlined the theological agenda as an effort to identify the Christologies that already exist in this nominally Christian continent. There was the normative question from the dogmatic perspective, "How is Jesus Christ correctly to be understood?" There was the descriptive and analytical question, "How is Jesus Christ *de facto* understood in Latin America today?" And there was the theological and confessional question: "How is the working efficacious power of Christ present in Latin America today?"[59] However, in the evangelical exploration to which we refer here there is a unique characteristic that has to be clarified and stressed. It is *the evangelistic thrust of evangelical theology,* which has been so aptly expressed by Orlando Costas:

> Theology and evangelization are two interrelated aspects of the life and mission of the Christian faith. Theology studies the faith; evangelization is the process by which it is communicated. Theology plumbs the depth of the Christian faith; evangelization enables the church to extend it to the ends of the earth and the depth of human life. Theology reflects critically on the church's practice of the faith; evangelization keeps the faith from becoming the practice of an exclusive social group. Theology enables evangelization to transmit the faith with integrity by clarifying and organizing its content, analyzing its context and critically evaluating its communication. Evangelization enables theology to be an effective servant of the faith by relating its message to the deepest spiritual needs of humankind.[60]

This emphasis makes evangelical theologizing different from the forms of Protestant theology that stem from churches that are not concerned with evangelization. The latter tends to focus more on the correction of abuses inside the existing churches, the search for a contextual identity, or the search for relevance in the sociopolitical struggles of our day.[61] It is also different from the Catholic approach, in which the sacramental dimension of the presence of the Roman Catholic Church in Latin America is taken as the basis for assuming that the population is already Christian. With that presupposition, evangelization is understood more as a call to commitment and discipleship than a call to conversion. What we find in authors like Padilla, Costas, and Núñez is a missiological thrust in which the evangelizing activity of the churches is a definite and influential presupposition and a prerequisite of theological discourse. It is the same conviction expressed by Emilio Castro, who writes, "Mission in the 1990s needs to concentrate on spreading the actual knowledge of the story of Jesus of Nazareth. 'Tell me the old, old story' is the refrain of an old hymn we used to sing in Sunday School. Yet the telling of that story is our most urgent mission challenge today."[62]

In this moment of transition in Latin America the search for a christological missiology has come from the crisis related to the traditional models of mission.

René Padilla has been the theologian who has worked consistently in the development of that agenda. He believes that there is a common christological concern in the work of theologians from Asia, Africa, Latin America, and the ethnic minorities of North America and Europe:

> The images of Jesus Christ imported from the West have on the whole been found wanting—too conditioned by Constantinian Christianity with all its ideological distortions and cultural accretions, and terribly inadequate as a basis for the life and mission of the church in situations of dire poverty and injustice. This has led to the search for a Christology which will have as its focus the historical Jesus and provide a basis for Christian action in contemporary society.[63]

The term "historical Jesus" for Padilla does not refer to the technical expression usually associated with the liberal theology of last century in a way that "historical" would mean "the product of the historical-critical method."[64] Evangelicals in Latin America would share what Padilla considers a fundamental premise of his Christology: "The Gospels are essentially reliable historical records and that the portrait of Jesus that emerges from them provides an adequate basis for the life and mission of the church today."[65]

The Latin American context forces the question of the need to rediscover and expound the concrete actions of Jesus as they were reported by the evangelists so that they may be grasped, contemplated, and understood as the shaping patterns for contemporary discipleship. This theological task goes to the wealth of biblical data that lies behind the creedal systematizations in which "the Christian message was cast into philosophical categories, and the historical dimension of revelation was completely overshadowed by dogma."[66]

To the degree to which the missionary movement and teaching in churches limit themselves to transmitting Christology mainly as propositional truth defined in the Nicene or Chalcedonian formulas, they transmit images of Christ that may be "useful for personal piety or civil religion, but . . . neither faithful to the witness of Scripture concerning Jesus Christ nor historically relevant."[67] The creedal formulations defining the deity and the humanity of Jesus Christ became obstacles to grasping those dimensions of the humanity that are very important for shaping life and mission today. Emilio Núñez in his study about liberation theologies acknowledges the fact that "this new emphasis on the humanity of Christ is a reaction to the lack of balance in a Christology that magnifies the deity of the Word incarnate at the expense of his humanity." He goes on to describe the way in which Latin American evangelicals received an Anglo-Saxon Christology that was the result of the liberal-fundamentalist debate:

> Thus what was emphasized in Evangelical conservative Christology was necessarily the deity of the Logos, without denying his humanity. We were presented with a divine-human Christ in the theological formula;

but in practice he was far removed from the stage of this world, aloof to our social problems.[68]

This biblical clarification does not dismiss the validity and usefulness of the traditional creedal statements, but it takes them as what they are, a form of Christian tradition that should always be open to confrontation with scripture, especially when tradition shows its limitations.[69] The confrontation of creeds with scripture, both understood within their historical context, helps us to appreciate the validity of the creeds, and at the same time to recover depths of meaning in scripture that might have remained in the shadows due to the historical relativity of the definitions.[70] This "recovery of memory" brought by a new reading of the gospels gives us a new perception of the importance of Jesus' teaching about the kingdom of God. Mortimer Arias finds that evangelization has to be understood from this perspective, from "the subversive memory of Jesus" that puts a question mark in much of our missionary and evangelizing practice.

One of the first illuminating questions becomes, Who was Jesus of Nazareth? Padilla has gathered material from the gospels around some features of Jesus' work that "could not but puzzle people in general, provoke suspicion in many and infuriate those who held positions of privilege in the religious-political establishment."[71] The picture obtained is eloquent and challenging: Jesus spoke with authority despite his lack of theological study; he claimed to be related to God in a unique way; he was a friend of publicans and sinners; he affirmed that God's kingdom was present in history and manifest in the healing of the sick; he concentrated his ministry on the uneducated, the ignorant, and the disreputable; he attacked religious oppression and rejected empty religious ceremonies; he condemned wealth and regarded greed as idolatry; he defined power in terms of sacrificial service and affirmed nonviolent resistance; and he summoned his followers to social nonconformity patterned after his own. For Padilla, the consequence is clear:

If the Christ of faith is the Jesus of history, then it is possible to speak of social ethics for Christian disciples who seek to fashion their lives on God's purpose of love and justice concretely revealed. If the risen and exalted Lord is Jesus of Nazareth, then it is possible to speak of a community that seeks to manifest the kingdom of God in history.[72]

A second important set of questions has to do with the way in which Jesus accomplished his mission. Bible exposition within the frame of missiological reflection was the agenda followed by Padilla as he explored the marks of Jesus' ministry. His basic assumption was that "to be a disciple of Jesus Christ is to be called by him both to know him and to participate in his mission. He himself is God's missionary par excellence, and he involves his followers in his mission."[73] Jesus' mission includes "fishing for the kingdom," in other words, the call to conversion to Jesus Christ as the way, the truth, and the life. This conversion stands as the basis on which the Christian community is formed. Mission includes also "compassion" as a result of immersion among the multitudes. Neither a sentimental burst of emotion nor an academic option for the poor but definite and intentional actions of service in order to "feed the multitude" with bread *for* life, as well as Bread *of* life. Mission includes "confrontation" of the powers of death with the power of the Suffering Servant, and thus "suffering" becomes a mark of Jesus' messianic mission and a result of power struggle and human injustice. Through creative contextual obedience Jesus' mission becomes not only a fertile source of inspiration but also has the seeds of new patterns that are being explored today through practice and reflection, such as simple lifestyle, holistic mission, the unity of the church for mission, the pattern of God's kingdom as a missiological paradigm, and the spiritual conflict involved in mission.

A third area of inquiry centers around the question, What is the Gospel? The most enthusiastic calls for missionary activism stem from sectors of evangelicalism in which this question seems irrelevant. As John Howard Yoder observed about one of the expressions of this sector, the Church Growth missiology, "It is assumed that we have an adequate theology that we received from the past. . . . We do not really need any more theological clarification. What we need now is efficiency."[74] One of the results of this assumption on the part of many evangelicals is that the quality and effectiveness of evangelism is measured only by quantifiable results, with no reference to faithfulness to the gospel in method, content, and style. This concern is not limited to Latin America. Missiologists who are exploring what it means to evangelize and be missionary in North America today also believe that the question is important. George R. Hunsberger says:

> The central question of theology—What is the gospel?—must be asked in more culturally particular ways. And the more particular the question the more will be our sense that the answer will emerge in unexpected ways. It will come more out of Christian communities which increasingly learn the habit of "indwelling" the Gospel story so deeply that it shapes their life of common discipleship.[75]

These important questions that should be asked with regard to the life and mission of the church today are related to the content of the gospel because "the *what* of the Gospel determines the *how* of its effects on practical life."[76] Grasping the wealth of meaning of the Gospel in the biblical revelation and the demands of the obedience of faith is the only way out of the prison of the predominant "culture Christianity" in North America, a culture that is also being exported through traditional evangelical missions, especially through the mass media. Padilla stresses the eschatological and soteriological dimensions of the Christian message centered in the person of Jesus Christ. In Jesus, through the pattern of promise and fulfillment, the Old and the New Testaments are related. From a careful exposition of the gospel centered on a solid christological core, Padilla concludes that "the apostolic mission is derived from Jesus Christ. He is the content as well as the model and the goal for the proclamation of the gospel."[77] Consequently, Christian preaching has to be molded by the word of God and not by a mere search for relevance:

> Preachers for whom relevance is the most basic consideration in preaching are frequently mistaken—they fail to see the link between relevance in preaching and faithfulness to the Gospel. . . . There is nothing more irrelevant than a message that simply mirrors man's myths and ideologies![78]

The consequence of this fact is critical in two ways. It rejects the unilateral stress on the humanity of Jesus that reduces Christian action to mere human effort. Thus it becomes necessary to criticize the Christology of some liberation theologians like Jon Sobrino for not taking seriously the wholeness of the gospel. "It is no mere coincidence that Sobrino should see the Kingdom of God as a utopia to be fashioned by men rather than as a gift to be received in faith."[79] Unacceptable also are liberation Christologies that overemphasize the political dimension of the death of Jesus at the expense of its soteriological significance. Padilla, for instance, accepts the truth based on examination of the texts of the gospels that the death of Jesus was the historical outcome of the kind of life he lived, and that he suffered for the cause of justice and challenges us to do the same. However, he thinks that warnings are necessary:

> Unless the death of Christ is also seen as God's gracious provision of an atonement for sin, the basis for forgiveness is removed and sinners are left without the hope of justification. . . . Salvation is by grace through faith and . . . nothing should detract from the generosity of God's mercy and love as the basis of joyful obedience to the Lord Jesus Christ.[80]

On the other hand, Padilla criticizes the managerial forms of missiology in evangelicalism, which, in their concern with methodology, disregard questions about the content of the gospel.[81] Serious work is needed in order to provide a contextual reading of scripture in response to the question, What is the Gospel? However, this is disregarded or overlooked by the Church Growth theory, which espouses what Charles Taber calls "a narrowed-down version of the evangelical hermeneutic and theology."[82] From the christological basis of his way of understanding the gospel, Padilla questions the rigidity of the structural-functional model of cultural anthropology used by Church Growth, because it produces a missiological approach "tailor made for churches and institutions whose main function in society is to reinforce the status quo."[83] He also questions the extreme individualism of missiologies that have lost the biblical wholeness:

The salvation that the Gospel proclaims is not limited to man's reconciliation to God. It involves the remaking of man in all the dimensions of his existence. It has to do with the recovery of the whole man according to God's original purpose for his creation.[84]

This holistic dimension of the gospel allows us to understand the New Testament teaching about the nature of human beings, which is offered within a missiological context. Christology is the key for anthropology because, to begin with, as Sidney Rooy says, "Everyone's relation to God in Christian anthropology is defined by each individual's relation to Jesus Christ."[85] This is the basis for important safeguards against the pitfalls of hermeneutical procedures such as those of the reductionist anthropology of the Church Growth school, which limits itself to read into the biblical text the values of contemporary American social sciences. Rooy elaborates this point:

The historical significance of the incarnation reaches backward and forward. Christ's life, death and resurrection mark the crucial point of human history—we might call them the mountain pass of creation's course. The same road stretches meaningfully back from the summit's pit to creation's beginning and continues its meandering progress to the destiny of humankind. The basic affirmations of humankind's identity as the one created in the image of God and responsible for the tending and development of natural reality remain valid. These affirmations are reconstituted in the reconciling work of Jesus Christ, the authentic image of God, the new person.[86]

In their debate with Church Growth missiology and its proposed method of "homogeneous units" based on race or class, Rooy and Padilla have insisted on the community dimension of the New Testament teaching about the new man, especially as Paul teaches it in his epistle to the Ephesians. They develop from this text an ecclesiology that derives from the work of Jesus Christ, because the new humanity is humankind in Jesus Christ: "The 'one new man' here is clearly a new humanity, the church composed of what was formerly two, that is Jews and Gentiles."[87] Through careful exegesis Padilla proves that apostolic missionary practice "aimed at forming churches that would live out the unity of the new humanity in Jesus Christ."[88] The "newness" that Paul is proclaiming is closely connected with his own missionary work as a Jewish man who happens to be a missionary to Gentiles. And precisely what he is doing is founding churches, communities of new people that are to express the novelty brought by the gospel, even if that novelty brings all the pastoral questions that fill his epistles. As Padilla concludes, "The impact that the early church made on non-Christians because of Christian brotherhood across natural barriers can hardly be overestimated."[89]

REDISCOVERY OF KINGDOM THEOLOGY

The pressures of social tension in the Latin American context as well as the growing involvement of evangelicals in the political arenas of their countries brought a new agenda to theological reflection.[90] Anyone who reads the gospels will find that the central theme of Jesus' teaching was the kingdom of God. However, as Mortimer Arias has pointed out, evangelical theologians in Latin America found that "the Kingdom of God theme has practically disappeared from evangelistic preaching and has been ignored by traditional 'evangelism.' The evangelistic message has been centered in personal salvation, individual conversion and incorporation into the church."[91] The kingdom of God became the theme of the second continental consultation of the Latin American Theological Fraternity in 1972. The reflection explored the Kingdom and the church, the kingdom and history, the kingdom as hermeneutical key to read the Bible, and the kingdom and social and political ethics.[92] The balance of the reflection emphasized the Kingdom as central to the gospel and a key for the evangelistic and missionary task of the churches in Latin America. It was another key point of the contribution of Latin America to the Lausanne Congress, forcefully expressed in the "Response to Lausanne":

> The Evangel is God's good news in Jesus Christ; it is good news of the reign he proclaimed and embodies; of God's mission of love to restore the world to wholeness through the cross of Christ and him alone; of his victory over the demonic powers of destruction and death; of his Lordship over the entire universe; it is good news of a new creation, a new humanity, a new birth through him by his life-giving Spirit. . . . It is good news of liberation, of restoration, of wholeness, and of salvation that is personal, social, global and cosmic.[93]

The theological work that followed dealt with issues related to social and political realities from the perspectives of the kingdom of God.[94] The approach to issues such as justice and power was basically christological in the work of Padilla that developed from the eschatological dimension of his Christology. This was operative in his critical evaluation of culture and the understanding of the forces hostile to the kingdom of God that presently enslave human beings and tend to undermine the church's identity and distort its mission. There is an Antichrist at work in the world that has to be named and unmasked at the same time at which Jesus Christ is proclaimed as Lord.

> The challenge of the moment is not to criticize the governments in religious language but rather to confront the values and attitudes that make it possible for our people to be domesticated by advertising; it is not to oppose the official myths with other secular myths but rather to point to the

judgement of God on every attempt to build the Kingdom of God without God. Since the coming of Christ, the key to history is to be found in his death and resurrection, and the proclamation of the Gospel places humanity face to face with only one alternative—Christ or Antichrist.[95]

From such a stance come the theological elements that will enable churches to avoid the corrupting comfort of the Constantinian pitfall in one extreme and the contradictions of otherworldliness in the other.

MISSION FROM THE PERIPHERY

Two significant trends at the beginning of a new century will have a bearing on the development of new missionary patterns, and part of the agenda for theology in the future will be to find out how they relate to become part of a coherent missiology with a global thrust. On the one hand, as Yoder has pointed out, "It is one of the widely remarked developments of our century that now one dimension, now another, of the ecclesiastical experience and the ecclesiological vision once called 'sectarian' are now beginning to be espoused by some within majority communions."[96] It may be that as Christians and churches search for more faithful patterns of obedience to Jesus Christ, they increasingly find themselves going through the experience of disestablishment in societies that hold some form of "official" Christian identity. They have discovered, like "sectarians" of the past, that they must learn to live as "resident aliens."

On the other hand, we have mentioned several times the massive southward shift of the center of gravity of the Christian world, in such a way that the lively and growing forms of Christianity now appear to be in Latin America, sub-Saharan Africa, and other parts of the southern continents. This being the case, the existence of thriving churches in what used to be called the Third World confronts the old European or North American churches with a new set of questions and new ways of looking at God's word. It is important to keep in mind what Andrew Walls deduces from this fact, even if some may consider what he says as an exaggeration,

> This means that Third World theology is now likely to be the representative Christian theology. On present trends (and I recognize that this may not be permanent) the theology of European Christians, while important for them and their continued existence, may become a matter of specialist interest to historians. . . . The future general reader of Church history is more likely to be concerned with Latin American and African, and perhaps some Asian, theology.[97]

With all their purported Latin Americanism most liberation theologies were still part of a western discourse, in tune with Marx and Engels, Moltmann, or the European theologians of Vatican II. Even though they were located in the frontier situations between affluence and misery, they still moved within the categories of Enlightenment theologizing. We must be prepared for something different if we are going to take seriously the emergence of new churches as part of the southward shift of the center of gravity of Christianity. The new pastoral situations and theological questions are coming from churches that move in the frontier between Christendom and Islam, churches surrounded by cultures shaped by animism or great ethnic religions, ethnic churches in the impoverished heart of secularized western cities, thriving Pentecostal churches in Latin America, or old churches in post-Marxist Eastern Europe. These are the missionary churches of today and tomorrow, and the ears of missiologists should be tuned to their message, their songs, and their groans, at the same time that they are attentive to the word of God.

The idea of a missiology that comes from the periphery of the modern world may have some merit as we explore the future. During a theological consultation about Christology, Argentinean Pentecostal Norberto Saracco explored the significance of the Galilean origin of Jesus' ministry.[98] His approach was not an effort to find situations in the context in which Jesus lived comparable to our contemporary ones, situations that would lend themselves to an "almost magical relationship that does not take seriously the text or our situation."[99] Saracco preferred to explore the meaning of the options chosen by Jesus for his own ministry, which were at the same time relevant to the context in which he ministered and consistent with his redemptive project.

Orlando Costas pursued this point in a more extensive reflection and developed a creative summary of a new dimension for a christological missiology.[100] Focusing on the Gospel of Mark, he explored a model of evangelization rooted in the ministry of Jesus. It could be characterized as an evangelistic legacy, "a model of contextual evangelization from the periphery." Costas placed special significance on Jesus' choice of Galilee, a racial and cultural crossroads, as the base for his mission. He explored also the significance of Jesus' identity as a Galilean, and of Galilee as an evangelistic landmark and the starting point of the mission to the nations, with its universal implications. Costas's understanding of his own contemporary context emphasized the "peripheral" nature of some of the points and places where Christianity is more dynamic today. His missiological proposal is that "the global scope of contextual evangelization should be geared first and foremost to the nations' peripheries, where the multitudes are found and where the Christian faith has always had the best opportunity to build a strong base."[101]

At some point the "sectarian" vision to which Yoder referred, coming from the periphery of official Catholic and Protestant versions of history, may have a fertile encounter with the theological questions coming from missionary churches in the peripheries of the contemporary world. As Jews and Gentiles came together through community events in the early church, new community events will be necessary on a global scale. Mission may facilitate such encounters, in which the reconciliation of Christians from the North and Christians from the South takes place as they experience what it means to become a "new humanity"—and theologize about it. As Padilla has stated:

The missiology that the church needs today is not one that conceives the people of God as a quotation taken from the surrounding society but one that conceives it as "an embodied question mark" that challenges the values of the world. . . . Only a missiology in line with the apostolic teaching and practice with regard to the extension of the Gospel will have a lasting contribution to make toward the building of this kind of church—the firstfruits of a new humanity made up of persons "from every tribe and tongue and people and nation" who will unitedly sing a new song to the Lamb of God.[102]

11

Mission Theology from Pentecost to the Twenty-First Century

In the New Testament, theology follows mission. The reflection about the faith and the church comes after the act of obedience of taking the gospel beyond the confines of the local church and planting the church elsewhere. When Jesus meets Paul on the road to Damascus, he calls the zealous Pharisee with an explicit missionary command, and it is in the course of going in obedience as a missionary to the Gentiles that Paul has to come to terms with all that is involved in the act of acknowledging Jesus as Lord. His missionary practice shows us a continuous reflection, placing it under the scrutiny of God's revealed word. Doing theology during the twentieth century in Latin America became an absorbing and challenging task when Christians started to think of the meaning of faith in Jesus Christ for them in their own context, in their own time and space, and to reflect on their own practice in the light of God's word. What makes New Testament theology exciting and refreshing is precisely the fact that it is forged in the heat of acts of obedience and engagement in mission. The questions are not academic, not just subjects for doctoral dissertations. They are vital questions, questions of life and death. The theologizing to which we have referred in this book thus far has been done with the enthusiasm and the sense of urgency that come from those dramatic points where faith and non-faith meet, where the question about the mission of the church has to do with the right of that church to exist under God's grace and judgment.

As a consequence, the missiological perspective is the one that allows us to perceive best the promise and the precariousness of Christian existence and of humanity's involvement in God's mission in the world. That explains why Protestantism in its different forms has been observed and evaluated better by Catholic missiologists, as we have seen in a previous chapter. That explains also why popular Protestantism's right to citizenship as part of the Protestant movement was first acknowledged by Protestants who were speaking and writing from a missiological perspective. One could say that the church administrator, as well as the systematic theologian, is concerned with tracing carefully the borders of orthodoxy, maintaining the limits of an acceptable expression of the faith that has been defined in a particular context. The missionary, on the other hand, embarks on the task of crossing borders and frontiers of all kinds, challenged many times to stretch to new limits the understanding of truth, to plumb into the depths of the revealed word with new questions from new contexts. From that ground the missiologist may grasp a new vision that will enrich the theological task but also help the church to extend the arms of fellowship to embrace the newcomers to the household of faith.

Moments of missionary advance and crossing of new frontiers have usually come from movements of spiritual renewal whose significance was first grasped by those concerned for the mission of the church. The growth of popular and evangelical Protestantism as a missionary force around the world continues to be a missiological challenge. With honesty and realism, Catholic missiologist Walbert Bühlmann perceived its significance when he wrote in the 1970s:

> Even in Latin America where 80% to 90% of the missionaries belong to radical evangelical groups distinguished by fierce anti-Catholicism, who call the Catholic Church the great harlot, contacts are being multiplied and a certain degree of cooperation is developing. At the very least acquaintance with their lively activity has shaken us up and helped to convert us from centralism, clericalism and parochial sacramentalism through a laity with Bible in hand.[1]

Looking at the situation from the perspective of a historian, Justo González reflected in the same decade about the growth of popular Protestantism in Latin America. He observed that "whereas twenty years ago Pentecostals were considered to be the fringe of Protestantism, now their numbers loom so large that in some countries they are the main body and the historic churches have become the fringe."[2] He predicted an important role for the historic Protestant churches in their interaction with the Pentecostal movement, to which they could make a significant contribution. But historical churches had to acknowledge that they could not envisage a massive numerical growth. "Religiously"—he wrote—"the future of Latin America is in a renewed Catholicism and/or a matured Pentecostalism. To both of these our seemingly insignificant historic churches are making an important contribution."[3] This interaction has been so intense that by 1999, in a very valuable interpretative book, Karl-Wilhelm Westmeier, a missionary and theologian in Colombia and Puerto Rico, argues that it is very difficult "to draw clear lines of demarcation between Pentecostalism as such and the more 'traditional' Protestant Christians and Evangelicals, especially if the latter have been impacted by the Pentecostal movement—and who can find a Latin Protestant that has not come under its spell?"[4]

This interaction did not always move along an easy path, and there are Protestants who have not yet come to terms with the reality of popular Protestantism in Latin America. However, Pentecostal theologian Juan Sepúlveda has witnessed a change of attitudes even in European Protestantism: "In the ecumenical movement one can perceive attitudes such as a radical criticism that sees in pentecostalism an intrinsically alienating religiosity centered in the proclamation of an ultramundane salvation, or the respectful appraisal that discovers in Pentecostals a defiant challenge."[5] He also observes that more recently "both Latin American and world ecumenism are increasingly focusing their attention on this issue and thinking about the possibility of a massive incorporation of pentecostalism in the ecumenical task."[6] Such change of attitude in ecumenical leadership could be read applying a hermeneutics of suspicion and asking if there may be reasons of ecclesiastical politics behind these new approaches to evangelicals and Pentecostals. But one could also apply a hermeneutics of charity[7] and see behind these new approaches a genuine missiological concern.

Some Pentecostals tend to stress their autonomy in relation to evangelicals and are critical of evaluations and analysis of the Pentecostal movement that use narrow evangelical categories as a frame. Douglas Petersen, an Assemblies of God missionary in Central America, reminds us that "although Pentecostals are certainly Evangelical in belief, they have been traditionally marginalized by other Evangelical groups as being unreliable, theologically suspect and unsophisticated."[8] Years of experience in interdenominational work across Latin America lead me to think that Westmeier's position better reflects the present situation. But there is an important clarification from Petersen that must be taken into account: "At its extreme Pentecostalism may be viewed as a creation of Latin American popular culture, an authentic expression of its ethos. . . . Despite having early foreign influences, Pentecostalism became indigenous and emerged as an authentic religious and social expression within the Latin American context."[9]

While Westmeier identifies the Pentecostal element as the whole of Protestantism in Latin America, other interpreters have taken different views. A critical Catholic scholar's massive interpretative study is entitled *Fundamentalist Protestantism in Latin America.*[10] The authors agree that there is a religious movement in Latin America with sufficient common characteristics to be identified as Protestant, and that Pentecostal churches are part of this movement. In order to convey the plurality and unity within the movement Míguez Bonino has used the image of "faces," and that is the title of his valuable interpretative work. He is quite aware of the ambiguity of the image with the possible reference to different faces of different subjects or different masks for the same subject.[11] He expresses a conviction, which I share, that we can properly talk about a Protestant movement in Latin America of which Pentecostals, evangelicals, liberal historical churches, and even ethnic transplanted churches are a part. All these types of Protestant churches would have as a shared conviction the idea that the Protestant presence in Latin America is essentially missionary:

> Therefore if we are to discover a "material principle"—that is a theological orientation which, as the best expression of the life and dynamic of the religious community, will give coherence and consistency to the understanding of the gospel and become a point of reference for the theological

building of the community—we must speak of mission as the material "principle" of a Latin American Protestant theology.[12]

The context in which mission has to take place now has changed significantly as the waves of postmodernity have affected Latin American societies. In liberation theologies and in evangelical theology the basic question that theologians have been asking was, What is the mission of the church in Latin America today? A search for light from the word of God was necessary to respond to the question, but the existence of the church was a given, and all questions about God, human beings, history, and Jesus Christ were posed from the ground of this initial reality about which there was no doubt. However, at this point, in the beginning of a new century, the question has taken a new turn. The question is still missiological, but the setting has changed. The frame of liberation discourse was the fact that officially the Roman Catholic Church had made a "preferential option for the poor," avowedly placing itself besides the masses and in a critical stance towards the dominant elites. That was a challenge not only for Catholics but also for Protestants of every kind.

What became evident in the 1990s was that the poor masses in Latin America were opting for the evangelical and Pentecostal churches, which had continued to grow at a significant pace and had become more visible actors in society. Not only is popular Protestantism growing, but several forms of spiritism, new and old forms of African and Eastern religiosity, are also flourishing, and there is also a nativist return to pre-Hispanic religions. Latin America faces now the religious explosion that is a mark of postmodernity and poses in a new way the question of religious pluralism. Theological reflection comes from the need of criteria for missiological discernment. Before we explore the theological questions posed by these missionary realities in Latin America, we must consider briefly what has developed as Pentecostals embarked in their own missiological reflection.

PENTECOSTAL MISSIOLOGY

Pentecostals have developed their own theological and missiological reflection, and this has been more evident in North America, where the movement became institutionalized first, in dialogue with evangelicalism and fundamentalism. The body of Pentecostal missiological reflection is evident in the entries about "mission" and "missiology" in the *Dictionary of Pentecostal and Charismatic Movements*.[13] An issue of *Pneuma*, the journal of the Society for Pentecostal Studies, was dedicated to Pentecostal missiology in 1994.[14] The variety and quality of the contributions prompted Assemblies of God historian Gary B. McGee to comment that that issue was evidence of "the emerging maturation of Pentecostal missiology." At that point the centennial of the Pentecostal movement was approaching and McGee warned that "missiological reflection is more necessary than ever for guiding and safeguarding the integrity of the mission enterprise."[15] There seems to be consensus among Pentecostal missiologists that though there had been a great deal of missionary activity at a global scale since the inception of the movement, there had been little theological reflection about it. When new generations of Pentecostals started to reflect about their practice, they related to already existing missiological material that seemed to express a theory that connected with their own experience, especially to material from evangelical sources. Writing in 1988, Pentecostal scholar Russell Spittler said that "an oral style coupled with historical recency and a strong anti-intellectual mood, means that much Pentecostal 'theology' is imported and absorbed from the surrounding culture."[16] He pointed out that in 1916 Assemblies of God, for instance, adopted a doctrinal statement from the Christian and Missionary Alliance, to which they added Pentecostal elements. In 1961, when they revised that statement, they adopted the language preferred by the National Association of Evangelicals, of which they were the largest member group.

The work of Melvin Hodges is a case that proves Spittler's observation. Hodges had been a missionary of the Assemblies of God in El Salvador, Central America, and later a mission executive with responsibilities in Latin America. His experience and reflection led him to emphasize the indigenous principles for mission that had been developed in the classic books of Roland Allen. Thus the teaching of a high Anglican connected with the practice of a Pentecostal. As a result, "Hodges, in fact, pentecostalized Allen's principles and rephrased them for his tradition."[17] He was able to fuse indigenous principles he had seen at work in the field with Pentecostal theology. Hodges wrote:

> The faith which Pentecostal people have in the ability of the Holy Spirit to give spiritual gifts and supernatural abilities to the common people . . . has raised up a host of lay preachers and leaders of unusual spiritual ability—not unlike the rugged fishermen who first followed the Lord.[18]

Hodges's more systematic book emphasizes what he calls basics for a theology of missions that are principles from classical evangelicalism: the authority of scriptures, the centrality of Christ, the dynamics of the Holy Spirit, the lostness of humankind apart from saving grace and the instrumentality of the church. His bibliography contains mostly conservative evangelical authors such as Peter Beyerhaus, Donald McGavran, and George Peters. Luther and Calvin are mentioned several times, but there is no reference to Pietism or the Holiness sources of the Pentecostal experience.[19] Hodges's work influenced the missionary policies of the Assemblies of God, especially in Latin America. However, he did not pursue a missiological reflection to incorporate the uniqueness of the Pentecostal experience.

In Paul Pommerville we find a more intentional effort in that direction starting from an avowedly evangelical and Pentecostal stance. Pommerville developed his missiology in dialogue with theological trends in North America but insists on processing theologically the meaning of the Pentecostal experience. He asks about the way in which Pentecostalism represents a potential correction for a distortion in twentieth-century missions.

The answer to this question is found in Pentecostalism's focus on the experiential dimension of the Christian faith. In terms of the dynamic and evidential experience of the Holy Spirit, Pentecostalism contrasts with the static intellectual-oriented expression of Christianity inherited from the post-Reformation period.[20]

An important aspect of his work is that it takes into account the experience and significance of the independent churches in Africa. The final chapter of the book deals with the kingdom of God and evaluates critically teaching about the kingdom that has separated it from the Holy Spirit. His concern has also been expressed by Pentecostal missiologists in Latin America.

Russell Spittler asked if there would be a way to "surface from the two-thirds world those who will become the Pentecostal theologians of the twenty-first century and be the first to express a truly indigenous Pentecostal theology." His conclusion is stated in a way similar to the proposals of other writers: "My hunch is that the first native theology of Pentecostalism will come from south of the equator. It will be written in Spanish. And it will have no footnotes."[21] That first native theology may be right now developing in Latin America, Asia, or Africa. However, I know two serious pieces of theological work that reflect the Pentecostal experiences of their authors. Both have been written in English and have many footnotes, but the authors are Hispanic preachers and scholars from the United States. I am thinking of *The Liberating Spirit* by Eldin Villafañe,[22] an urban missiologist and theological educator, and *Orthopathos* by Samuel Solivan,[23] a systematic theologian and also a theological educator.

These are not exactly Latin American theological essays, but they are born from the Latino experience in the United States, from the Hispanic margin, and the authors deal honestly and creatively with their Pentecostal experience. In both works there is a section of sociohistorical analysis of the church reality in which their reflection is grounded, an effort to define the Latino Pentecostal experience as a minority within the context of American culture. In questions of spirituality Villafañe enters into dialogue with Hispanic spirituality in both the Catholic and Protestant traditions, with an ecumenical and irenic attitude that would be more difficult to find among Latin American Pentecostals. Both works are missiological in method and content.

Villafañe and Solivan have significant points of departure from the more general missiological thinking that developed among North American Pentecostals. There is a critical edge in their approach to the theological task that comes precisely from the awareness of a condition of marginality and suffering that generates an amount of cultural criticism not evident in the Anglo Pentecostal missiology of the United States. The critical approach of these Hispanic missiologists contrasts with what Gary B. McGee calls "dangerous levels of inculturation of Charismatics and Pentecostals in the materialistic quagmire of American society."[24] One can find the same critical edge in the theological reflection developing among Pentecostals in Latin America, and we will move now to outline in more detail the missiological questions at this point.

Posing it in its simplest form, the missiological question becomes a search for discernment: Are these new missionary facts the work of the Holy Spirit? The question may be disclosed in a threefold manner: First, is the emergence of these new forms of popular Protestantism a sign of God's Spirit moving within the social realities of our times? Is this the new wine of the Spirit reviving the church from below? This would be the pneumatological question. Second, are the new structures of mission, new forms of worship, and new ways of communication that are typical of this popular Protestantism the new wineskins that the Spirit will use in the twenty-first century? This would be the ecclesiological question. Third, is this religious revival going to bring transformation so that the evil forces that are disintegrating postmodern societies will be controlled and human life preserved? This is the eschatological question.

THE PNEUMATOLOGICAL QUESTION

In a previous chapter we referred to the origins of Latin American Protestantism and the roots of the missionary movement among the Wesleyan revivals and the Moravian pioneers of mission. The dynamism of missionary Protestantism came from those renewal movements of the eighteenth and nineteenth centuries. Popular Protestantism is also related to them, though the links are not always direct or explicit. Those parents in the faith had grasped truth about the Holy Spirit that now starts to make sense as Latin American Protestants try to figure out their identity in order to engage in mission and theologize about mission in the postmodern world. The readiness of those like Wesley or Zinzendorf to abandon old church structures and their creativity in developing new structures for mission were possible because they were open to the movements of the Spirit. This is the double task mentioned by Steuernagel: perceiving the breath of the Spirit in history and moving in the direction the Spirit is bearing us. The discernment of the breath of the Spirit requires an open attitude and the sensitivity to acknowledge that behind facts something as new and unusual as the strength and vigor of the Spirit may be at work. The act of obedience demands creativity in order to shape new structures that will be adequate instruments for missionary action in a particular historical moment.

Even in the Pauline missionary practice we find the same discernible pattern. Paul's missionary strategy may be understood in reference to the ministry models that preceded his work. Thus, for instance, in Romans Paul uses the model of the priest in the Old Testament to describe his own missionary work, but he puts new content in the definition of the task, new content that corresponds to the new covenant (Rom. 15:15-16). His patterns of travel, financial support, and style of proclamation correspond to the urban world of the main centers of the empire, and in that way they are different from the pattern of the itinerant preachers that we find in Jesus and the initial mission in Judea, Galilee, and Samaria. The Book of Acts shows that Paul follows a certain logic in the different steps of his missionary work (for instance, Acts 14:21-28), but at the same time he is open to new initiatives from the Spirit that are different from his original plans (Acts 16:6-10).

Paul's Christology is the development of pastoral, doctrinal, and ethical teaching that stems from the fact of Christ. Paul elaborates his Christology as he responds to the needs and the questions of churches that were born from the Spirit and had the signs of new life but had not yet articulated their belief in a meaningful way. The receivers of these letters were people who had grasped the Lordship of Christ and whose eyes had been opened by the Spirit to see the glory of God in the face of Jesus Christ, but they did not have yet a clear conceptual Christology (2 Cor. 4:5-6). By contrast, in many places in the world today we have churches in which people repeat weekly the minutiae of a christological creed but do not have the new life in Christ that the Spirit begets. On the other hand, we have growing churches where there are the signs of the power of the Spirit at work but where a basic theological task is necessary, one along the lines of what Paul did in his ministry.[25]

Both as we look back to historical models and as we look around us to what is taking place in churches around the world, the question of how the Spirit of God moves through the missionary initiative of those popular and grassroots churches becomes a decisive question. Asking it with honesty may cast a critical light on the life of our own churches when they lack the missionary dynamism that should be part of their normal life. Here I find specially relevant what missiologist Lesslie Newbigin wrote at the middle of the twentieth century. Pointing to some deadlocks in the ecumenical conversations of the 1950s between Catholics and Protestants, he wondered if

> the way forward may be found in a new understanding of the doctrine of the Holy Spirit. But of course that illumination which is needed will never come as a result of purely academic theological study. May it not be that the great Churches of the Catholic and the Protestant traditions will have to be humble enough to receive it in fellowship with their brethren in the various groups of the Pentecostal type with whom at present they have scarcely any fellowship at all?[26]

This is the kind of dialogue that has been taking place recently in the doing of theology in Latin America, but it still has a long way to go. Pentecostals who have taken part in the Lausanne movement and in the reflection within the Latin American Theological Fraternity have found acceptable the christological and soteriological basis of these movements as a frame of reference. They did not have to abandon their basic convictions, and they forcefully conveyed them in a way that influenced the reflection of other Protestants. In doing this they were faithful to their tradition and missionary practice. Many of them kept from their Holiness background the fourfold Christology expressed in the simple formula that refers to Christ as Savior, Sanctifier, Healer, and Coming King. This conviction is found in the hymns that Pentecostals sing, in their sermons and in their stories. I have heard Pentecostal theologian Norberto Saracco from Argentina saying that the fourfold formula is shared by Pentecostals with other evangelicals, but that the difference is that Pentecostals believe that Christ is all that *here and now*, not in a distant future.

This immediacy of the experience of Christ by the power of the Holy Spirit is one of the distinctive notes of popular Protestantism. Reflecting about the experience of Pentecostals in Chile, Sepúlveda has pointed out the conflictive element at the point of their emergence in 1910: "the conflict between a religiosity centered in the objectivity of dogma, in which faith consisted in the formal, conscious and rational acceptance of doctrine; and a religiosity which gave priority to the subjective experience of God, in which faith is a response to a kind of possession of the being by the Divine One."[27] The christological criterion allows us to discern the work of the Holy Spirit. The uniqueness of this religious experience is that it converts people into disciples of Jesus Christ who dedicate their life to the worship, exaltation, and proclamation of Jesus Christ.

The work of Karl-Wilhelm Westmeier about popular Protestantism in Colombia offers carefully gathered sociological data to show the way in which religious experience related to Christ has ethical consequences that eventually bring upward social mobility.[28] His social analysis shows the sociological potential of conversion to Pentecostalism, including an emphasis on some qualities of character as an indication of "a change of life." Westmeier views this important component of the Pentecostal experience as evidence of Christ's redeeming power. Like evangelical Protestants, the Pentecostals presented the convert with a series of specific prohibitions against the use of alcohol and tobacco. But what was especially significant in Pentecostal practice was that the prohibitions were accompanied by a strong emphasis on an emotional conversion experience, being touched by the joy and the mystery of God's power, which in some cases was the decisive moment for breaking away from the old habits like alcoholism, so prevalent among the urban poor and lower-middle classes.[29] The joy of this initial ecstatic moment is also kept in a celebrative type of worship that emphasizes joy and is conducive to it. Thus self-discipline is here accompanied by joy and celebration.

For Catholic observers, it has taken the sensitivity that comes from a missiological stance to appreciate the significance of the effects of popular Protestantism among the poor in Latin America. There have been dialogues between Catholics and Pentecostals[30] and between Catholics and evangelicals,[31] and the documents that provide an account of the dialogues report clearly a consensus about this christological foundation. In an account of the dialogue Kilian McDonnell writes:

Over the years since 1972, we have discovered that Pentecostals and Catholics agree on a number of first order realities: common faith in an experience of Jesus Christ as lord and saviour and his all-sufficient death and resurrection. God as Father, the power of Pentecost, the forgiveness of sins and the promise of eternal life. This means that even now Pentecostals and Catholics enjoy a measure of common faith and experience of Jesus as Lord.[32]

A more complex question is to what degree policies of Catholic and Pentecostal leaders in Latin America are shaped by the conclusions of these dialogues. My observation is that the news about these events does not seem to reach the Catholic media in Latin America, and the results of those dialogues do not inform the official documents of the Catholic church from that region or about it.[33]

Catholic missiologists have to deal with the more basic question of how the Holy Spirit is moving through the growth of evangelicals and Pentecostals in Latin America. In the final analysis the question is also whether the Reformation of the sixteenth century was a work of the Holy Spirit to renew God's church. Besides the dogmatic, theological, and canonical issues at stake in responding to this question, a missiological stance may help to nuance the question and clarify the issues at stake. From my missiological perspective the Reformation had not only a reforming and evangelistic dimension but also a contextual thrust. With its emphasis on Bible translation to the language of the people, it was the way in which Europe was re-evangelized, and in some cases evangelized, as it came out of the womb of the Latin imperial mold into the modern world of nationalities.

By the same token, we Latin American Protestants have to ask ourselves how God's Spirit is moving today in our continent. In the past we emphasized a radical discontinuity between the established Roman church and the evangelical communities. Now we have to ask ourselves if the Spirit of God is moving through the changes brought to the Catholic church not only by Vatican II but also by the very presence and growth of Protestantism in Latin America. And if the Spirit is moving through those events, how are we going to relate to them? It is from the ground of missiology that we may answer better these questions.

For Catholics, evangelicals, and Pentecostals the criteria for evaluating religious phenomena has to be theological more than sociological. Numerical growth or spectacular healings or multitudes that fall on the ground at the word of a charismatic speaker are not the criteria to discern the work of the Holy Spirit in Christian missionary work. Movements are to be measured by their ability to communicate the word and life of Jesus Christ to people and by the degree to which the religious experiences produce in people a Christlike character. Jesus' teachings about the Holy Spirit in the Gospel of John point to the work of the Holy Spirit as the one who keeps alive the memory of Jesus Christ, glorifies him, and convinces the world about the truth of his message. Paul's teaching in his epistles refers to the signs and wonders that accompany the proclamation of the gospel when it is carried on in the power of the Spirit. But he also emphasizes the fruit of the Spirit in the character and the transformation of persons as their lives are modeled on Jesus Christ.

ECCLESIOLOGY, SOCIAL ANALYSIS, AND MISSIOLOGY

A second set of questions has to do with the renewal of church structures for mission. Regarding this ecclesiological question Orlando Costas's missiological reflection summed up well the variety of theological concerns that evangelical theology faced and developed after Lausanne (1974). Costas tried to articulate a vision of what he called "the integrity of mission" through an approach that was both critical and constructive. The critical dimension came in some cases from the use of social analysis to grasp the patterns of social and political practice of people in churches. In *Liberating News* Costas raised the issue of a need for a contextual evangelistic practice:

> Unfortunately the evangelistic practice of many churches, both in the Americas and elsewhere, has suffered from the absence of a clear vision of their sociohistorical contexts. Consequently, their evangelistic practice has been contextually shallow. Recognizing this we have been arguing not so much for a new type of evangelization as for a new way of understanding and practicing contextual evangelization. This implies a sociohistorical approach to the biblical roots of evangelization, a communal theological ground and an ecclesial vision informed by the theological and social base of the church.[34]

The missiological focus of some recent trends in New Testament study is showing the relevance of the agenda described here by Costas and the deepening of our understanding of the early church as a result of what he calls a sociohistoric approach to biblical sources.[35] Anthropological and sociological research about the Mediterranean basin in the first century has shed light on the context of the New Testament so that we see more clearly and precisely the nature of mission, its methods and effects in the apostolic age, the worldviews of the main actors in this drama, the way in which the fact of Christ influenced human history at that time.[36] Similarly the social sciences have helped provide a better understanding of the current sociohistoric context in Latin America, that is, the framework with which today's Christian mission has a dialectical relationship.

The social sciences contribute to the work of theologians by providing a better understanding of the church as a social group and of how its structures operate. The information gathered by social scientists about the way churches operate as communities can serve to open the eyes of theologians. The growth of the popular Protestant churches in Latin America brought them under the sometimes hostile scrutiny of social scientists from outside. We have already seen how in the first sociological studies of popular churches Willems and Lalive showed some characteristics that are very important in terms of ecclesiology, especially how these churches facilitated people's participation and how a liberating experience thereby took place and enabled simple men and women to practice the priesthood of all believers.

There was an element of protest at the emergence of popular Protestantism in different parts of the world. What Sepúlveda writes about in Chile may be applied as a general principle in several other cases. He points to

> the conflict between a religion mediated by specialists of a cultured class (a specialized clergy) and by an enlightened culture; and a religion in which the poor people have direct access to God and in which the relationship with the sacred can be communicated legitimately in the language of the culture itself, and in popular language.[37]

The promise of the movement was precisely this accessibility to simple people of the experience not only of being possessed by truth but also becoming communicators of truth to others: true missionaries. Growth in numbers as well as the leadership patterns among the popular classes in Latin America brought to the fore the issue of pastoral styles. Outside observers such as Peter Wagner related success in numerical growth to authoritarian leadership styles and proposed them as a pattern that others should imitate.

Pentecostal theologians have expressed the need to develop a theology of power for both the pastoral and the political dimensions of the faith. Among them, Norberto Saracco of Argentina and Ricardo Gondim Rodrigues of Brazil have been exploring the questions about church structures and the pastoral situation of popular Protestantism from within. This was their valuable contribution to CLADE III under the theme "The Gospel of Power," a reflection rooted in the ministerial experience of the authors in Pentecostal church circles.[38] Both were reflecting critically about their pastoral experience in an effort to shed light on it by biblical and theological reflection.

Saracco offered a careful analysis of biblical texts showing that the gospels have a great deal of material proving how the proclamation of the gospel takes place in the midst of conflicts over power; hence, it is impossible to understand the ministry of Jesus except within the framework of profound controversy. This is said to distinguish the teaching of Jesus, in whose person the reign of God was present in the world, from the teachings of the rabbis or the Greek philosophers who gave speeches on good habits, or speculations on the past, present, and future of humankind.

Gondim's approach also explored the biblical vocabulary on *power*, but he delved further into the analysis of the manifestations and the use of power within Latin American society and the Pentecostal churches that have grown within it. He pointed out:

> In pentecostal eyes, power has primarily a supernatural dimension. From church institutions built on "divine revelation" to the day-by-day exercise of the charismatic gifts, Latin American pentecostals have perceived the gospel as a charismatically practicable power.[39]

Gondim is very critical of the caudillo-style leadership resulting from emphasis on this conception of power. For him, Pentecostal leadership often becomes sick and suffers under the weight of this excessive load of responsibility: "Leaders come to act not only as codifiers but also as inspectors of Christian behavior. In pentecostalism they are the ones who determine what is sin and what is not, legislating on matters from female garb to leisure."[40] Gondim also referred to the local church basis of political participation and the key role played by pastors who "are politically the owners of votes in the church, and negotiate blatantly with them. Besides having proven extremely sensitive to possible heresies, such behavior places an excessively heavy responsibility on a single person."[41]

Both Pentecostal theologians are explicit about the need to overcome the insufficiencies displayed by various theologies circulating in Latin America. Gondim devotes several paragraphs to analyzing two theological lines: on the one hand, liberation theologies, which according to him lost their transcendent reference points and became horizontalist; and on the other hand, "prosperity theologies," which even though they speak of God's power are nothing more than "consumerist materialism dressed up in biblical teaching." Within the tension of these extremes Gondim found that the theology of a holistic gospel in the sense of the Lausanne Covenant seemed to represent one of the most healthy evangelical movements in recent years. What this "holism" was missing, according to Gondim, was a move from a rhetorical prophetic stance to a committed militancy.

Situating themselves within the spirit of CLADE III, Saracco and Gondim also agreed on the need for a theology of the gospel of power to have a missiological dimension. For Saracco,

> This power or authority conferred only makes sense in the setting of the Reign. It is the divine authority to act and it takes place in relationships that reflect God's lordship. In other words, power is seen to be subordinated to mission. It is not power for power's sake, nor is its purpose to accumulate control over certain persons or structures.[42]

For Gondim,

> In order for the gospel to be one of power its preaching must be embodied in a committed life. . . . The gospel of power recognizes that without love faith is dead; the charismatic gifts, cymbals clanging without the preaching of love, mutilate the gospel; and the mission of the church is dishonored.[43]

The critical comments of these missiologists about the accumulation of power in the person of the minister shows the trend to a development of clericalism in established Pentecostal churches. This would take them eventually to the same patterns of church organization and life against which Pentecostalism developed as a movement of protest that succeeded in empowering the poor for mission.[44]

We pointed out earlier the way the issues of justice and power were approached from a christological perspective. The starting point was the eschatological dimension of Christology applied in a critical evaluation of the culture and the forces against the reign of God that are currently enslaving human beings and tend to undermine the identity of the church and distort its mission. The anti-Christ acting in the world must be named and unmasked at the same time that Jesus Christ is proclaimed as Lord. The christological key is also very important when we look within the church's structures. If the end product of Christian ministry is lives shaped by the example of Jesus Christ and by the demonstration of the fruits of the Spirit, that fact gives us valuable missiological keys. In refining our christological evaluation, sociological analysis helps us to understand what is really happening, for example, in the internal life of popular Protestant churches and their projection into the societies of which they form a part.

GOSPEL AND POWER: CHURCH FACING THE WORLD

As we move into the eschatological question we ask if this religious revival is going to bring transformation so that the evil forces that are disintegrating postmodern societies will be controlled and human life preserved. For Saracco, we need to use the category of the reign of God in order to understand the missionary model of Jesus Christ and the way it throws light on our contemporary situation. The gospels make it very clear that Jesus, anointed by the Spirit, engaged in a ministry that from the start faced opposition. The atmosphere of conflict was the context within which the reign of God and the power of the gospel are to be understood. The source of conflict was the fact that Jesus' ministry touched all aspects of life. The material and spiritual needs of people were not seen as mutually exclusive. The evil spirits that oppressed people resisted Jesus, but resistance also came from those persons or social groups that had political or religious power and were oppressing the people.

Today's mission in Latin America also confronts the powers of darkness and needs the same empowering that made possible the mission of Jesus. Saracco is posing a critique to the conformist stance in political matters that at present characterizes popular Protestant preaching, which avoids conflictive issues and stances and suspects any critical attitude of being "leftist," "liberationist" or "Marxist." Such an attitude comes from a reductionist theology that Saracco has identified:

> Unfortunately, contemporary evangelicals, especially in Latin America, have been influenced by a dispensationalist theology that has given them a Gospel without Kingdom, and by a Western worldview that has deprived them of a holistic understanding of human beings and the world.[45]

The task of the theologian is to recover a biblical dimension of the gospel as the gospel of the kingdom and to see how the Holy Spirit today transforms persons in all the dimensions of their humanity. Led inevitably to political action by numerical growth and upward mobility, evangelicals had to pay attention to the theological task of reflecting on the political realm. During the 1970s such evangelical reflection was done within the theological framework of the kingdom of God.[46] By 1983, at a consultation focused on the issue of political power,[47] Latin American evangelicals active in the political arena in their countries brought a new agenda for theological reflection.[48] In 1990, at the consultation held to celebrate the twenty-year anniversary of the founding of the Latin American Theological Fraternity, the reflection was deliberately set up around two issues: justice and power. In the series of regional consultations preceding that celebration, poverty and terrorism were also studied. For evangelicals in Latin America these are not theoretical issues. Many of the authors of the presentations reflected on their own experiences as politicians, human rights advocates, defense lawyers, pastors in areas where wars of insurgency and counterinsurgency were decimating the population, or denominational leaders who had to provide guidance during presidential elections in which evangelicals had a decisive vote.[49]

Where this reflection connected with the Pentecostal leadership that entered in politics in the decade of the 1980s, they contributed their presence and enthusiasm to the work of the churches for justice and human rights and presented an articulate protest against social evils and dictatorships. Darío López, a Peruvian Pentecostal pastor and scholar, has written a book about the struggle of evangelicals and many Pentecostals during the crisis of violent guerrilla warfare and military repression unleashed by the Shining Path movement in Peru (1980-92). Records show that 529 evangelicals were killed, among them 49 pastors of popular churches.[50] The National Evangelical Council, which represents more than 90 percent of the evangelical and Pentecostal churches, responded with relocation of thousands of victims, a pastoral of comfort and material help, concerted action with human rights organizations, and consistent public denunciation of abuses in remote areas of the country. This had to be accompanied by an educational task for the leadership of churches, especially in the areas of conflict. The theological reflection that had taken place in the previous decade was the basis for the public expression of evangelicals and Pentecostals. López thinks that "beyond its limitations, this social experience led by *a prophetic minority within a religious minority* in a nominally Roman Catholic country has great theological signification for the holistic mission of the church in other historical contexts."[51]

In my sociohistorical interpretation of Latin American Protestantism I have proposed that it initially had an ability to challenge the status quo and make a social critique as a committed minority within a context of nominal Christendom. In this sense it had a stance, that is, an attitude or disposition, similar to that of the Anabaptists of the Radical Reformation in the sixteenth century. In their preaching they did not shy away from conflict or social criticism because they were convinced of a committed and self-sacrificing discipleship, which can be identified with the "following of Christ," a central theme in the Anabaptist life and message.[52] This interpretation refers especially to the historical Protestantism that came mostly during the first part of the twentieth century. In their origins Pentecostals also had a critical stance in relation to society at large, coming from their social origin in the margins of society and their eschatological perception of the world. Juan Sepúlveda has described in a precise way the evolution from this initial attitude:

> When a Pentecostal says "This world offers nothing, only perdition," he is not making a dogmatic statement but simply giving form to his own experience: the world in which he has lived is a world of misery. To the degree that the causes of this situation are not transparent, it is seen to be permanent: it is not that this world *might be* evil, it *is* evil. All one can do is wait for better days in the kingdom of God.[53]

Social evolution of Pentecostals or the practice of service to the needs of people brings a change of attitude and the radical opposition between church and world is replaced by "the idea that though the world is unjust and foreign to the will of God, there can and should be changes on behalf of those who suffer."[54] However, sometimes the early dualism of church-world is kept, but in a new form, when Pentecostals enter politics and adopt simplistic radical positions. The church-world dualism became anti-communism at the time of Pinochet's military coup in 1973. We have already seen that in countries where the growth of grassroots Protestantism has been most visible, sociological analysis examined the evolution of these churches; there are valuable studies encompassing several decades in Chile and Brazil. In recent years evangelical theologians have developed more sophisticated sociotheological research in an effort to plumb the social life of the churches and their structures by connecting facts to beliefs.[55] Paul Freston, a Brazilian sociologist and evangelical scholar, has carried out the most exhaustive and systematic examination of Brazilian Pentecostalism and its politically related expressions.[56] Summarizing information from a variety of sources, he concludes: "The new evangelical political participants in Brazil do not have a project, they only feel, and perhaps justifiably, that the future belongs to them."[57] This situation openly contrasts with the situation in the early twentieth century, when Protestantism presented itself as the bearer of modernization and had a defined social project; at present, "the current majority political project of Brazilian Protestants, that of the Pentecostal leadership, far from being the future opening up before the nation, is somber, tinged with apocalyptic chaos, and barely goes beyond a church-growth strategy."[58]

On the other hand, an analysis of the current activities of Pentecostal politicians shows that they seem to be placing themselves at the service of political conservativism, Freston quotes an observer who concludes: "Conservative Protestantism in its search for visibility is implementing a new strategy of presence and influence in society. It provides a phenomenal contribution of cultural and rhetorical resources ('Christian values') and enviable human and organizational base resources."[59] Thus it becomes a new religious right comparable to the Moral Majority in the United States. What is worse, some of these politicians have fallen into corrupt practices that non-evangelicals are quick to criticize. What Freston describes as the lack of a political project to guide the political action of Pentecostals comes from their extremely individualistic concept of the work of the Holy Spirit in the world. Hence, this evangelical sociologist thinks that it is urgent that evangelicals in Brazil work seriously on the ethical issues now challenging them.

In moving from social analysis to raising ethical and theological issues, Freston uses the account of the temptations that the devil presents to Jesus (Matt. 4:1-11; Lk. 4:1-13) as the key for understanding the temptations now faced by the large Pentecostal churches in Brazil. Within the framework of a missiological Christology, it is possible to understand that in this New Testament story we have a reference for the perennial temptations the church will face in carrying out its mission in any age. The temptation to possess the kingdoms of the world and their splendor is the temptation of triumphalism and the search for visibility that especially affects a religious minority on the rise. The temptation to change stones into bread is the temptation of a hedonistic gospel that seeks quick quasi-magical answers to the material expectations of its followers. So-called prosperity theology is an example of how it is possible to fall into this temptation. Finally, the temptation to throw oneself from the pinnacle of the temple is the temptation that seeks to impress the world with a spectacular demonstration of power and is well portrayed in the so-called Spiritual Warfare, with its technical answers for the spiritual dimensions of mission. These temptations militate against the ethical renewal that the popular churches in Brazil urgently need.[60] Freston poses the need to develop a theology of power that will help to overcome the temptation to an idolatry of power in church and politics, and "an ethic of renunciation motivated by the Kingdom of God in place of our predominant legalism."[61]

ESCHATOLOGY, THE SPIRITUALITY OF *MAÑANA*

The way in which eschatology relates to a renewed biblical understanding of the Holy Spirit has been forcefully presented by Justo L. González in his beautiful book *Mañana: Christian Theology from a Hispanic Perspective.*[62] From his rich background as a historian of the church and Christian doctrine and sociohistoric perception of the place of the Hispanic minority in the United States, González offers us a fresh formulation of basic Christian doctrines. In the chapter entitled "Life in the Spirit" he addresses the deeply felt malaise that affects many mainline Protestant denominations in North America and discards easy prescriptions that look for structural matters and constitutional revisions as a solution. For him, "the problem really has to do with the meaning of the Gospel and how we apply it, not only in our individual lives but also in the communal and structural life of the church," and consequently "the solution to our present malaise will not be found until we deal with issues of spirituality and come to a spirituality that is both deeply grounded in Scripture and radically relevant to today's world."[63]

In order to guide us through the understanding of biblical spirituality, González reminds us of the way in which Christian thinking became influenced by Hellenistic religiosity and adopted its contrast between matter and spirit. That distinction, however, is not central to the biblical understanding of reality and should not be at the center of our understanding of spirituality.

> The basis for Christian spirituality is not "the spiritual" in the sense of the non-material. The basis for Christian spirituality is the Spirit—the Holy Spirit of God. Therefore in biblical parlance one is "spiritual" not because one is primarily concerned with "spiritual" things in contrast to the "material" but because of the presence of the Holy Spirit. A "spiritual person" is not one who flexes and develops his or her spirit, as an athlete flexes and develops muscles, but one in whom the Spirit of the Lord dwells.[64]

As we look at the totality of scripture, from creation to consummation, all that God has done, is doing, and will do is done through the Spirit: "Through the power of the Spirit, the world is created out of the void. Through the power of the same Spirit, the 'natural human being'—the 'old,' 'soulish,' 'unspiritual' human being—is created anew, so that sinful nature no longer holds sway."[65] There is here a discontinuity because the spirit of the world only sees "that which naturally follows from the present order, while the Spirit of God allows us to see 'what has been bestowed on us (1 Cor. 2:12),' the coming Reign, the new order, our inheritance, the promise."[66] What González finds in the Book of Acts is that "part of the function of the Spirit is to allow the believing community to live already, at least partially, in the 'not yet' of the Reign."[67]

> On this basis, being "spiritual" means living out of the future we have been promised, precisely because that promise has been sealed and guaranteed by the Holy Spirit. What this means is that Christian spirituality— that genuinely Christian spirituality that is based not on our own "spiritual" or "soulish" powers but on the presence of the Holy Spirit—is eschatological in nature. It is future oriented. It is life lived out on an expectation, out of a hope and a goal. And that goal is the coming Reign of God. To have the Spirit is to have a foot up on the stirrup of the eschatological future and to live now as those who expect a new reality, the coming of the Reign of God.[68]

What González proposes is a stance and a theology that can well be described by the Spanish word *mañana*. This word not only means "tomorrow," and, as many Anglo-Saxons would be prompt to remind us, "the indolent response of people too lazy to make any kind of effort." *Mañana* is the radical questioning of today; unlike today, "it is a time of a new reality, not the outcome of today's disorderly order but the outcome of other factors that bring about a breach with an unbearable today." Gambling or drugs are the ways in which some poor people try to get into that *mañana*.

Then there are those who capture the *mañana* vision of Scripture. The world will not always be as it is. It will not even be an outgrowth of what is. God who created the world in the first place is about to do a new thing—a thing as great and as surprising as that first act of creation. God is already doing this new thing, and we can join in it by the power of the Spirit. *Mañana* is here! True, *mañana* is not yet today, but today can be lived out of the glory and the promise of *mañana*, thanks to the power of the Spirit.[69]

PART FOUR

MISSION *FROM* LATIN AMERICA

12

Mission from Latin America

Latin America is now the base for a growing Christian missionary movement to other parts of the world. Among the more lively and vigorous Protestant churches that have developed in Latin America there is a vigorous willingness to assume responsibilities in Christian mission on a global level. An estimated four thousand missionaries are sent from Latin American churches or missionary organizations to other parts of the world. It should be noted at the outset, however, that this vision did not begin in the closing decades of the twentieth century. Denominations like the Baptists, Methodists, and Assemblies of God have been sending missionaries to other Latin American countries and to Africa and Europe for almost a century. A few examples will suffice. The Baptist churches in Paraguay arose from the work of the Argentinean missionaries Maximino Fernández, Enrique Molinas, and Celestino Ermili, who began to work there in 1919.[1] In the 1930s Argentinean and Uruguayan Methodist missionaries were working in Bolivia and Peru.[2] Starting in 1930, Chilean Pentecostal emigrants went to Argentina with a missionary vision and became established in various cities, sometimes receiving missionary support from Chile, sometimes as bivocational missionaries, earning their living with their own trade or business.[3]

In these instances obedience to the missionary impulse did not have to wait until the churches were numerically strong or economically powerful. In some cases these churches were just beginning or were still in the process of being formed, but they had a global vision that went beyond their national boundaries. In this sense they looked more like the New Testament churches, such as the one in Antioch, which shortly after its founding and establishment was ready to send two of its well-known leaders to preach the gospel elsewhere (Acts 11:19-30; 13:1-4). The idea that only rich and large churches are able to take part in the global mission is the result of the Constantinian paradigm in which mission is carried out from the top down, from the center of economic and political power. A vision and missionary drive in which it becomes possible for the churches to "give out of their poverty" is now being retrieved in Latin America.

The events and movements that we are going to discuss in this chapter are simply illustrations of a much broader and richer movement whose history remains to be discovered and researched.

YOUTH, PIONEERS IN THE HISTORY OF MISSION

As at other moments in Christian history, it has been young people who have pioneered the recovery of missionary vision and practice in Latin America. We are particularly thinking of what has happened in student circles. A constant note in the history of mission has been youth participation at critical steps. Young people who become aware of their privilege and potential open up to hearing the call of Jesus Christ and charge forward to cross borders with the gospel. However, there is an important point to keep in mind. It would be wrong for us to think that the decisive events in mission are those in which educated and privileged persons were the protagonists, simply because we have a record of their activities through the centuries. There are many anonymous stories that may be more decisive, and the historian as well as the missiologist has to be sensitive to that fact. It is people with the privilege of a certain degree of education who can write letters, send reports, keep diaries, write books, attend conferences, and put together manifestos, thus becoming prominent in recorded history. But for every person mentioned in missionary history there are thousands whose names are never chronicled, though they are equally important. One effect of the idea of looking at history and at scripture through the eyes of the poor will be the development of a new way of writing missionary history and evaluating missionary activity.

Even before the universities as we now know them existed, young people of student age and similar educational level were playing an important role in missions. The kind of people that would gather around scholars to form the guilds out of which the oldest colleges and universities in Europe developed were the kind of people that gathered around spiritual teachers and formed the great missionary orders of the Middle Ages. That was the case for the Franciscans and the Dominicans, for instance. The itinerancy of these orders developed at a crucial moment and became the new focus of missionary activity; it replaced the stability and permanence of the monastery, which for the previous five centuries had been "the heart of the missionary enterprise."[4]

As historian Stephen Neill points out, the two orders were very different in style and in the way in which they formulated their specific call. But a genuine missionary impulse lived in each. Before the end of the thirteenth century, Franciscans were found at the ends of the known earth. And about 1300 the Dominicans formed the *Societas Fratrum peregrinantium propter Christum inter gentes* (The company of brethren dwelling in foreign parts among the heathen for the sake of Christ). Two centuries later the Jesuits, in whose ranks we find mainly college and university people who had gathered around Loyola, became heavily involved in missionary action in Asia and in the continents that today we call the Americas. Religious from these orders not only evangelized the natives, established new churches, and ministered to the conquerors, but a few among them also used their education and influence to defend the new Christians from the exploitation and oppression of the European colonial enterprise. Bartolomé de Las Casas (1474-1566), a Dominican, combined his missionary practice in what today is Mexico and Guatemala with his voluminous writings and his academic debates in the University of Salamanca to prove the humanity of the natives and the need for a missionary methodology patterned after the example of Jesus Christ.[5]

The first permanent missionary impulse on the Protestant side came from Moravian Pietists from Central Europe in the mid-eighteenth century. Along with a spiritual revival and the disciplined cultivation of evangelical piety, they had a global vision with a sense of missionary obligation and a rigorous academic training center, the University of Halle.[6] Pietism connects with other renewal movements during the post-Reformation period, including the student societies for spiritual revival in the English world of the sixteenth century. Moravians were also influential in the spiritual awakenings of the eighteenth century in England and North America, and in the development of grassroots evangelical student movements in the nineteenth century. In each of these movements, universities and colleges became centers where young people were challenged to consider the call of Jesus Christ to missionary service, both at home and abroad.[7]

In the English-speaking world the Student Volunteer Movement (SVM) arose in the nineteenth century. It can be traced back to the Haystack prayer meeting in Williams College, Massachusetts, in August 1806, a meeting that has become a milestone of missionary history. Clarence P. Shedd's classic work has documented the development of the student societies that spread out from the centers at Andover, Brown, and Dartmouth.[8] Four students from that Haystack prayer meeting presented a petition to the General Assembly of the Congregational Churches on June 27, 1810. It was the enthusiasm of those thousands of young people who wanted to serve in the evangelization of the world that eventually forced the churches to form mission boards to channel their ardent vocations. The word *volunteer* in the movement's name is a good description of its nature. It was a movement that erupted spontaneously in campuses across North America and the world.

The eagerness among the students to band together to pray for mission, to offer their lives, to write, and to travel at their own expense in order to promote their vision marked the beginning of the SVM. A Catholic student by the name of Mary Josephine Rogers was inspired by the SVM when she was a student at Smith College. She dedicated her life to mission and became the right hand of James E. Walsh, the founder of the Catholic Foreign Mission Society of America, better known as Maryknoll. Angelyn Dries says that Rogers "proved an invaluable leader in spiritual formation, in practical organization and as a coworker with Walsh in the development of Maryknoll."[9] Dries also traces back to the influence of the SVM the development of the Catholic Students Mission Crusade, which was to have a decisive influence in motivating and educating for mission several generations of young Catholics in the United States.[10]

It is surprising to see the echo that the original vision of the SVM had not only in the regions where the church had been established for centuries, but also in other parts of the world where it had just arrived. After a trip around the world in which the famous mission statesman John R. Mott traversed sixty thousand miles and visited 22 different countries and 144 universities, colleges, and schools, he could report about the wave of missionary concern that he found: "About three hundred students have volunteered, that is dedicated their lives to Christian work. More than five sixths of this number are students in mission lands."[11]

A brief reflection about the history of the SVM shows some characteristics of its initial stages. They are points about which there seems to be consensus among historians and scholars, though there may be different criteria about which points were more decisive for the success of the movement. In the first place the SVM was a *spontaneous* movement. It was not promoted by any church agency, but it was influential in the development of mission agencies. Second, it had a definite *evangelical character* in its spirituality and in the basic theological convictions that nurtured the missionary vision. Third, a net of *personal relationships* structured it; I noticed this as I became familiar with the life stories of those such as Robert Speer, John R. Mott, and John A. Mackay, whose correspondence reflects a common vision and a sense of mutual belonging nurtured by faith. Fourth, its leaders put amazing *organizational ability* to the service of their vision. At a time in which travel and communication were not as developed as they are now, the movement was a global network with a truly ecumenical thrust. And fifth, the movement played a *fermenting role* for the renewal of the church. Its adherents became leaders in the mainline denominations and were able to communicate their missionary vision.[12] When the SVM declined in the 1930s, the movement that continued its missionary vision was the InterVarsity Christian Fellowship, which has motivated and educated several generations of university students for mission up to the present, especially through the triennial Urbana Missionary Convention.[13] The same patterns may be observed in the development of missionary vision among young people in Latin America.

MISSIONARY VISION IN BRAZIL, THE CONGRESS OF CURITIBA (1976)

Brazil is one of the countries in which Protestantism had a more rapid and sustained growth. It was also one of the first countries to send missionaries abroad. The Brazilian Baptist Convention organized a foreign mission board as early as 1906 and sent missionaries to neighboring countries such as Bolivia and Paraguay, to Portuguese-speaking countries in Africa, and to Portugal. More recently the student movement in Brazil has been a source of missionary vocations. Starting in 1958 various evangelical student movements worked in Latin America in cooperation with the International Fellowship of Evangelical Students. Latin American universities were considered a strategic but difficult mission field.[14] Since the early 1950s the Alianca Biblica Universitaria (ABU) from Brazil was one of these movements that grew rapidly among university and high school students as a creative indigenous force. At a crucial point, in 1972, Neuza Itioka, a Brazilian teacher of Japanese background, became the general secretary of the movement. She was invited to attend an Asian missionary conference in Baguio, the Philippines (1973), and also the Lausanne Congress on Evangelism (1974). She returned with the vision of challenging Brazilian students with the missionary demands of Jesus Christ, and in 1976 the ABU organized a missionary congress. The spontaneous response was unexpected. ABU could only accommodate five hundred students, but there were more than two thousand requests for registration. So the organizers were able to select the most committed students by demanding that attendants take a Bible course and read some pieces of contemporary missionary literature.

The congress became a milestone in the history of student groups in Latin America. Besides the Brazilians, fifty students and graduates from all over Latin America attended. Held on the campus of the University of Paraná in Curitiba during the month of July 1976, its motto was "Jesus Christ: Lordship, purpose, and mission." It was a call to see every structure of Brazilian life and every country of the world as a mission field. The "Declaration of Curitiba" summed up the presentations, discussions, and group work of those attending.[15] This document reflects well the initial missionary awareness of a generation of Latin American men and women.[16] The "Declaration of Curitiba" sums up biblical convictions and expresses an awareness of history: "We humbly thank God for what has been done thus far, acknowledging the work of those who brought the gospel to Latin American lands and the great challenge that their evangelical legacy represents for us" (par. 3). It then affirms belief in the sovereignty of God, God's intention to bless all nations, the reality of Jesus Christ as key to history, and the role of the church: "We believe that being church becomes real along the road, in carrying out the missionary task, in direct dependence on the Lord who sends, as it bears the message of the Reign of God" (par. 7).

One specific feature of this movement is that it does not reduce the notion of mission to the transcultural activity of those fully devoted to this task in faraway lands. There is a clear consciousness that the missionary challenge today is present in every corner of Latin America just as much as in lands overseas:

> We recognize that mission cannot be an isolated department in the life of the church because it forms part of its very essence, for "the church that is not missionary is not church." Thus mission commits all Christians in the entirety of their lives. The priesthood of all believers cannot be replaced by the mistaken exclusive notion that considers only professional missionaries. We are deeply concerned about the lack of this missionary vision in the Latin American church (par. 8).

The end of so-called Christian society, the process of secularization, and social changes as well as the rise of non-Christian religions are also recognized.

Within this framework the permanent nature of the call of God in Christ is likewise recognized: "We recognize that God has placed us at this particular moment of history as his witnesses in Latin America" (par. 12). Following the example of Jesus, witness must be given by opening our eyes to the needs of the "suffering, abandoned, and exploited" Latin American masses, by crossing geographical, sociological, cultural, and religious barriers, and by praying and acting.

The declaration did not remain on paper but was followed by actions of obedience to specific calls. Among the organizers and leaders of the congress Tacito and Glacy Pinto went to work in student circles in Italy; Neuza Itioka did specialized missiological studies about Brazilian popular religiosity at Fuller Seminary in California and returned with a doctorate to lead a program for the training of Brazilian missionaries; Antonia Leonora Van der Meer, a translator, left her diplomatic career to do theological training and then went as a missionary to Angola; Dieter Brepohl and his family served as missionaries in Ecuador; Valdir Steuernagel, a Lutheran pastor, earned the doctorate in missiology in Chicago and returned to found and direct a missionary institute within the Lutheran church of Brazil. The student movement also mobilized Brazilian students for mission in Italy and Bolivia and provided scholarships for students from Portuguese-speaking Africa, so that while at the university they could also be trained as missionaries with the movement in Brazil. Eleven years after the Curitiba congress, during a meeting on mission and holistic transformation[17] attended by ninety people from all over Latin America and with thirty service projects represented, many acknowledged that their experience as disciples in the university and the student congress in Curitiba had been key moments of inspiration and decision for carrying out their missionary vocation.

One way of explaining why student movements have been a source of missionary vocations through history could be summarized in a word that has both sociological and theological connotations: *privilege*. University students are privileged people everywhere. In spite of the abysmal economic differences between a student in Europe or North America and one in Africa or Latin America, in North and South, the student is a privileged person in relation to the rest of the population. Privilege can be translated in terms of more mobility than other segments of the population; more choices in relation to work and life options; more training that enables articulation of views, desires, and expectations; and more exposure to global realities and the consequent awareness of them. In the clear terms of Jesus' teaching, privilege brings responsibility and becomes a call to commitment: "From everyone who has been given much, much will be demanded; and from the one who has been entrusted with much, much more will be asked" (Lk.12:48).

EMERGENCE OF COMIBAM (1987)

Eleven years after the Curitiba congress, other youth circles connected to the conservative organization known as CONELA (Confraternity of Evangelicals of Latin America) organized an Ibero-American Missionary Congress (Congreso Misionero Iberoamericano—COMIBAM) that was also held in Brazil, this time in São Paulo (November 1987). The congress was attended by thirty-one hundred delegates representing all the Latin American countries and twenty-five other nations of the world. As William Taylor describes it:

> [The congress] was both an event and proof of a missionary ethos rippling through the churches in Latin America. The emphasis of COMIBAM has not been so much evangelism within one's culture—a perennial spirit of these churches—but rather cross-cultural evangelism and church planting both across Latin America's thousands of cultural lines as well as to the entire world.[18]

Organizers of COMIBAM were enthusiastic about their vision. The coordinator of the conference, Luis Bush, said, "In 1918 Latin America was declared a mission field. In 1987 Latin America declares itself a mission force." But there was also awareness about the difficulties of supporting mission along traditional lines for churches that primarily ministered among the poor. Rudy Giron, a pastor from Guatemala, said, "Missions from Latin America will be sacrificial. We don't have computers; we don't have dollars; but 'By my Spirit, says the Lord.'"[19] Speakers during the congress warned against the dangers of sending out missionaries without adequate training, as well as the need to develop adequate infrastructure for support. A remarkable fact of the congress was that almost 70 percent of the expenses were paid with funds from Latin American participants and mission organizations. As a continuation of the congress, a network of loosely coordinated missionary efforts developed and the initial "C" standing for "Congress" in the acronym was changed to "Cooperation." COMIBAM has drawn in many participants, a new generation eager to participate in mission on a world scale,[20] especially in those places on the globe where there is little or no Christian presence, such as the Muslim world.[21]

At first COMIBAM was strongly influenced by "managerial missiology" from the United States; Latin Americans adopted missiological concepts and methodologies such as "unreached peoples," "10-40 window," and "adopt-a-people." The pragmatic bias of this missiology probably explains why the program of the initial congress reflected a reluctance to deal with some important theological issues that Latin American missiologists had been exploring since the 1960s. In recent years the leadership of COMIBAM and the FTL have come to an agreement on how to work together in order to complement an emphasis on action with a critical reflection in good biblical fashion. Publications of COMIBAM include informative and statistical catalogues about Latin American involvement in global mission[22] but also a dictionary of missiology[23] and a two-volume work about mission theology.[24]

At the second COMIBAM congress, held in Acapulco in 1998, progress in evangelical missionary work from Latin America was plain to see. In 1982, it has been estimated, 92 Protestant organizations were sending a total of 1,120

Latin Americans as missionaries to other parts of the world. By 1988 the numbers had grown to 150 organizations and 3,026 missionaries.[25] Figures published in 1997 indicate that there are 3,921 Latin American missionaries elsewhere in the world, sent by 284 organizations.[26] These figures, compiled by scholars, are generally conservative estimates and do not include many spontaneous movements that are hard to document. Nor do they include migrants with no ties to established agencies who on their own do missionary work elsewhere in the world. Even so, the statistics are evidence of a missionary drive that is on the rise.

MISSIONARY CONCERN IN CATHOLIC CIRCLES

Today Latin American Catholics are also raising the question of their responsibility for the mission of evangelizing elsewhere in the world. As has been indicated, there are weighty demographic and historic reasons for this. During the Fourth Latin American Missionary Conference (COMLA-4) Catholic leaders portrayed the situation in a striking way: "Even though 42 percent of the world's Catholics are in Latin America and the evangelization of the continent began five hundred years ago, Latin Americans do not make up even two percent of the missionaries in the world."[27]

It is acknowledged that in order to be able to keep its presence and ministry in Latin America, the Catholic church needs a continual influx of missionaries from other continents. Over 60 percent of the priests and nuns in Peru, for example, are foreign.[28] This creates a dilemma: how to set off to do mission in other lands when there is so much to do right here?

The bishops at Puebla (1979) had already noted this when they presented the need for greater Latin American participation in world mission: "Finally the time has come for Latin America to intensify works of mutual service between local churches and to extend them beyond their own frontiers 'ad gentes.' True, we ourselves are in need of missionaries; but we must give from our own poverty."[29] The reason for urgency of missionary participation is repeated in the COMLA-4 "Final Message" with a line that looks as though it were taken from Protestant missionary literature:

> As the year 2000 draws near, only a third of the world population (close to six billion inhabitants) has been reached by the gospel. In this situation, the Latin American church, which encompasses almost half of all the Catholics in the world, is making only a tiny contribution to missionary presence beyond its boundaries.[30]

This concern for the evangelization of the "unreached" is in line with the most recent teaching of Pope John Paul II, especially in his 1990 encyclical *Redemptoris Missio (The Mission of the Redeemer)*. This may seem surprising in Latin America, where, as a majority church, Catholics have been primarily concerned about keeping their faithful in the sheepfold and holding onto their political privileges as a religious majority; emphasis on evangelization has been more characteristic of Protestants. Nonetheless, the series of missionary congresses known as COMLA started in November 1977 when the National Missionary Congress of Mexico became the First Latin American Missionary Congress. It is acknowledged that *Evangelii Nuntiandi* (1975) about evangelization from Pope Paul VI was influential in this starting point. COMLA-2 was held in Tlaxcala, Mexico, in 1983, with the motto "With Mary, missionaries of Christ," which reflects the teaching of Pope John Paul II. COMLA-3 was held in Bogotá, Colombia, in 1987, with the motto "America, your time has come to be an evangelizer"; it was followed by COMLA-4 in Lima, Peru, in 1991, with the motto "Latin America, from your faith send missionaries," and COMLA-5 in Belo Horizonte, Brazil, in 1995, with the motto "I came, I saw and I proclaimed." According to the present secretary general of the Pontifical Missionary Union:

> The entire series of these congresses were inspired and organized by the Pontifical Mission Societies. Their purpose is to foster the missionary responsibility of local churches both old and new, and to invite them to cooperate more fully both at home and beyond their own frontiers, also including evangelization *ad gentes*.[31]

The idea of "giving out of our poverty" expressed at Puebla reflects the realization on the part of Catholic scholars of the defects in the Constantinian mission. The Swiss missionary Roger Aubry, who headed the CELAM Missions Department, has been one of the most enthusiastic proponents of Catholic missionary work toward nonbelievers. In the specialized language of Catholic missiology this is the mission *ad gentes*. Aubry has eloquently expressed the new Catholic view:

> Mission from poor to poor purifies the image of every mission. The new style is the absence of political support, economic domination, and cultural superiority, so as not to have any support other than the power of the gospel, Good News for these peoples. This style does away with many *facilities* which in other circumstances may have made it possible to maintain a very high rate of baptisms. But it also does away with certain *ambiguities*. The power of the evangelizer is the Word of God present in Jesus crucified, bereft of any human power, and in the risen Jesus, rich only in the power of God.[32]

The most recent development after COMLA-6 in Parana, Argentina, 1999, was the effort to connect the missionary effort of Latin American Catholics with the activity of Catholics in the United States and Canada. The new series of congresses will be called CAM (American Missionary Congresses) and the word *American* will embrace both Latin America and North America. This strategy corresponds to the new organizational scheme that developed after the American Synod of Churches, in which we have seen the beginning of new patterns for sharing human and material resources between Catholics from the North and the South.[33]

TWO MODELS OF MISSION OUT OF POVERTY

For many Protestants the economic situation is a major obstacle on the road to the Latin American missionary vocation. Protestant churches are a minority, those that have grown most are churches among the poor, and the continent is now in a phase in which more and more people are poor. Missionary zeal and vision abound, but material resources to mobilize human resources are lacking. Within this context of poverty two models of missionary activity have been developed. First, there is the *cooperation model* led by European and North American churches that add their material resources to the human resources of Latin American churches in order to engage in missionary endeavor outside the Americas or within them. Various missionary organizations are moving in this direction. But the model raises some practical issues for which there are no easy answers.

The churches that provide material resources want to prevent the creation of a spirit of dependence that ends up crushing the stewardship capability of Latin American churches to sustain their own missionaries. With money from rich churches it is possible to set up expensive missionary enterprises that will not last because they will not be able to take root in poor countries. Yet missionary education in wealthy countries has led people to think that what is given for the missions is "their money" and should go to support "their missionaries," that is, those of their own nationality. It is hard to realize that what is given to the missions belongs to the Lord and could be used with greater generosity and imagination.

The longstanding traditional missionary orders in the Roman Catholic Church, such as the Franciscans, Jesuits, and Dominicans, are international bodies and do not bear the stamp of any nationality. One who enters an order, regardless of the country from which he or she comes, will be sustained by the order's resources. To that we have to add that the vows of chastity, poverty, and obedience along with training in a well-defined spiritual discipline prepare the members of these orders to carry out their missionary task even under conditions of poverty and insecurity or social tension. Protestants naturally have very different ideas of ministry and church order.

We have noted how pioneers of missionary participation have come from university classrooms. Because students are young and willing to take risks, Protestant youth movements have created models of socially and transculturally sensitive missionary teams. Often those who have participated in them have been enabled to see their own social condition and culture from a critical distance. This has also been facilitated by the mobility and simple lifestyle of the teams. In organizations as different as the Mennonite Central Committee, Youth with a Mission, International Fellowship of Evangelical Students, and Operation Mobilization, through experience and reflection in the light of God's word, a training space for mission has been created. In these movements there are intentional forms of cultivating community through commitment requirements, spirituality, and prayer, the real kind of fellowship out of which mission comes. There is a team spirit that allows for growth from individualism to awareness of the body of Christ and a disciplined life as part of a team with a sense of purpose. A simple lifestyle allows volunteers to immerse themselves more fully among those with whom they work in ministry. I would venture to say that this kind of experience enables participants to try out some of the characteristics of traditional monastic orders that have remained as mission tools across cultural and social borders.

Second, there is the centuries-old *migratory model* of mission. The founders of the church at Antioch in the New Testament were Christians who had to emigrate as a result of religious persecution. Of this difficult initial stage Justo González says:

> Most of the expansion of Christianity in the centuries before Constantine took place not as a result of the work of people dedicated solely to this task, but thanks to the ongoing witness of hundreds of millions of merchants, slaves, and Christians condemned to exile, who went about giving witness to Jesus Christ wherever life led them, thereby setting up new communities in places where "professional ministries" had not yet arrived.[34]

In our time as well, travelers from poor countries who migrate for economic survival bring the Christian message and missionary initiative with them. Moravians from Curaçao have gone to Holland, Baptists from Jamaica emigrated to Central America and to England, Christian women from the Philippines work in Muslim countries, Haitian believers have gone to Canada, and Latin American missionaries are going to Japan, Australia, and the United States. This missionary presence and activity has been significant even though it rarely reaches reports and stories in the media of institutional missionary activity.

CHURCHES IN TIME OF MISSION

A remarkable event in Latin American Protestantism made it possible to experience the degree to which many Protestant churches in Latin America are sharing missionary dynamism. It is no exaggeration to say that the Third Latin American Congress on Evangelization (CLADE III), organized by the FTL, was the most representative assembly of Latin American Protestantism in the twentieth century. The 1,008 participants who met in Quito from August 24 to September 4, 1992, represented a major portion of the Protestant churches working in the Spanish- and Portuguese-speaking world of the Americas. For the first time in meetings of this nature aboriginal communities speaking Quechua, Aymara, Mapuche, and other languages were adequately represented. Also present were the presidents and executive secretaries of the two organizations of Protestant cooperation in the continent, CLAI and CONELA, and leaders and representatives of a wide range of Protestant bodies. Theologian José Míguez Bonino has pointed out that CLADE III "went beyond the limits of the Latin American Theological Fraternity to become a truly 'Latin American Protestant Congress' as much due to the breadth of its representation as to the wealth of materials and freedom of debate."[35]

The program was built around an eloquent slogan: "The whole gospel, for all peoples from Latin America." A strong note at CLADE III was the realization that Latin America is not merely a mission field where Latin American churches and missionaries from elsewhere witness their faith and evangelize. The action of the Holy Spirit, the strength of the evangelical churches, and the historic moment that our peoples are undergoing have made Latin America even now a base from which missionaries are sent to other places in the world. "The whole gospel" emphasizes the rediscovery of a comprehensive and holistic sense of mission that was an important part of the agenda of congresses that preceded this one (CLADE I, in Bogotá, 1969, and CLADE II, in Lima, 1979). "For all peoples from Latin America" is the expression of a new awareness that points to already existing practice among Protestants and to the renewal of the sense of mission. It also expresses the renewed search for biblical and theological prin-ciples that will allow for the creation of mission models more suited to the possibilities of the new ministries and to the new world situation.

At this congress it was obvious that there is already a Latin American mis-sionary movement that is involved in mission around the world and reflecting theologically about it. Giving testimony from the podium were Antonia Leonora Van der Meer, a Brazilian missionary who had returned from Angola, and Mirta Marengo, an Argentinean physician who had returned from working in Spain and North Africa. These testimonies were moving, with no hint of triumphalism; they were self-critical but based on the deep conviction that today God is call-ing Latin Americans to cross new borders. A profusion of missionary models could be seen and heard at CLADE III. In a single day one could meet a young Mexican lay minister of the Mennonite church who developed a tent-making model for establishing churches in marginal populations of Mexico; a Colom-bian nurse who with her husband, a Peruvian medical doctor, were working in a Presbyterian mission in the jungle of Peru; a Lutheran minister who has moved with several families of business and professional people from a coastal city in Brazil to a jungle town in order to establish new, self-supporting churches; and Peruvian musicians in the AMEN movement, who have sent Andean missionar-ies and music groups to various European countries.

The experience of one of the speakers illustrates the cycle of missionary history that is developing in Latin America. Key Yuasa is a pastor of a Holiness church and a missiologist in São Paulo, Brazil. His family migrated from Japan to Brazil in the early decades of the twentieth century; the migrants came as communities of believers with their pastors. The upsurge of Japan as an eco-nomic power in recent decades, as well as the deterioration of the Brazilian economy, has caused a migration of Brazilians of Japanese descent to Japan in search of jobs. Key Yuasa's church has now sent a couple to Japan as missionaries to work among these migrant workers, who are marginalized and work in abject conditions.

The 1970s and 1980s in Latin America were a time in which evangelicals engaged in theological reflection about their presence and history, and rediscovered the "whole gospel" and new forms of evangelization. The agenda and content of the first and second congresses of evangelism (CLADE I and II) register this process. In the 1990s mission *from* Latin America became part of the agenda, which included a self-critical evaluation of the forms of Catholic and Protestant mission that were based on the military, economic, or political power of the era of Christendom. In one of the theological papers of CLADE III, missiologist Valdir Steuernagel examined the missiological consequences of this new awareness at the same time that he affirmed the universality of mission. It is the universal character of the Christian faith that gives it its missionary dimension:

Faith in Jesus does not confine itself within geographical, ethnic, racial, political or social and economic borders. Because of its fundamental relevance for all human beings in all places and all generations it is a faith without frontiers. The confession of the universal character of the lordship of Jesus Christ takes a deeply missiological dimension.[36]

However, Steuernagel reminds us that in the history of missions, affirmation of the universality of faith in Christ has gone hand in hand with the military or economic conquest by the "Christian" empires or nations. Therefore, we need an incarnational theology as a principle that will give direction to the Latin American missionary practice. The universality of Jesus Christ has been for too long conveyed in the philosophical categories of western culture. Therefore we need a commitment to express and practice our faith in a contextual manner and to empower others to do the same when we move on in mission. The mark of the Christendom model of mission has been to be served. But we know that Jesus taught us to serve by word and deed.

We must return to the model of Jesus. The principle of universality cannot lead to arrogance or be clothed in the mantle of superiority. This is the model that we are invited to follow, whether in the church, the neighborhood, or far off lands.[37]

It is precisely in order to grasp some contours of the nature of the missionary challenge as Latin Americans move to take part in global mission that we are going to propose a brief agenda for the formation of missionaries.

13

Formation of the Transcultural Missionary

In the light of five centuries of Christian mission in Latin America, we may ask how the Latin American missionaries of this new century are going to be formed. In describing the task of missiology in chapter 2, we were also posing an agenda that we have followed in this effort to understand mission on our continent. This agenda may also be taken as an outline of the components that ought to be part of any training program for missionaries in the future. It is no longer any use to us simply to imitate and translate missionary methods worked out in the wealthy countries from which the missionary force used to set out. We are thankful for the vocation and commitment of thousands of men and women who understood that God was calling them to mission and responded to that call. But we also have to acknowledge that in some aspects the methods they used were marked by a certain triumphalism and dependency on abundant material means, and even on marketing and persuasion techniques. What is needed, in the first place, is a return to the biblical models. The fundamental principles of mission in the New Testament, rooted in the Old Testament, must be reread. We then need a missionary-training curriculum in which the biblical portion is reinforced, not simply as pure scholarly learning but with a missiological thrust. A good part of this chapter is devoted to outlining elements of the biblical formation. Other aspects of a formative agenda are mentioned briefly at this point.

Second, we must reexamine the historic models to see how mission was carried out before the church became an ally of empire and a tool for colonization. For instance, we must rediscover how the poor have been missionaries at different moments in history, from below, in the Galilean manner. We must apply the same curious and critical eye that we apply to reading history to *observing* the present in order to see how the dynamic churches that carry out their mission among the poor are carrying out mission today. Our effort must be toward a missiological reading of history. For instance, the way Eduardo Hoornaert reads early church history from the perspective of his experience with Base Ecclesial Communities among the poor in Brazil is especially helpful.[1]

Third, the social sciences are helpful for understanding today's cultures and societies. They have to be employed with a missiological criterion, not allowing them to impose their ideological and political program but using them as tools for a better understanding of the world in which we live. It is interesting to see the contribution that many missionaries have made to anthropology and linguistics. A solid biblical grounding in the vision of the human being and society can help us to discern what to accept and reject from tools of the social sciences. For instance, many Latin Americans have found helpful the work of Eugene Nida, who applies anthropology and sociology to the understanding of religious realities in Latin American societies.[2] Jacob Loewen has used anthropological insights for a courageous and humble evaluation of missionary experiences in several Latin American settings.[3] Paul Hiebert has been very explicit about the missiological use of the social sciences and some of the questions it poses.[4] These are just a few examples from among those who have written from the ground of both their own missionary experience and their scientific formation.

Fourth, there is the value of learning from practice. Working with and under the guidance of missionaries, pastors, and evangelists, we can complement and energize what we learn in books. One only learns to cross cultures by crossing them, so training centers have to be located in places where cultures are continually being crossed. Almost any Latin American city is in some way an ongoing melting pot of cultures, but certain cities like Santa Cruz (Bolivia), Asunción (Paraguay), New York (United States), and Montreal (Canada) are true laboratories of cultural pluralism and crossing of ethnic boundaries. In my own teaching I encourage students to embark on different forms of missionary practice and to learn how to reflect about that practice. I have found Paulo Freire a valuable source of ideas about reflection on practice; his whole career as an educator modeled this continuous reflection.[5]

Five, there is no substitute for spiritual discipline. The great missionary movements have occurred in the midst of the renewal of spiritual life. The school of prayer, biblical meditation, mutual exhortation, and waiting on the Lord has shaped the core of the missionary vocation, the spirit of service, learning how to get along with others, and devotion to Christ who sustains missionaries in the midst of the conflicts and difficulties of their service. Without intentional and constant spiritual discipline, there is no missionary formation. I am convinced that missionary teams have to express the kind of companionship and mutual belonging described in the New Testament as *koinonia*. In decades of observation and experience I have become convinced that this is the weakest point of Protestant missions from English-speaking countries. This is so especially in the independent faith missions, in which frequently there is no common spirituality, no sense of being part of a body, and even a passive acceptance of the competitive mentality of the secular culture. We have much to learn from the Catholic missionary orders.

BIBLICAL FORMATION FOR MISSION

Those missionaries whose action involves crossing from one culture to another in obedience to God's call sooner or later find themselves facing their own cultural baggage in encounter or conflict with the culture to which they have gone with the gospel. It then becomes necessary to distinguish between the biblical core of their faith and Christian life, and the cultural clothing in which they are wrapped. This distinction requires an act of reflection on one's own practice and the development of a discernment that is illuminated by the word of God. For missionaries seeking authentic immersion in another culture, this experience is very often tense, humiliating, and painful; at the same time it is enriching because it leads to maturity. On the other hand, some missionaries do not survive the traumas of their first experience and soon return defeated. Others prefer to minister from a distance, and even while physically present somewhere, they never reach the kind of identification Paul describes: "I have become all things to all people, that I might by all means save some" (1 Cor. 9:23). Here I am going to limit myself to examining briefly the role played by biblical and theological training to make transcultural missionary work possible.

THE BIBLE IN PROTESTANT MISSIONARY PRACTICE

A distinctive note in missionary practice has been emphasis on biblical translation. The great missions started by Protestants flourished particularly in the nineteenth century, and a fundamental component of their practice was the translation of the Bible into vernacular languages of the lands in which missionaries were planting churches. Historian Stephen Neill highlights the contrast between Catholic and Protestant missionary practice.[6] In places like the Philippines and Latin America, Catholic missionaries in the sixteenth century studied the native languages, compiled dictionaries, and translated catechisms into the local languages. But it was only with the arrival of Protestants in the nineteenth century that the Bible was translated into the native languages of the people. In the case of the Spanish language, only with their arrival did the Bible begin to be widely distributed.

The incredible work of Bible translation in the last two centuries represents the Protestant conviction that those who hear the message of Christ for the first time ought to be able to read the Bible in their own language. Translating the Bible was considered indispensable for the formation of a native pastorate as an immediate step after evangelization. Hence, primary schools and literacy work were also logical necessities; if the Christian people must be nourished by the word of God, they have to be able to read it. All this reflects the Protestant convictions that the Word of God is the authority for the church's faith and practice and that we are all priests in the people of God. Here we have a case of how theological convictions shape missionary practice.

Another significant fact revealed by the biographies and autobiographies of the missionaries is that the impulse to devote oneself to mission often comes from convictions on the missionary obligation of believers, springing from reading the Bible. For the Pietists, among whom the Protestant missionary movement began, the discipline of daily Bible reading was part of the life of home and church. Small-group Bible study and Pietist prayer contributed to mutual pastoring and to the personal edification of believers. This discipline then passed over into the Methodist movement and the revivals in the English-speaking world, from which the Protestant missionary movement has drawn nourishment up to our own time. The diaries, reports, and letters of Protestant missionaries show that these disciplines of spiritual life were sustaining them in the vicissitudes, sadnesses, and joys of their labors. Protestant missionary spirituality has always been deeply biblical.[7]

Moreover, when Protestants began to reflect systematically on their missionary practice, the Bible was again the inevitable reference point. Today Gustav Warneck is recognized as founder of missiology, the theological discipline that systematically studies mission. In his excellent historical study of missionary models, Valdir Steuernagel writes:

> For Gustav Warneck it was absolutely essential that his theology of mission have a solid biblical foundation. Regarding the Bible as an authority was part of a Pietist legacy that he inherited. In defending biblical authority, he was in constant conflict with liberalism, whose biblical debility he detected and denounced. However, for him the Bible was not only authoritative, it was missionary.[8]

From the outset Protestant missiology was an effort to understand and analyze missionary practices in the light of the word of God. In the nineteenth century Protestant mission bore the mark of the imperial presence of Europe and the United States. In the twentieth century the breakup of European empires, the anti-colonial struggle, and the emergence of new nations have made it necessary to reexamine the methods and styles of Christian mission. Thus, over the course of the twentieth century a new reading of the word of God has sought to correct aspects of the missionary enterprise that reflected the culture and imperialist assumptions of the West more than the biblical models of missionary action. In a time of transition and change, Protestants are seeking to reread the scripture rather than going to the treasure of the Protestant missionary tradition. While this tradition may be valuable and serve as a reference point, it is not authoritative.

In this regard it is important to note that Catholic practice has been influenced by that of Protestants. After Vatican II the official documents on missionary issues, such as the papal encyclicals, seek to be grounded in scripture and not only in tradition, as in pre-conciliar times. In this regard the rate of change within Catholicism was incredible. In fact, during the 1980s and 1990s the systematic work by the Catholic biblical scholars Donald Senior and Carroll Stuhlmueller, *The Biblical Foundations for Mission,* was used as a textbook (in English and Spanish) in a number of Protestant seminaries, given the lack of an equivalent evangelical work.[9] The appearance of an excellent work edited by René Padilla is an important step in the effort to provide a solid foundation for Latin American missionary activity.[10]

The continuity of Christian missionary action in the new century demands that the new generations of missionaries be trained biblically and theologically for their endeavors for several reasons: (1) in order to understand their own calling in the light of the word of God and to develop a missionary way of life nourished by the totality of the word; (2) so that the content of their missionary action will be to communicate the word of God to human beings, guiding them to a responsible discipleship through direct personal contact with the word, and founding communities rooted in the word; and (3) so that upon reflecting systematically and critically on their missionary practice, they may be able to go to the word and find not only inspiration but guidance so as to have missiological discernment.

FORMATION OF VOCATION AND MISSIONARY STYLE

The everyday life of the church is the cradle of future missionaries. In it what must be emphasized is the importance of teaching the word, taking into account the missionary direction of its teaching. We never tire of insisting that the New Testament is fundamentally a missionary document. Paul's letters are not theological treatises to be taught as texts in a seminary, analyzed, and memorized; they are letters to living churches that have particular pastoral and missionary problems. The entire New Testament was written within the context of the passage of Christian faith from the Jewish world to the Gentile world. That is, the context of the New Testament is missionary, and its teaching can be captured better when we approach the text with the questions and concerns that come from a vital interest and a practice of obedience to mission. A whole new world of missiological light came to me when I learned from Paul Minear how to read the Epistle to the Romans as a missiological document.[11]

The vocation or calling of persons to mission must take into account that the life and witness of the major Old Testament figures also have a missionary dimension. The very existence of a chosen people has its origin in God's call to Abraham, who is chosen to receive God's blessing so that he and his posterity will become a blessing for all nations. Other biblical figures such as Joseph, Esther, Daniel, and Nehemiah are models of missionary life in pagan and hostile societies. They are illustrations of God's blessings and providence so that these men and women of God will be instruments of blessing in the societies where they are active. Likewise, Jonah is a paradigm of Israel's temptation to reject fulfillment of its mission.

In the Bible, obedience to God's missionary call draws nourishment from a piety rooted in the word. This can clearly be seen in stories like those of Zechariah, John the Baptist, the Virgin Mary, and Jesus himself in the gospels. Life itself, response to God, and style of life are explicated or celebrated with Old Testament texts. This rootedness in the totality of God's word, which shows God's missionary purpose, gives depth to the missionary call of individual people. God's compassion for all creatures and for all humankind, the faithful suffering of God's servants under the most varied circumstances, faithfulness to divine

Providence in the midst of personal and historic adversities, the power of obedience to the divine word vis-à-vis the forces of evil—all form part of the character of future missionaries when Christian education and the pulpit communicate the whole word. They are also obligatory elements in any missionary formation program.

The training of future missionaries does not simply transmit to them intellectual contents about the word of God, neutral information such as a computer could communicate. The *purpose of information is formation* of truly Christian attitudes, values, virtues, and way of life, that is, life according to the pattern of Christ. This formation includes training so that the person learns to be regularly nourished on the word and prayer in the search for a constant source of strength that makes possible the (almost always painful and difficult) exercise of the missionary vocation. Training often has to include correcting attitudes, prejudices, feelings of superiority, and spiritual pride within the community of disciples. *Information* and *formation* are thus combined for a constant *transformation* into the pattern of "a perfect humanity that is shaped to the full stature of Christ" (Eph. 4:13).[12] This process never takes place in a "solo" way. It always happens in community—in small groups around God's word, taking time to pray, to listen to the Spirit, to be led by the Spirit through the varied insights of the community and the ups and downs of efforts at obedience.

THE BIBLICAL CONTENT OF MISSIONARY ACTION

The word of God is central in the content—the *what*—of missionary action. Underlying any missionary work are certain explicit or implicit theological convictions. In the case of Latin America, while the different missions have transmitted certain predominant theological lines, such as Reformed, Anabaptist, or Dispensationalist theologies, there has also been an effort to find a biblical foundation for all these traditions. Today, biblical theology is to some degree favored over systematic theology, especially with regard to Christian mission. Evangelical theology in Latin America has found a notable convergence in which the approach proper to biblical theology is paramount.

The biblical and theological framework provided to transcultural missionaries ought to help them situate their own practice within a coherent understanding of the faith and of the message that they are communicating. There is a great variety of specific forms of mission, such as evangelization and planting churches, serving human needs through medicine or economic development, translating the Bible, theological education, Bible teaching, and training leaders. Nevertheless, each specific activity can be related to biblical teaching, and a basic theological formation helps missionaries to make the connection. A biblical worldview must be developed so that within it can fit the broad range of types of missionary action. Nevertheless, the best thing that missionaries share in the field of work to which they go is what is rooted in the word of God, so that those who receive the benefit of this action are in turn able to read and understand the word by themselves, thereby establishing continuity.

In the nineteenth century Protestant missiologists formulated the goal of missionary action in terms of helping the emergence of a local church that would reach the point of *self-propagation, self-support,* and *self-government,* avoiding a permanent dependence on missionaries. In more recent times theological activity has been added to these three classic elements. A church should be able to *self-theologize,* to find an expression of its faith in response to the demands of its own context. Communication of the word is essential for the emergence of such churches. It is my conviction that every missionary ought to be able to connect his or her own practice—whatever it may be—to the teaching of the word. Such a worldview cannot be built without having grasped and reached a command of the major lines of biblical teaching extending over both testaments.

Training along these lines should provide future missionaries with tools for biblical study that will enable them to refer continually to the word of God. Not every missionary is going to be a Bible scholar who needs to know the biblical languages, the art of interpretation, church history, and dogmatic theology. But certainly every missionary must be able to read the text intelligently and honestly, connect his or her action with the broad range of biblical revelation, and pass on to those with whom he or she works an attitude of respect—indeed enthusiasm—for the Bible. Years of experience in a variety of mission fields have shown me that whatever a missionary's specialization may be, for edification of lives and churches, he or she will always have chances to share the word, and what the missionary does in this regard will always be gratefully remembered.

Missionaries whose specific task has to do with training leaders or biblical and theological teaching must have a greater mastery of biblical matters and of the tools for understanding and presenting the text. This means advanced biblical studies in the classic subjects of introduction to the Bible, content of each book, biblical languages, methods of exegesis and interpretation, and familiarity with the context of the cultures of the biblical period. At the same time, however, missionaries must be provided with the capabilities and pedagogical tools that will enable them to translate the wealth of the content provided by scholarship into the simple language of ordinary people and the conceptual categories of other cultures. Biblical and theological training must include the modeling of accessible kinds of communication. It is distressing to see people who are unable to translate biblical erudition at the pastoral level and who end up alienating their hearers rather than communicating to them the wealth and beauty of the biblical message. Sometimes what they do is simply imitate the communication style of their seminary or university professors at an academic level.

The training of transcultural missionaries must include stimulating the critical capacity to pose with courage the questions emerging from practice. At the same time there must be training for creative missiological reading of the word. The best biblical training for missionaries in the future will not be handing them a ready-made packaged theology, no matter how evangelical it might look or sound, but to provide the tools so that going back to the wealth of the biblical text and continually drawing nourishment from it, these missionaries may respond to the new situations that come up in their field of work. It must not be forgotten that "indeed the word of God is living and active, sharper than any two-edged sword" (Heb. 4:12). Any theology is but an effort to articulate the truth of the word in a particular context, a fallible and limited human effort. It is useful for the people of God at a particular time, helping it to formulate its belief with a sense of identity. But crossing borders in mission always shows the limitations of theologies—and it also shows the inexhaustible wealth of the word.

The Holy Spirit presses the people of God to missionary action, and mission is only carried out if there is a people obedient to this impulse. The foundation and pattern for missionary action is the word of God, which reveals to us the Creator's saving will for human creatures, and the missionary model par excellence is the person and work of Jesus Christ. Mission history is a history of lights and shadows because it has a human dimension. Only by divine initiative and action can it be explained that the gospel has come down to us as a "treasure in clay vessels," despite the imperfections and limitations of those vessels. Biblical and theological training of future missionaries will make it possible for the gospel to continue its course to the ends of the earth.

CHRISTIAN MISSION AND CULTURES

It is characteristic of Christian faith that it is constantly crossing cultures. It began in Palestine in the Jewish world, and its center is the person of Jesus Christ. Even so, the documents known as the gospels are not written in the Hebrew or Aramaic spoken by Jesus but in Greek, that is, they are a translation of what Jesus said. The gospel message did not remain in its original Jewish setting but went out to make its way into the Greek and Roman world, this world that the Jews called Gentile.

The Christian message has a drive that impels it forward, wending its way from one culture to another. Its fundamental characteristic is this "translatability"; hence, the Christian message has been able to be presented in an incredible variety of cultures. There is no tongue into which the Christian message cannot be translated. The Bible, a book whose central theme is Jesus Christ, has been translated into more languages than any other book; as the century ended it had been translated completely or partially into twenty-two hundred languages.

This means, therefore, that any language is a good vehicle for the gospel. There is no language more sacred than the others, although with certain religions (such as Islam), someone who wishes to understand in depth must learn the language of the religion. The masters of the Qur'an, the sacred book of Muslims, have to learn to read in Arabic in order to be legitimate masters of that faith. By contrast, the Christian faith can be interpreted or preached in Quechua, Aymara, or Guaraní as well as in Hebrew, Spanish, Russian, or Chinese. In any language a person can delve into the depths of the thought of Jesus Christ and his teachings. This message can be translated into all languages.[13]

This explains the tremendous cultural impact of the Christian faith; translatability of the message has ennobled all the cultures that it has touched. In this way a Cashibo or Aguaruna person in the Peruvian jungle can say "God speaks my language"; we who read the Bible in Spanish, English, or French can say the same thing. In many instances, Bible translation has not only led to the enhancement of cultures in every corner of the globe but also to a revitalization of cultures. This runs counter to the claims of some anthropologists who have accused missionaries of destroying the cultures of indigenous peoples. This view, caused by prejudice and ignorance, must be corrected.

It is wrong to generalize and accuse all missionaries of destroying cultures. For example, many of the Catholic missionaries who came to Latin America in the sixteenth century learned Quechua, Aymara, and the language of the Moxos in Bolivia. The first book in Peru was a Christian catechism printed in the sixteenth century in Quechua. The fact is that the missionaries were motivated by the Spirit of Jesus Christ and tried to imitate him; they showed a desire and willingness to listen to people before communicating the faith. Of course there were other kinds of missionaries in the sixteenth century who instead followed the philosophy of "first conquer, then convince," which was the philosophy of religious warfare and of wiping out idolatry.

The same is true about when Protestant missions began to go to different parts of the world, especially in the eighteenth century. William Carey, an English cobbler who went to India in 1792, immediately began to translate the Bible into some of the languages of India. Although he was not university educated, Carey learned Sanskrit and eventually a total of sixteen languages spoken in India. He had to prepare a dictionary of some of these languages, and hence the very existence of some of them was first known in Europe thanks to his work. The same thing is happening today with those who are translating the Bible into the languages of native communities in the Bolivian, Peruvian, and Ecuadorian Amazon. They are also creating dictionaries and sometimes collecting folklore, legends, and literature that would otherwise be lost. These things are being preserved as a contribution to universal culture, thanks to this work that goes along with mission and that is ennobling each culture while spreading the message of Christ.

Yet missionary action also relativizes every culture. No culture can claim to be sacred. In the Bible there is no effort to impose Jewish culture. Saint Paul, the great missionary in the New Testament, had to wage his great missionary battle to communicate the message of Jesus—a Jew—to Greeks and Romans without imposing Jewish customs on them. Some Christian believers from Jewish backgrounds wanted the requirements of Jewish culture like circumcision, and ways of eating, dressing, and relating to be imposed on the Gentiles. The apostle Paul insisted on proclaiming Christ while giving his hearers the freedom to live Christian faith within the framework of their own culture. Thus, century after century, Christianity has managed to cross cultures, to transcend from one culture to another, and in this process it has contributed unbelievably to enriching the memory of humankind. Humankind today appreciates much better the multiplicity of cultural creations that displays the creativity God has placed in us human beings. For twenty centuries Christian mission has enabled an astonishing variety of cultures to exist together.

A PROFOUND CHANGE OF ATTITUDE

The key that connects biblical formation with the ability to appreciate and transcend cultures in Christian mission is the central truth of the incarnation: "And the Word became Flesh and lived among us, and we have seen his glory, the glory as of a father's only son, full of grace and truth" (Jn. 1:14). This presence of the Word in the very midst of historic human reality is a model of the way missionaries must live and proclaim the truth of Jesus Christ in the midst of the communities to which they are sent. Becoming aware of the urgency of these questions about missionary presence and style has been a leaven of creativity in circles where Christian mission is studied and reflected upon.

In more recent decades this has meant a refreshing return to sacred scripture. "Mission in Christ's way" is the agenda that has forcefully developed in the evangelical world. We have a classic missionary passage in the Protestant world, namely, the Great Commission in Matthew 28:18-20. This passage summed up well the christological impulse ("All authority in heaven and on earth has been given to me"), fullness of content ("Go therefore and make disciples . . . baptizing them . . . and teaching them to obey") and the transcultural scope of mission ("of all nations"). Now, at the beginning of a new century, we have rediscovered the almost forgotten text of John 20:21: "As the Father has sent me, so I send you." In this text we not only have a mandate for doing mission but also a model of how to go about it. Before seeking methods and tools to help us communicate a verbal message, we have to seek a new style of missionary presence relevant to this moment in human history. When we understand the text of the Great Commission by placing it in the context of the entire Gospel of John, the model of Jesus takes on clear and concrete characteristics that oblige us to revise our current models.

Essentially, the turn toward the missiological model of the apostle John and the return to the whole of biblical teaching mean abandoning an imperialist mentality in mission. Such a shift is better suited to a post-imperial age. During the height of empire, mission was carried out always from a position of superiority in political, military, financial, and technological realms. "Cross and sword" was the expression that summed up the spirit of the Catholic and Iberian mission at its high point in the sixteenth century. "Trade and Christianity" was the symbolic phrase at the high point of European Protestant mission in the nineteenth century. "Information, technology, and gospel" seems to sum up well the spirit of mission in the most recent period. The change of mindset required by mission in the post-imperial age has strong implications for the Protestant missionary enterprise today. A change of method will not be enough. What is needed is a change of spirit that consists in recovering the priorities of the person of Jesus. We can sum it up by paraphrasing Paul in his letter to the Philippians:

Let there be in us the same feeling and mind that was
    also in Christ Jesus,
Who in order to reach us crossed the border between
    heaven and earth.
He crossed the border of poverty to be born in a stable
    and live without knowing where he was going to
    rest his head at night.
He crossed the border of marginalization to befriend
    women and embrace publicans and Samaritans.
He crossed the border of spiritual power to free those
    afflicted by legions of devils.
He crossed the border of social protest to sing truths to
    the Pharisees, scribes, and traffickers in the
    temple.
He crossed the border of the cross and death to help us
    all pass over to the other side.
Risen Lord, who therefore awaits us there, at every
    border that we have to cross with his gospel.

Notes

1 Christian Mission Today

1. I am aware that many have stopped using term *Third World,* and others are replacing it with the expression *two-thirds world.* I continue to use it for convenience, and by it I mean Latin American countries and the new nations of Asia, Africa, and Oceania.

2. Justo L. González, *Historia de las Misiones* (Buenos Aires: La Aurora, 1970), 23.

3. For this translation biblical quotations are primarily from the New Revised Standard Version; translation may be modified or others may be used in order to reflect Escobar's text, which uses primarily the Nueva Versión Internacional.—TRANS.

4. "And the Word became flesh and lived among us" (Jn. 1:14).

5. David B. Barrett, a widely known statistical expert, publishes yearly a statistical table on the state of Christianity in the *International Bulletin of Missionary Research.*

6. Walbert Bühlman, O.F.M. Cap., *The Church of the Future: A Model for the Year 2001* (Maryknoll, N.Y.: Orbis Books, 1986), 5-6.

7. The International Missionary Council was a Protestant body that brought together the missionary boards of Europe and North America and sought to coordinate missionary action as well as information exchange and research on Christian mission.

8. Timothy Yates, *Christian Mission in the Twentieth Century* (Cambridge: Cambridge University Press, 1994), 136.

9. Lesslie Newbigin, *Foolishness to the Greeks* (Geneva: World Council of Churches; Grand Rapids, Mich.: Eerdmans, 1986).

10. Bühlman, *The Church of the Future,* 5.

2 Mission Today: Practice and Reflection

1. Statistical data taken from the annual table published by David B. Barrett in the *International Bulletin of Missionary Research* 25/1 (January 2001).

2. For information on the Lausanne movement and its relationship to the study of mission in Latin America, see the studies collected in *Boletín Teológico* 67/68 (July-December 1995).

3. For a brief history of these CLADE meetings, see *Iglesia y Misión* 67/68 (January-July 1999).

4. My studies reflect the tensions of doing theology within this framework (see *Evangelio y Realidad Social* [El Paso: Casa Bautista de Publicaciones, 1988]. From an ecumenical standpoint, see Mortimer Arias, *Salvación es Liberación* (Buenos Aires: La Aurora, 1973).

5. Roland Allen was one of the first missionary-missiologists of the twentieth century to examine creatively the Pauline corpus and the Book of Acts seeking the keys to missionary methodology in order to shed light on his own practice.

6. Dieter Georgi, *The Opponents of Paul in Second Corinthians* (Edinburgh: T. & T. Clark, 1987). See also my chapter on Paul as a model of mission in René C. Padilla, *Bases Bíblicas de la Misión* (Buenos Aires: Nueva Creación; Grand Rapids, Mich.: Eerdmans, 1998), 307-50.

7. David Bosch offers a valuable missiological summary of some authors who have carefully examined the material in Luke-Acts (see *Transforming Mission: Paradigm Shifts in Theology of Mission* [Maryknoll, N.Y.: Orbis Books, 1992]).

8. David Bosch, "Reflections on Biblical Models of Mission," in *Towards the Twenty-First Century in Christian Mission,* ed. James M. Phillips and Robert L. Coote (Grand Rapids, Mich.: Eerdmans, 1993), 177.

9. Some of these ideas are developed further in the last chapter of this book, which is devoted to the training of missionaries.

10. CEHILA is the Spanish acronym for the Commission for the Study of the History of the Church in Latin America, established by Argentinean historian Enrique Dussel. A number of volumes of the fundamental work of this commission has already appeared, and some include brief sections and appendices on the history of Protestants.

11. For example, Pedro Borges, *Misión y Civilización en América Latina* (Madrid: Alhambra, 1987); older works such as that of Vicente D. Sierra, *El Sentido Misional de la Conquista de América,* 4th ed. (Buenos Aires: Ediciones Dictio, 1980); and several of the studies published by CELAM in the series "Colección V Centenario."

12. John A. Mackay, *The Other Spanish Christ* (New York: Macmillan, 1933).

13. W. Stanley Rycroft, *Religion and Faith in Latin America* (Philadelphia: Westminster Press, 1958).

14. Justo L. González, *Historia de las Misiones* (Buenos Aires: Methopress, 1970).

15. Hans Jürgen Prien, *Historia del Cristianismo en América Latina* (Salamanca: Ed. Sígueme, 1985).

16. Pablo Deiros, *Historia del Cristianismo en América Latina* (Buenos Aires: FTL, 1992).

17. For example, the early works of Carmelo Alvarez and Jean Pierre Bastian.

18. Michael Green, *Evangelism in the Early Church* (Grand Rapids, Mich.: Eerdmans, 1970), chap. 1.

19. Eduardo Hoornaert, *The Memory of the Christian People* (Maryknoll, N.Y.: Orbis Books, 1988).

20. Enrique Dussel, *A History of the Church in Latin America* (Grand Rapids, Mich.: Eerdmans, 1981), 38.

21. Mackay, *The Other Spanish Christ,* 24-26.

22. A summary of this process can be found in Brian Stanley, *The Bible and the Flag* (Leicester, England: Apollos, 1990).

23. The best treatment of this topic thus far can be found in Joel Carpenter and Wilbert Shenk, eds., *Earthen Vessels* (Grand Rapids, Mich.: Eerdmans, 1990).

24. Gustavo Gutiérrez, *The Power of the Poor in History* (Maryknoll, N.Y.: Orbis Books, 1983).

25. Francis Fukuyama, "The End of History," in *The National Interest* 16 (Summer 1989), 3-18.

26. Gustavo Gutiérrez, *The Truth Will Make You Free* (Maryknoll, N.Y.: Orbis Books, 1990), 53-84.

27. Scott Mainwaring, *The Catholic Church and Politics in Brazil 1916-1985* (Stanford, Calif.: Stanford University Press, 1986), chap. 1.

28. A work summarizing the controversy is Pablo Richard and Diego Irarrázabal, *Religión y Política en América Central* (San José: DEI, 1981). See also the questions raised by José Luis Idígoras, S.J., in *La Religión Fenómeno Popular* (Lima: Ediciones Paulinas, 1991).

29. We have summarized this question in *Los Evangélicos: ¿Nueva Leyenda Negra en América Latina?* (México: Casa Unida de Publicaciones, 1991); see also, Carlos Martínez García: "Secta: un concepto inadecuado para explicar el protestantismo mexicano," in *Boletín Teológico* [Buenos Aires] 41, 55-72.

30. See, for example, studies on the issue collected in *Misión* 8/1 (March 1989).

31. See, for example, *Boletín Teológico* 31 of the FTL (September 1988), which is devoted to this topic, with the studies from the consultation "Fe cristiana y ciencias sociales en América Latina hoy" [Christian faith and social sciences in Latin America today].

32. That was established by the famous book *France, Pays de Mission?* by H. Godin and Y. Daniel (Paris: Editions du Cerf, 1943).

33. Peter L. Berger, *The Noise of Solemn Assemblies* (Garden City, N.Y.: Doubleday, 1961).

34. Roger Mehl, *Sociology of Protestantism* (Philadelphia: Westminster Press, 1970).

35. Ibid., 2.

36. Ibid., 1.

37. Ibid., 5.

38. For example, see *Colonialism and Christian Missions* (New York: McGraw Hill, 1966).

39. Especially his book *Social History and Christian Mission* (London: SCM Press).

40. Especially his recent book *The Missionary Movement in Christian History* (Maryknoll, N.Y.: Orbis Books, 1996).

41. The development of this school and some of the features I comment on here may be seen in the works of Peter Wagner, Larry Pate, George Otis, and others. See my article "Evangelical Missiology: Peering into the Future at the Turn of the Century," in *Global Missiology for the Twenty-First Century*, ed. William D. Taylor (Grand Rapids, Mich.: Baker, 2000), 101-22; see also the response by David Tai-Woong Lee, 133-48.

42. On this aspect, see a critical evaluation in *Poder y Misión: Debate Sobre la Guerra Espiritual en América Latina* (San José: IINDEF, 1997).

43. In this regard, see the critique of the concept of "homogeneous units" in C. René Padilla, *Mission between the Times* (Grand Rapids, Mich.: Eerdmans, 1985).

44. See an evaluation along these lines in Tito Paredes, *El Evangelio en Platos de Barro* (Lima: Ediciones Presencia, 1989).

3 Latin America: Mission Land

1. In this chapter I have used, in part, updated and amplified material published in James M. Phillips and Robert Coote, eds., *Toward the Twenty-First Century in Christian Mission* (Grand Rapids, Mich.: Eerdmans, 1993), and *Latin America: Mission Field and Mission Base* (Livingston Memorial Lecture, Belfast Bible College, 1998).

2. Information taken from the U.S. Catholic Mission Association, *U.S. Catholic Mission Handbook: Mission Inventory 1996-1997* (Washington, D.C., July 1997). This figure includes Belize, but not all English- or French-speaking countries in the Caribbean.

3. Data compiled from John A. Siewert and Edna G. Valdez, eds., *1998-2000 Mission Handbook, U.S. and Canadian Ministries Overseas* (Monrovia, Calif.: MARC Publications, 1997).

4. Franz Damen, "Las sectas ¿avalancha o desafío?" *Cuarto Intermedio* [Cochabamba, Bolivia] 3 (May, 1987), 45.

5. See a history of this process in Norman Goodall, *The Ecumenical Movement* (New York: Oxford University Press, 1961).

6. Gonzalo Báez-Camargo, "Mexico: A Long Stretch from Edinburgh," *Ecumenical Review* 14 (October 1963–July 1964), 267.

7. Gonzalo Báez-Camargo, "The Place of Latin America in the Ecumenical Movement," *The Ecumenical Review* 1 (1948-49), 311.

8. Robert E. Speer, *South American Problems* (New York: Student Volunteer Movement for Foreign Missions, 1913), 145.

9. Juan Kessler and Wilton M. Nelson, "Panamá 1916 y su impacto sobre el Protestantismo latinoamericano," *Pastoralia* 2 (November 1978), 5-21.

10. This has been noted particularly by the Catholic historian Prudencio Damboriena, S.J., *El Protestantismo en América Latina* (Bogotá-Friburgo: FERES, 1962), 1:23.

11. Speer, *South American Problems.*

12. John A. Mackay, *That Other America* (New York: Friendship Press, 1935), 69-73; 107-16. For a brief appraisal of Mackay's work, see Samuel Escobar, "The Missionary Legacy of John A. Mackay," *International Bulletin of Missionary Research* 16/3 (July 1992), 116-22.

13. John A. Mackay, "The Power of Evangelism," in *Addresses and Other Records, Report of the Jerusalem Meeting of the International Missionary Council* (London: Oxford University Press, 1928), 8:121.

14. Báez-Camargo, "Mexico," 267.

15. Ibid., 268.

16. José Míguez Bonino, "Latin America," in *The Prospects of Christianity throughout the World*, ed. M. Searle Bates and Wilhelm Pauck (New York: Charles Scribner's Sons, 1964), 168.

17. John McCoy, "La embestida evangélica," in *Noticias Aliadas* [Lima] 26/24 (June 29, 1989), 2.

18. Erasmo Braga, *Panamericanismo: aspecto religioso* (New York: Sociedade de Preparo Missionario, 1916), 195.

19. Roger Greenway, *An Urban Strategy for Latin America* (Grand Rapids, Mich.: Baker, 1973), 236, emphasis added.

20. For a carefully documented summary of the Colombian case, see Elizabeth E. Brusco, "Colombia: Past Persecution, Present Tension," in *Religious Freedom and Evangelization in Latin America*, ed. Paul E. Sigmund (Maryknoll, N.Y.: Orbis Books, 1999), 235-52.

21. A careful study of the development of missiological concepts in Latin America is found in Juan Gorski, M.M., *El desarrollo Histórico de la Misionología en América Latina* (La Paz, Bolivia, 1985).

22. In Gerald M. Costello, *Mission to Latin America* (Maryknoll, N.Y.: Orbis Books, 1979), 276.

23. Angelyn Dries, O.S.F., deals with this and several related issues in her exhaustive study *The Missionary Movement in American Catholic History* (Maryknoll, N.Y.: Orbis Books, 1998). See also two other important works in this regard: Gerald M. Costello, *Mission to Latin America* (Maryknoll, N.Y.: Orbis Books, 1979), and Mary M. McGlone, C.S.J., *Sharing Faith across the Hemisphere* (Maryknoll, N.Y.: Orbis Books, 1997).

24. Gorski, *El desarrollo Histórico de la Misionología en América Latina*.

25. Roger Aubry, *La Misión Siguiendo a Jesús por los Caminos de América Latina* (Buenos Aires: Ed. Guadalupe, 1990).

26. Manual M. Marzal is author of many works, including *La Transformación Religiosa Peruana* (Lima: Pontificia Universidad Católica, 1983).

27. Dries, *The Missionary Movement in American Catholic History*, 97.

28. Raymond McGowan, quoted in ibid., 98.

29. Dries, *The Missionary Movement in American Catholic History*, 99.

30. William J. Coleman, *Latin American Catholicism: A Self-evaluation,* Maryknoll Study Series (Maryknoll, N.Y.: Maryknoll Publications, 1958), 33.

31. Dries, *The Missionary Movement in American Catholic History*, 181.

32. Ibid., 213.

33. Ibid., 181.

34. Ibid., 213.

35. *Puebla Document*, par. 342. See text in John Eagleson and Philip Scharper, *Puebla and Beyond: Documentation and Commentary* (Maryknoll, N.Y.: Orbis Books, 1980), 172.

36. Aubry, *La Misión Siguiendo a Jesús por los Caminos de América Latina*, 93.

37. Segundo Galilea, *Evangelización en América Latina* (Quito: CELAM-IPLA, 1969); see also idem, *La Responsabilidad Misionera en América Latina* (Bogotá: Ediciones Paulinas, 1981).

38. Alfred T. Hennelly, S.J., ed., *Santo Domingo and Beyond* (Maryknoll, N.Y.: Orbis Books, 1993), 48.

39. Edward L. Cleary, "John Paul Cries 'Wolf,'" *Commonweal* (November 20, 1992), 7.

40. William D. Taylor and Emilio A. Nuñez, *Crisis in Latin America* (Pasadena, Calif.: William Carey Library/World Evangelical Fellowship [WEF], 1996), 183.

41. Ibid., 183-84.

42. Costello, *Mission to Latin America*, 5.

43. Quoted in ibid., 41.

44. Stephen Judd, M.M., "The Seamy Side of Charity Revisited: American Catholic Contributions to Renewal in the Latin American Church," *Missiology* 15/2, 7.

45. Acronym of the Cooperación Missionera Iberoamericana [Iberoamerican Missionary Cooperation], a Protestant body set up in 1987.

46. Acronym of Congreso Misionero Latinoamericano [Latin American Missionary Congress]. These events are inspired and promoted by the Pontifical Mission Societies of the Roman Catholic Church. The first was held in Torreón, Mexico, in 1977, and the fifth in Belo Horizonte, Brazil, in 1995.

4 Lessons from Missionary History

1. Emilio Antonio Núñez, "Posición de la iglesia frente al 'aggiornamiento,'" in CLADE I *Acción en Cristo para un continente en crisis* (San José and Miami: Editorial Caribe, 1970), 39.

2. Emilio Antonio Núñez, *Conciencia e Identidad Evangélica y la Renovación Católica* (Guatemala: Grupo Evangélico Universitario, n.d.), 9.

3. Ibid., 10.

4. Ibid.

5. I am here following the advice of those who took part in three meetings between evangelicals and Catholics between 1977 and 1984 (see Basil Meeking and John Stott, eds., *The Evangelical-Roman Catholic Dialogue on Mission 1977-1984: A Report* [Grand Rapids, Mich.: Eerdmans, 1986]).

6. On this point see the work of a Spanish author who cannot be suspected of partisanship, Conde de Canilleros, *Tres testigos de la conquista del Perú* (Buenos Aires: Espasa Calpe, Colección Austral, 1955).

7. Justo L. González, *Historia de las Misiones* (Buenos Aires: La Aurora, 1970), 158-59.

8. Juan B. A. Kessler, *Historia de la Evangelización en el Perú* (Lima: El Inca, n.d.), 50.

9. Instituto Teológico de Vida Religiosa, *Gracia y Desgracia de la Evangelización de América* (Madrid: Editorial Claretiana), 1992. [Note that the primary meaning of *desgracia* is not "disgrace" but "disaster" or "misery."—Trans.]

10. On Acosta, see Ronan Hoffman, *Pioneer Theories of Missiology* (Washington, D.C.: The Catholic University of America Press, 1960). Protestant scholar Stuart McIntosh, a missionary in Peru, did a full translation of Acosta's book *De Procuranda* into English.

11. In *La Historia del Cristianismo en América Latina* (Salamanca: Sígueme, 1985), Hans Jürgen Prien has made good use of modern research. Another recent work is that of Pedro Borges, *Misión y Civilización en América Latina* (Madrid: Alhambra, 1987). A very valuable interpretation from a missiological standpoint is Ivan Vallier, *Catholicism, Social Control and Modernization* (Englewood Cliffs, N.J.: Prentice Hall, 1970).

12. Norman Horner, *Cross and Crucifix in Mission* (Nashville, Tenn.: Abingdon Press, 1965).

13. Kenneth Scott Latourette, *A History of the Expansion of Christianity* (New York: Harper & Row, 1939, 1943), see vol. 3, chaps. 3-6; vol. 5, chap. 4.

14. Stephen Neill, *A History of Christian Missions* (New York: Penguin Books, 1986). In this revised edition see chapters 6 and 8 in particular.

15. González, *Historia de las Misiones,* chaps. 5, 6 and 9.

16. Robert Ricard, *La Conquista Espiritual de México* (Mexico: Fondo de Cultura Económica, 1991), 21, emphasis added.

17. A study on the relationship between Catholic ecclesiology and mission is found in *La Misionología Hoy,* edited by Obras Misionales Pontifícias in Spain (Estella: Ed. Verbo Divino, 1987). See especially chapters 6 and 9.

18. Ricard, *La Conquista Espiritual de México,* 21.

19. Ibid., 22.

20. W. Stanley Rycroft, *Religion and Faith in Latin America* (Philadelphia: Westminster Press, 1958).

21. Gonzalo Báez-Camargo, *Hacia la Renovación Religiosa en Hispanoamérica* (Mexico, 1929).

22. José Míguez Bonino, "El testimonio cristiano en un continente descristianizado," in *Testimonium*, vol. 9, Fasc. 1, first quarter 1961. Míguez nuances his judgment but maintains his critique in *Protestantismo y Liberalismo en América Latina* (San José: DEI, 1983).

23. Juan Luis Segundo, *De la Sociedad a la Teología* (Buenos Aires: Ed. Carlos Lohle, 1970), 37.

24. Gustavo Gutiérrez, *Líneas pastorales de la Iglesia en América Latina* (Lima: CEP, 1970), 17.

25. Ibid., 16-17.

26. Ibid.

27. Vallier, *Catholicism, Social Control and Modernization*, 7.

28. Ibid., 8.

29. González, *Historia de las Misiones,* 18.

30. William D. Taylor and Emilio A. Nuñez, *Crisis in Latin America* (Pasadena, Calif.: William Carey Library/World Evangelical Fellowship [WEF], 1996), 403.

31. The term *caudillo* refers to a political or military strongman, like the regional leaders who dominated post-independence politics in the nineteenth century, and by extension it is applied to dictators, populist leaders, and political bosses to the present.—TRANS.

32. This problem was partly what prompted Juan Kessler to undertake the research in the previously cited work on Protestant missionary history in Peru and Chile.

33. W. Dayton Roberts, *Strachan of Costa Rica: Missionary Insights and Strategies* (Grand Rapids, Mich.: Eerdmans, 1971). See my brief appraisal of Strachan in "The Two Party System and the Missionary Enterprise," in *Reforming the Center: American Protestantism, 1900 to the Present*, ed. Douglas Jacobsen and William Vance Trollinger (Grand Rapids, Mich.: Eerdmans, 1988), 349-58.

34. Kenneth Strachan, *The Missionary Movement of the Non-historical Groups in Latin America* (New York: Committee of Cooperation in Latin America, 1957).

35. Ibid., 12.

36. The most outstanding works in this regard are René Padilla's studies of Pauline ecclesiology in *Mission between the Times* (Grand Rapids, Mich.: Eerdmans, 1985); and those of Juan Driver on Anabaptist ecclesiology in *Contracorriente: Ensayos sobre Eclesiología Radical,* 3d ed. (Guatemala: Semilla, 1998).

37. Emilio A. Núñez, *Caminos de Renovación* (Grand Rapids, Mich.: Portavoz, 1975), 103.

38. José Luis Perez Guadalupe, *Las Sectas en el Perú*, 2d ed. (Lima: Conferencia Episcopal Peruana, 1992), 11.

5 The Social Impact of Mission

1. See, for example, Wayne A. Meeks, *The First Urban Christians: The Social World of the Apostle Paul* (New Haven, Conn.: Yale University Press, 1983); and John E. Stambaugh and David L. Balch, *The New Testament in Its Social Environment* (Philadelphia: Westminster Press, 1986).

2. Acts 16:1-40; see also my notes in "Las ciudades en la práctica misionera del Apóstol Pablo: el caso de Filipos," *Misión* 31 (1990), 6-13.

3. Acts 19:23-41.

4. A description and interpretation of this process can be found in Justo L. González, *Historia de las Misiones* (Buenos Aires: La Aurora, 1970), esp. chaps. 1-5.

5. Gustavo Gutiérrez provides a careful study of this process and on how theological reflection offers explanations and justifications, in *Las Casas: In Search of the Poor of Jesus Christ* (Maryknoll, N.Y.: Orbis Books, 1993), chaps. 4, 5.

6. Pedro Borges, *Misión y civilización en América* (Madrid: Alhambra, 1986), 1.

7. On missionary opinions of this moment and its consequences, see the Introduction in Manuel M. Marzal, et al., *The Indian Face of God in Latin America* (Maryknoll, N.Y.: Orbis Books, 1996).

8. Stephen Neill, *A History of Christian Missions,* rev. ed. (Middlesex: Penguin Books, 1986), 194-96.

9. James S. Dennis, *Christian Missions and Social Progess: A Sociological Study of Foreign Missions,* 3 vols. (Edinburgh and London: Oliphant, 1897, 1899, and 1906).

10. Vicente D. Sierra, *El Sentido Misional de la Conquista de América,* 4th ed. (Buenos Aires: Ediciones Dictio, 1980).

11. John 20:21.

12. William Axling, *Kagawa* (New York: Harper, 1932).

13. Viv Grigg, *Companion to the Poor* (Monrovia, Calif.: MARC Publications, 1990).

14. Such was the case of Regions Beyond Missionary Union in the early twentieth century in Peru or of the Bolivian Indian Mission.

15. John B. A. Kessler, Jr., *A Study of the Older Protestant Missions and Churches in Peru and Chile* (Goes: Oosterban and le Cointre, 1967), 184-93.

16. Luis E. Valcárcel, *Memorias* (Lima: Instituto de Estudios Peruanos, 1981), 71.

17. Frederick A. Stahl, *In the Land of the Incas* (Mountain View, Calif: Pacific Press Publishers, 1920).

18. José Antonio Encinas, *Un ensayo de Escuela Nueva en el Perú* (Lima: Imprenta Minerva, 1932; facsimile edition, Lima: Centro de Investigación y Desarrollo de la Educación, 1986), 148.

19. Ibid.

20. Kessler, *A Study of the Older Protestant Missions and Churches in Peru and Chile,* 235-40.

21. Luis E. Valcárcel, *Tempestad en los Andes* (Lima: Editorial Universo, 1972; first edition, 1928).

22. Such is the case in Philippi (Acts 16), and Ephesus (Acts 19), and in his defense when he is arrested and imprisoned in Jerusalem (Acts 21 to 27). In all these cases Paul's evangelizing action encounters resistance and stirs up trouble.

23. Norman Goodall, *Christian Mission and Social Ferment* (London: Epworth Press, 1964), 21-23.

24. The data summarized here are taken from David Phillips, "Protestantism in Bolivia to 1952," master's thesis, University of Calgary, Alberta, Canada, 1968; see also Samuel Escobar, "The Bolivian Baptist Story: Context and Meaning in Latin America," in *Bridging Cultures and Hemispheres: The Legacy of Archibald Reekie and Canadian Baptists in Bolivia,* ed. William H. Brackney (Macon, Ga.: Smyth and Helwys, 1997), 111-23.

25. Norman Dabbs, "Why the Condor," in *The Enterprise* [Toronto], magazine of the Canadian Baptists Overseas Mission Board (January 1974), 5-6.

26. Jean Pierre Bastian, *Los disidentes: sociedades protestantes y revolución en México (1872-1911),* (Mexico: Fondo de Cultura Económica, 1989).

27. Ibid., 313.

28. Rubén Ruiz Guerra, *Hombres nuevos: Metodismo y modernización en México (1873-1930)* (Mexico: CUPSA, 1992).

29. Ibid., 106.

30. Ibid., 11.

31. I do not share the common tendency of Latin American theologians to condemn the relationship between Protestantism and liberalism out of hand, although I think it has to be assessed critically. From a missiological standpoint, it is possible to appreciate actions of service and transformation motivated by Christian love, while not agreeing with the political framework surrounding them.

32. Bastian, *Los disidentes,* 313.

33. Anabaptist theologians have emphasized the significance of this New Testament pattern. See especially John Howard Yoder, *The Politics of Jesus: Vicit Agnus Noster* (Grand Rapids, Mich.: Eerdmans, 1994).

34. A fascinating study along these lines is Rodney Stark, *The Rise of Christianity: A Sociologist Reconsiders History* (Princeton, N.J.: Princeton University Press, 1996).

35. Emilio Willems, *Followers of the New Faith: Culture Change and the Rise of Protestantism in Brazil and Chile* (Nashville, Tenn.: Vanderbilt University Press, 1967), 13.

36. Emilio Willems, "Protestantism and Culture Change in Brazil and Chile," in *Religion, Revolution and Reform: New Forces for Change in Latin America*, ed. William V. D'Antonio and Frederick B. Pike (New York: Frederick A. Praeger, 1964), 106-7.

37. Ibid., 107.

38. Willems, *Followers of the New Faith*, 251.

39. Blanca Muratorio, *Etnicidad, evangelización y protesta en el Ecuador* (Quito: CIESE, 1982).

40. Ibid., 82.

41. Ibid., 86.

42. Ibid., 89.

43. Ibid., 89.

6 From Mission to Liberation

1. Robert Speer, *South American Problems* (New York: Student Volunteer Movement for Foreign Missions, 1913), 237.

2. William J. Coleman, M.M., *Latin American Catholicism: A Self-Evaluation* (Maryknoll, N.Y.: Orbis Books, 1958), 20.

3. Speer, *South American Problems*, 237.

4. John A. Mackay, *The Other Spanish Christ* (New York: Macmillan, 1933), 264.

5. Hans Jürgen Prien, *La Historia del Cristianismo en America Latina* (Salamanca: Sigueme, 1985).

6. For a brief, helpful, interpretative account of this wave, see Kenneth Strachan, *The Missionary Movement of the Non-Historical Groups in Latin America* (New York: Committee of Cooperation in Latin America, 1957).

7. Besides Prien, see Guillermo Cook, ed., *New Face of the Church in Latin America* (Maryknoll, N.Y.: Orbis Books, 1994); Daniel R. Miller, ed., *Coming of Age: Protestantism in Contemporary Latin America* (Lanham, Md.: University Press of America, 1994); and Joel Carpenter and Wilbert Shenk, eds., *Earthen Vessels* (Grand Rapids, Mich.: Eerdmans, 1990). A very promising analysis by Costa Rican historian Arturo Piedra is in the process of being published, *Evangelización Protestante en América Latina* (Quito: CLAI). Volume 1 was published in 2000.

8. For North America, see Gerald M. Costello, *Mission to Latin America* (Maryknoll, N.Y.: Orbis Books, 1979); Mary M. McGlone, C.S.J., *Sharing Faith across the Hemisphere* (Maryknoll, N.Y.: Orbis Books, 1997); and Angelyn Dries, O.S.F., *The Missionary Movement in American Catholic History* (Maryknoll, N.Y.: Orbis Books, 1998).

9. John J. Casey has provided an analysis of the crisis from the perspective of the Maryknoll order in his article "Doing Mission: The Catholic Experience," *Missiology* 14/4 (October 1986).

10. Coleman, *Latin American Catholicism*, chaps. 1, 2.

11. McGlone, *Sharing Faith across the Hemisphere*, esp. chaps. 1, 2.

12. Franklin Hamlin Littell, *From State Church to Pluralism: A Protestant Interpretation of Religion in American History* (Garden City, N.Y.: Doubleday, 1962), 29, 148-49.

13. Jeffrey Klaiber, S.J., *The Catholic Church in Peru 1821-1985* (Washington, D.C.: The Catholic University of America Press, 1992), 254.

14. For instance, German Doig Klinge, *De Río a Santo Domingo* (Lima: Vida y espiritualidad, 1993) or Alberto Methol Ferré et al., *CELAM Elementos para su historia* (Bogotá, Colombia: CELAM, 1982).

15. Costello, *Mission to Latin America*, 29.

16. Prien, *La Historia del Cristianismo en America Latina*, 856ff.

17. Hernán Parada, *Crónica de Medellín* (Bogotá: Indoamerican Service, 1975), 25.

18. Ibid.

19. Costello, *Mission to Latin America,* 275.

20. Ibid., 281.

21. McGlone, *Sharing Faith across the Hemisphere*, 94.

22. Ibid., 107.

23. Costello, *Mission to Latin America*, 70.

24. Prien, *La Historia del Cristianismo en America Latina*, 1040-45.

25. Jorge Alvarez Calderón, "Peruvian Priest Recalls Origins of the Church of the Poor," interview in *Latinamerica Press* [Lima] (March 31, 1983), 23.

26. From the complete text of the article by Illich published as appendix II in Costello, *Mission to Latin America*, 284.

27. Prien, *La Historia del Cristianismo en America Latina*, 1042-45.

28. Peruvian Bishops' Commission for Social Action, *Between Honesty and Hope* (Maryknoll, N.Y.: Orbis Books, 1970), 246.

29. Jeffrey Klaiber, S.J., *The Church, Dictatorships, and Democracy in Latin America* (Maryknoll, N.Y.: Orbis Books, 1998), 5.

30. Alfonso López Trujillo, *Hacia una Sociedad Nueva* (Bogotá: Ediciones Paulinas, 1978).

31. Enrique Dussel, *La Iglesia Latinoamericana de Medellín a Puebla* (Bogotá: CEHILA-Codecal, 1979).

32. Coleman, *Latin American Catholicism.*

33. Prudencio Damboriena, S.J., *El Protestantismo en America Latina*, 2 vols. (Bogotá, Columbia-Friburgo, Suiza: FERES, 1962).

34. Ireneo Rosier, *Ovejas Sin Pastor* (Buenos Aires: Carlos Lohle, 1960), 103.

35. Gustavo Gutiérrez, *Lineas Pastorales de la Iglesia en America Latina* (Lima: Centro de Estudios y Publicaciones, 1970).

36. *Between Honesty and Hope,* xiii.

37. Gustavo Gutiérrez, "Church of the Poor," in *Born of the Poor: The Latin American Church since Medellín*, ed. Edward Cleary (Notre Dame, Ind.: University of Notre Dame Press, 1990), 18.

38. Samuel Escobar, *Liberation Themes in Reformational Perspective* (Sioux Center, Iowa: Dordt College Press, 1989), 25.

39. John A. Mackay *The Other Spanish Christ* (New York: Macmillan 1933), xii.

40. See, for instance, the writings of José H. Prado Flores of Mexico.

41. See chapter 10 herein.

42. Sante Uberto Barbieri, *Land of El Dorado* (New York: Friendship Press, 1961), 51.

43. For Protestant missiology, see Stephen Neill, *A History of Christian Missions* (New York: Penguin Books, 1964), 195 ff.; for the role of the Bible in missions to Latin America, see Prien, *La Historia del Cristianismo en America Latina*, 710-16.

44. In John J. Considine, ed. *The Religious Dimension in the New Latin America* (Notre Dame, Ind.: Fides, 1966), 205.

45. Walter M. Abbott, "Bible Needs of Roman Catholics," *United Bible Societies Bulletin* 71/3 (1967), 103.

46. Emilio A. Núñez, "Posicion de la Iglesia frente al Aggiornamento," in CLADE I *Acción en Cristo para un Continente en Crisis* (San José and Miami: Editorial Caribe, 1970), 40.

47. C. René Padilla, "Liberation Theology: An Appraisal," in *Freedom and Discipleship: Liberation Theology in Anabaptist Perspective*, ed. Daniel S. Schipani (Maryknoll, N.Y.: Orbis Books, 1989), 40.

48. See my article "Panorama religioso de America Latina" and English abstract in *Bulletin of the United Bible Societies* 174/175 (1995), 130-43.

49. Rosier, *Ovejas Sin Pastor,* 107.

50. Peadar Kirby and David J. Molineaux, "CEBs Promote New Ministries, New Model of Church," *Latinamerica Press* 17/24 (June 27, 1985), 1.

51. Ibid.

52. Juan Luis Segundo, *The Hidden Motives of Pastoral Work in Latin America* (Maryknoll, N.Y.: Orbis Books, 1978), 2.

53. A fundamental book about this issue is C. R. Boxer, *The Church Militant and Iberian Expansion 1440-1770* (Baltimore: The Johns Hopkins University Press, 1978).

54. Ivan Illich, quoted in ibid., 286.

55. Kenneth Scott Latourette, *A History of the Expansion of Christianity* (New York: Harper & Row, 1941), 4:48.

56. Stephen Neill, *A History of Christian Missions,* 2d ed., rev. Owen Chadwick (Harmondsworth: Penguin 1986), 177.

7 Popular Protestantism: A Missiological Perspective

1. The Lutheran theologian Rudolf Obermüller wrote about "Pentecostal sects" in his report *Evangelism in Latin America: An Ecumenical Survey* (London: Lutterworth, 1957), 19.

2. See the proceedings of this congress in Carl F. H. Henry and W. Stanley Mooneyham, eds., *One Race, One Gospel, One Task,* 2 vols. (Minneapolis, Minn.: World Wide Publications, 1967).

3. William J. Martin, *A Prophet with Honor: The Billy Graham Story* (New York: William Morrow and Co., 1992).

4. Jean Pierre Bastian, "Protestantism in Latin America," in *The Church in Latin America 1492-1992,* ed. Enrique Dussel (Maryknoll, N.Y.: Orbis Books, 1992), 346. Bastian nuances his judgment in a more recent work, *La Mutación Religiosa de América Latina* (Mexico: Fondo de Cultura Económica, 1997).

5. David B. Barrett, "Statistics, Global," entry in *Dictionary of Pentecostal and Charismatic Movements*, ed. Stanley M. Burgess and Gary B. McGee (Grand Rapids, Mich.: Zondervan, 1988), 810-30.

6. Ronald Knox in his classic work *Enthusiasm* (New York: Oxford University Press, 1961), showed that over the centuries glossolalia has appeared in movements that were often regarded as sectarian by established churches.

7. For a recent work of history, description, and interpretation, see Walter Hollenweger, *Pentecostalism: Origins and Developments Worldwide* (Peabody, Mass.: Hendrickson, 1997). For a classic history of the movement in the United States, see Robert Mapes Anderson, *Vision of the Disinherited: The Making of American Pentecostalism* (New York: Oxford University Press, 1979). On Latin America, see Benjamín Gutiérrez and Dennis Smith, eds., *In the Power of the Spirit: The Pentecostal Challenge to Historic Churches in Latin America* (Drexell Hill, Pa.: Skipjack Press, 1996), and Karl-Wilhelm Westmeier, *Protestant Pentecostalism in Latin America* (Madison, N.J.: Fairleigh Dickinson University Press, 1999).

8. Gary B. McGee, "Pentecostals and Their Various Strategies for Global Mission: A Historical Assessment," in *Called and Empowered: Global Mission in Pentecostal Perspective*, ed. Murray A. Dempster et al. (Peabody, Mass.: Hendrickson, 1991), 203-4.

9. See the history of the movement in Hans Jürgen Prien, *La Historia del Cristianismo en América Latina* (Salamanca: Sígueme, 1985), 825 ff.; for further details, see Paul Freston, *Protestantes e Política no Brasil: da Constituinte ao Impeachment* (Ph.D. thesis, Universidad Estadual de Campinas, Brazil, 1993).

10. J. B. Kessler, *A Study of the Older Protestant Missions and Churches in Peru and Chile* (Goes: Oosterban & le Cointre, 1967), chap. 9; see also Corporación Iglesia Evangélica Pentecostal, *Historia del Avivamiento Origen y Desarrollo de la Iglesia Evangélica Pentecostal* (Santiago, 1977).

11. Donald W. Dayton, *Theological Roots of Pentecostalism* (Metuchen: The Scarecrow Press, 1987).

12. Bastian, *La Mutación Religiosa de América Latina*, chap. 7.

13. Demos Shakarian, *The Happiest People on Earth* (Old Tappan, N.J.: Fleming Revell, 1975).

14. Bastian, *La Mutación Religiosa de América Latina,* 204.

15. I have studied this theme more extensively in "Conflict of Interpretations of Popular Protestantism," in *New Face of the Church in Latin America,* ed. Guillermo Cook (Maryknoll, N.Y.: Orbis Books, 1994), 112-34.

16. Walter Hollenweger's book mentioned above and his classic *The Pentecostals* (Minneapolis, Minn.: Augsburg, 1972), are based on a mass of documented research. Hollenweger is a Swiss Pentecostal and probably the most recognized expert on the subject. More than any other scholar he has paid attention to the missiological significance of Pentecostalism.

17. Juan Sepúlveda, "Pentecostal Theology in the Context of the Struggle for Life," in *Faith Born in the Struggle for Life,* ed. Dow Kirkpatrick (Grand Rapids, Mich.: Eerdmans, 1988), 298.

18. Bernardo Campos, "En la Fuerza del Espíritu: Pentecostalismo, Teología y Etica Social," in *En la Fuerza del Espíritu,* ed. Benjamin Gutierrez (Mexico: Guatemala: AIPRAL-CELEP, 1995), 58.

19. The Brazilian sociologist Emilio Willems specialized in social change; within that framework he studied Brazilian and Chilean Pentecostalism (see *Followers of the New Faith* [Nashville, Tenn.: Vanderbilt University Press, 1967]).

20. Lalive D'Epinay, a Swiss sociologist, spent time in Chile researching in depth the attitudes of Chilean Pentecostalism toward social reality and then wrote *Haven of the Masses* (London: Lutterworth Press, 1969).

21. I have studied interpretative keys in "Conflict of Interpretations of Popular Protestantism," in *New Face of the Church in Latin America,* ed. Guillermo Cook (Maryknoll, N.Y.: Orbis Books, 1994), 112-34.

22. Andrew Walls, "The Mission of the Church Today in the Light of Global History," in *Mission at the Dawn of the Twenty-First Century,* ed. Paul Varo Martinson (Minneapolis, Minn.: Kirk House Publishers, 1999), 384.

23. W. J. Hollenweger, "Towards an Intercultural History of Christianity," *International Review of Mission* 76/304 (October 1989), 526.

24. David B. Barrett, ed., *World Christian Encyclopedia* (Nairobi: Oxford University Press, 1982), 17.

25. Mike Berg and Paul Pretiz, *Spontaneous Combustion: Grassroots Christianity Latin American Style* (Pasadena, Calif.: William Carey Library, 1996).

26. Ibid., 12.

27. Ibid., 17.

28. David B. Barrett, *Schism and Renewal in Africa: An Analysis of 6,000 Contemporary Religious Movements* (Nairobi: Oxford University Press, 1968).

29. William R. Read, Victor M. Monterroso, and Harmon A. Johnson, *Latin American Church Growth* (Grand Rapids, Mich.: Eerdmans, 1969).

30. Peter Wagner, *Look Out! The Pentecostals Are Coming* (Carol Stream, Ill.: Creation House, 1973).

31. W. Dayton Roberts, *Strachan of Costa Rica* (Grand Rapids, Mich.: Eerdmans, 1971).

8 Popular Protestantism and Catholic Missiology

1. Jeffrey Klaiber, S.J., *La reacción católica ante la presencia protestante durante la república aristocrática* (Lima: Seminario de Historia del Protestantismo en el Perú, 1995).

2. Franz Damen, "Las sectas ¿avalancha o desafío?" *Cuarto Intermedio* [Jesuit magazine, Cochabamba] (May 1987), 45. Damen is a Passionist priest, has been a missionary in Bolivia, and has published several works on Protestants in Latin America.

3. Roger Aubry, *La misión: siguiendo a Jesús por los caminos de América Latina* (Buenos Aires: Ed. Guadalupe, 1990), 105-15. Monsignor Aubry, a Swiss Redemptorist priest, was president of the CELAM Department of Missions from 1974 to 1979 and has been a missionary in the interior of Bolivia since 1970.

4. Aubry, *La misión,* 105.

5. Ibid., 106.

6. Osvaldo Santagada, "Caracterización y situación de las sectas en América Latina," in *Sectas en América Latina* (CELAM). There is no indication of place or date of publication, but it is number 50 in the series published by CELAM in Bogotá, and in the introduction, Archbishop Antonio Quarracino mentions a 1981 meeting that led to the book.

7. I Conferencia General del Episcopado Latinoamericano, *Documento de Río* (Lima: Vida y Espiritualidad, 1991). The original document reprinted in this new edition dates back to 1955.

8. See *Medellín: Conclusiones,* nos. 2:26 and 30; 5:19; 8:11; 9:14.

9. *Puebla Conclusions,* 1107, 1109, in *Puebla and Beyond: Documentation and Commentary,* ed. John Eagleson and Philip Scharper (Maryknoll, N.Y.: Orbis Books, 1979).

10. *Puebla Conclusions,* 1109.

11. Opening Address of the pope in Santo Domingo, paragraph 12, in Alfred T. Hennelly, S.J., *Santo Domingo and Beyond: Documents and Commentaries from the Historic Meeting of the Latin American Bishops' Conference* (Maryknoll, N.Y.: Orbis Books, 1993), 47-48.

12. Ibid., 48.

13. Ignacio Vergara, *El Protestantismo en Chile* (Santiago: Editorial del Pacífico, 1962); Ireneo Rosier, *Ovejas sin Pastor* (Buenos Aires: Ed. Carlos Lohlé, 1960).

14. José Comblin, "Brazil: Base Communities in the Northeast," in *New Face of the Church in Latin America,* ed. Guillermo Cook (Maryknoll, N.Y.: Orbis Books, 1994), 217.

15. Phillip Berryman, *Religion in the Megacity: Catholic and Protestant Portraits from Latin America* (Maryknoll, N.Y.: Orbis Books, 1996), 148.

16. See chapter 6. See also Samuel Escobar, *La fe evangélica y las teologías de la liberación* (El Paso, Tex.: Casa Bautista de Publicaciones, 1987), chaps. 2, 3, 4.

17. Here I am using, in part, material from my article "Conflict of Interpretations of Popular Protestantism," in Cook, *New Face of the Church in Latin America,* 112-34.

18. Damen, "Las sectas ¿avalancha o desafío?," 52.

19. Ibid., 58.

20. Aubry, *La misión,* 111.

21. Ibid., 112.

22. Damen, "Las sectas ¿avalancha o desafío?," 60-61.

23. Ibid.

24. Comblin, "Brazil," 219.

25. John Gorski, M.M., *El desarrollo histórico de la misionología en América Latina* (La Paz, Bolivia, 1985), 283.

26. José Luis Idígoras, S.J., *La religión fenómeno popular* (Lima: Ediciones Paulinas, 1984), 236.

27. Ibid., 238.

28. Ibid., 245.

29. Ibid., 245-46.

30. Angel Salvatierra, "Retos y características especiales de la nueva evangelización," in *Nueva Evangelización* (Bogotá: CELAM, 1990).

31. Comblin, "Brazil," 218.

32. I have dealt with this issue also in Cook, *New Face of the Church in Latin America,* and also in *Historia y Misión: revisión de perspectivas* (Lima: Ediciones Presencia, 1994).

33. Thomas J. Reese, "The Synod Points Out Needs," *America* (January 3, 1998), 3.

34. John Paul II, *Ecclesia in America,* Post Synodal Apostolic Exhortation (Washington, D.C.: United States Catholic Conference, 1999), no. 73.

35. Ibid.

36. Ibid.

37. Ibid.

9 *Missiological Reflection on Belief, Experience, Structure*

1. Donald W. Dayton, *Theological Roots of Pentecostalism* (Grand Rapids, Mich.: Francis Asbury Press, 1987).

2. Howard A. Snyder deals with this issue in *The Community of the King* (Downers Grove, Ill.: InterVarsity Press, 1977), chap. 5.

3. Justo L. González, *Historia de las Misiones* (Buenos Aires: La Aurora, 1970), 187-88 (emphasis added).

4. Ibid.

5. Ibid., 203.

6. Kenneth S. Latourette, *Desafío a los protestantes* (Buenos Aires: La Aurora, 1957), 78.

7. Kenneth S. Latourette, *The Prospect for Christianity* (London: Eyre and Spottiswoode, 1949), 150.

8. Latourette, *Desafío a los protestantes*, 78.

9. Emil Brunner, *The Misunderstanding of the Church* (Philadelphia: Westminster Press, 1953), 47-48.

10. Ibid., 48.

11. Ibid.

12. Ibid., 52.

13. See the articles on these figures in Gerald H. Anderson, ed., *Biographical Dictionary of Christian Missions* (New York: Macmillan, 1998).

14. Roland Allen, *The Spontaneous Expansion of the Church* (London: World Dominion Press, 1956).

15. Roland Allen, *Missionary Methods: St.Paul's or Ours*, 3d ed. (London: World Dominion Press, 1953).

16. Harry Boer, *Pentecost and Mission* (Grand Rapids, Mich.: Eerdmans, 1961).

17. Ibid., 12.

18. Howard Snyder, "The Church as God's Agent in Evangelism," in *Let the Earth Hear His Voice*, ed. J. D. Douglas (Minneapolis, Minn.: World Wide Publications, 1975), 327-60.

19. Howard A. Snyder, *New Wineskins* (Downers Grove, Ill.: InterVarsity Press, 1975).

20. Howard A. Snyder, *The Radical Wesley and Patterns for Church Renewal* (Downers Grove, Ill.: InterVarsity Press, 1980).

21. Gonzalo Báez Camargo, *Genio y espíritu del metodismo wesleyano*, 2d ed. (Mexico: Casa Unida de Publicaciones, 1981), 94.

22. Kenneth Strachan, *Desafío a la evangelicación* (Buenos Aires: Logos, 1970), 28.

23. Orlando Costas, *La Iglesia su misión evangelizadora* (Buenos Aires: La Aurora, 1971), 105-6.

24. Ted Limpic, *Catálogo de organizaciones misioneras iberoamericanas* (Miami: Comibam-Unilit, 1997), 191.

25. Valdir Steuernagel, *Obediencia missionária e prática histórica: Em busca de modelos* (São Paulo: ABU Editora, 1993), 92.

26. Ibid., 93.

27. Here I am summarizing from Steuernagel, *Obediencia missionária e prática histórica*, 101-11.

28. See chapter 11.

29. José Comblin, *The Holy Spirit and Liberation* (Maryknoll N.Y.: Orbis Books, 1989).

30. Ibid., 27.

31. Ibid.

10 From Mission to Theology

1. See, for instance, Mortimer Arias, *Announcing the Reign of God* (Philadelphia: Fortress Press, 1984); and Emilio Castro, *Freedom in Mission* (Geneva: World Council of Churches, 1985).

2. Orlando Costas, *Theology of the Crossroads in Contemporary Latin America* (Amsterdam: Rodopi, 1976).

3. See Samuel Escobar, "The Search for the Missiological Christology in Latin America," in *Emerging Voices in Global Christian Theology*, ed. William F. Dyrness (Grand

Rapids, Mich.: Zondervan, 1994), 199-227. I am incorporating in this section parts of that chapter.

4. Stanley Hauerwas and Will Willimon, "Why *Resident Aliens* Struck a Chord," *Missiology* 19/4 (October 1991), 419-29.

5. In this regard the meeting of the International Missionary Council in Jerusalem in 1928 was one of the first instances in which awareness about the need to consider Europe and North America mission fields became public. This was not unrelated to the fact that it was also at that meeting that the validity of Protestant missionary work in Latin America was acknowledged by the ecumenical movement (see the observations of Báez-Camargo in chapter 3 herein).

6. See chapter 6 herein.

7. Samuel Escobar, "Biblical Content and Anglo-Saxon Trappings in Latin American Theology," *Occasional Bulletin* [Latin American Theological Fraternity] 3 (October 1972); Samuel Escobar and John Driver, *Christian Mission and Social Justice* (Scottdale, Pa.: Herald Press, 1978).

8. Escobar, "Biblical Content and Anglo-Saxon Trappings in Latin American Theology," 2.

9. C. René Padilla, "Biblical Foundations: A Latin American Study," *Evangelical Review of Theology* 7/1 (1983), 86.

10. Samuel Escobar, "Evangelical Missiology: Peering into the Future at the Turn of the Century," in *Global Missiology for the Twenty-First Century*, ed. William D. Taylor (Grand Rapids, Mich.: Baker, 2000), 101-22.

11. For a brief evaluation of this movement, see James A. Scherer, *Gospel, Church, and Kingdom* (Minneapolis, Minn.: Augsburg, 1987), chap. 5. For a brief history and documents of the movement, see John Stott, ed., *Making Christ Known: Historic Mission Documents from the Lausanne Movement 1974-1989* (Grand Rapids, Mich.: Eerdmans, 1996).

12. See especially the contributions of Orlando Costas and René Padilla in *Down to Earth*, ed. John Stott and Robert Coote (Grand Rapids, Mich.: Eerdmans, 1980).

13. Stott and Coote, *Down to Earth*, 334.

14. See, for instance, the confluence of fifteen authors from around the world in their commentary on the Lausanne Covenant in *The New Face of Evangelicalism*, ed. C. René Padilla (Downers Grove, Ill.: InterVarsity Press, 1976).

15. See especially, John Howard Yoder, *The Original Revolution* (Scottdale, Pa.: Herald Press, 1972); idem, *The Politics of Jesus* (Grand Rapids, Mich.: Eerdmans, 1972). For an explanation of the relevance of the Anabaptist position for Latin America, see Samuel Escobar, "The Kingdom of God, Eschatology and Social and Political Ethics in Latin America," *Theological Fraternity Bulletin* [Buenos Aires] 1 (1975), 1-42.

16. The relevance of Ellul's insights for Latin America comes from his effort to read scripture and the Christian tradition from his French context, subject to the same ideological influences prevalent in Latin America. Ellul was a lay theologian who had not lost his Protestant identity.

17. For a description of post-imperial missiology and its sources, see chapter 2 herein.

18. In the Spanish language the word *evangélico,* the literal translation of *evangelical,* is used as a synonym of *Protestant.* However, since the 1960s church life and theology have developed in two streams within the Protestant minority: "Ecumenical Protestantism" for some of the oldest churches related to the conciliar ecumenical movement, and "Evangelical Protestantism," which in its ethos and theology is closer to the position to which we usually refer with the term *evangelical* in English. This position is also shared by some of the largest Pentecostal communities.

19. For a history of the Latin American Theological Fraternity, see Anthony Christopher Smith, *The Essentials of Missiology from the Evangelical Perspective of the "Fraternidad Teologica Latinoamericana"* (Ph.D. dissertation, Southern Baptist Theological Seminary, Louisville, 1983). Smith's work focuses on the fraternity's missiology.

20. Brazilian missiologist Valdir Steuernagel (1988) has documented the debates and the hostility of North American missiologists from the Church Growth school against Latin American evangelical theologians in *The Theology of Mission in Relation to Social Responsibility within the Lausanne Movement* (Ph.D. dissertation, Lutheran School of Theology, Chicago, 1988), esp. 164ff. and 224ff.

21. Stott and Coote, *Down to Earth*, 334.

22. Protestant antecedents of liberation theologies are studied by Alan Neely in *Protestant Antecedents of the Latin American Theology of Liberation* (Ph.D. dissertation, American University, Washington, D.C., 1976). Several Latin American evangelicals offer a critical approach in *Fe Cristiana y Latinoamerica Hoy,* ed. C. René Padilla (Buenos Aires: Ediciones Certeza, 1974).

23. Andrew Kirk, *Liberation Theology* (Atlanta, Ga.: John Knox Press, 1979).

24. Emilio A. Núñez, *Liberation Theology* (Chicago: Moody Press, 1985).

25. Samuel Escobar, *La fe evangelica y las teologias de la liberación* (El Paso, Tex.: Casa Bautista, 1987); idem, *Liberation Themes in Reformational Perspective* (Sioux Center, Iowa: Dordt College Press, 1989).

26. Daniel Schipani, ed., *Freedom and Discipleship* (Maryknoll, N.Y.: Orbis Books, 1989).

27. See especially the contributions of René Padilla, Sidney Rooy. and Orlando Costas in *Exploring Church Growth,* ed. Wilbert Shenk (Grand Rapids, Mich.: Eerdmans, 1983).

28. C. René Padilla, *Mission between the Times* (Grand Rapids, Mich.: Eerdmans, 1985).

29. Orlando Costas, *Christ outside the Gate* (Maryknoll, N.Y.: Orbis Books, 1982).

30. Orlando Costas, *Liberating News* (Grand Rapids, Mich.: Eerdmans, 1989).

31. Costas's doctoral dissertation dealt with the missiology of the ecumenical theologians of Latin American Protestantism *(Theology of the Crossroads in Contemporary Latin America).*

32. José Míguez Bonino, *Faces of Latin American Protestantism* (Grand Rapids, Mich.: Eerdmans, 1997), 112.

33. See Samuel Escobar, "The Missionary Legacy of John A.Mackay," *International Bulletin of Missionary Research* 16/3 (July 1992), 116-22.

34. John A. Mackay, *The Other Spanish Christ* (New York: Macmillan, 1933).

35. Ibid., 110.

36. Ibid., 98.

37. John A. Mackay, *Mas yo os digo . . .* (Mexico: Casa Unida de Publicaciones, 1964); idem, *El Sentido de la Vida* (Lima: Ediciones Presencia, 1988).

38. Mackay, *The Other Spanish Christ*, 110-11.

39. Ibid., 112.

40. Ibid., 117.

41. John A. Mackay, *A Preface to Christian Theology* (New York: Macmillan, 1941), 50.

42. Mackay summarized his missionary theology in a book that is still relevant, *Ecumenics: The Science of the Church Universal* (Englewood Cliffs, N.J.: Prentice-Hall, 1964).

43. Pedro Gringoire (Gonzalo Báez-Camargo), *Las Manos de Cristo,* 2d ed. (Mexico: Casa Unida de Publicaciones, 1985 <1950>).

44. The Spanish version of *Jesus Christ Liberator: A Critical Christology for Our Time* by Leonardo Boff (Maryknoll, N.Y.: Orbis Books, 1978), appeared in 1974. In the preface of the Spanish version Héctor Borrat presents it as "the first systematic Christology published in Latin America," and he acknowledges that Protestants were far ahead of Catholics in the study of that theme (in Leonardo Boff, *Jesucristo el liberador* [Buenos Aires: Latinoamerica Libros, 1974], 11).

45. Amado Anzi, S.J., *El Evangelio Criollo* (Buenos Aires: Editora Patria Grande, 1964).

46. The historical and theological processes of these years have been covered extensively by Emilio A. Núñez, *Liberation Theology,* and Samuel Escobar, *La fe evangelica y las teologias de la liberación.*

47. Justo L. González, *Revolución y Encarnación* (Rio Piedras, P.R.: La Reforma, 1965).

48. Justo L. González, *Jesucristo es el Señor* (Miami: Editorial Caribe, 1971).

49. Justo L. González, *A History of Christian Thought*, 3 vols. (Nashville, Tenn.: Abingdon Press, 1987).

50. Padilla, *Fe Cristiana y Latinoamerica Hoy,* 166.

51. Justo L. González, *Mañana: Christian Theology from a Hispanic Perspective* (Nashville, Tenn.: Abingdon Press, 1990), 143.

52. Samuel Escobar, *Diálogo entre Cristo y Marx* (Lima: AGEUP, 1967); Samuel Escobar, Edwin Yamauchi, C. René Padilla, *¿Quién es Cristo Hoy?* (Buenos Aires: Certeza, 1970).

53. The text of this presentation was published in English as part of a symposium (*Is Revolution Change?,* ed. Bede Griffiths [London: InterVarsity Press, 1972]).

54. The complete text of the declaration can be found in CLADE I *Acción en Cristo para un Continente en Crisis* (San José and Miami: Caribe, 1970), 134-35. Quoted in William D. Taylor and Emilio A. Núñez, *Crisis and Hope in Latin America* (Pasadena, Calif.: William Carey Library, 1996), 414.

55. For a development of these themes with a more contemporary key, see Mortimer Arias, *The Great Commission* (Nashville, Tenn.: Abingdon Press, 1992).

56. For a careful chronicle and analysis of the Lausanne process and the Latin American participation in it, see Steuernagel, *The Theology of Mission in Relation to Social Responsibility within the Lausanne Movement,* 124-69.

57. See Samuel Escobar, "The Social Impact of the Gospel," in Griffiths, *Is Revolution Change?*

58. C. René Padilla and Mark Lau Branson, eds., *Conflict and Context: Hermeneutics in the Americas* (Grand Rapids, Mich.: Eerdmans, 1986), 83.

59. José Míguez Bonino, ed., *Faces of Jesus* (Maryknoll, N.Y.: Orbis Books, 1984), 1.

60. Costas, *Liberating News,* 2.

61. This is, for instance, the general thrust of the writings of many of the Protestant authors from Latin America in a valuable anthological volume, *Faith Born in the Struggle for Life,* ed. Dow Kirkpatrick (Grand Rapids, Mich.: Eerdmans, 1989).

62. Emilio Castro, "The Old Old Story and Contemporary Crisis," in *Mission in the 1990s,* ed. Gerald Anderson (Grand Rapids, Mich.: Eerdmans; New Haven, Conn.: OMSC, 1991), 56.

63. C. René Padilla, "Christology and Mission in the Two Thirds World," in *Sharing Jesus in the Two Thirds World: Evangelical Christologies from the Contexts of Poverty, Powerlessness, and Religious Pluralism,* ed. Vinay Samuel and Chris Sugden (Grand Rapids, Mich.: Eerdmans, 1983), 13.

64. Walter A. Elwell, ed., *Evangelical Dictionary of Theology* (Grand Rapids, Mich.: Baker, 1984), 584.

65. Padilla and Lau Branson, *Conflict and Context,* 81.

66. Ibid.

67. Ibid., 83.

68. Núñez, *Liberation Theology,* 236.

69. For this point, see the debate about Padilla's christological proposal in Padilla and Lau Branson, *Conflict and Context,* 92-113.

70. For a recent exploration along these lines, see González, *Mañana: Christian Theology from a Hispanic Perspective.*

71. Padilla and Lau Branson, *Conflict and Context,* 87.

72. Ibid., 89.

73. C. René Padilla, "Bible Studies," *Missiology* 10/3 (1982), 319-38.

74. John Howard Yoder, "Church Growth Issues in Theological Perspective," in *The Challenge of Church Growth,* ed. Wilbert Shenk (Elkhart, Ind.: Institute of Mennonite Studies, 1973).

75. George R. Hunsberger, "The Newbigin Gauntlet: Developing a Domestic Missiology for North America," *Missiology* 19/4 (1991), 406.

76. Padilla, *Mission between the Times,* 62.

77. Ibid.

78. C. René Padilla, "God's Word and Man's Myths," *Themelios* 3/1 (1977), 3.

79. Padilla, "Christology and Mission in the Two Thirds World," 28.

80. Ibid.

81. I have described managerial forms of missiology in chapter 2 herein.

82. Charles Taber, "Contextualitzation," in Shenk, *Exploring Church Growth*, 119.

83. C. René Padilla, "The Unity of the Church and the Homogeneous Unit Principle," in Shenk, *Exploring Church Growth,* 301.

84. Padilla, *Mission between the Times,* 79.

85. Sidney Rooy, "A Theology of Humankind," in Shenk, *Exploring Church Growth,* 198.

86. Ibid.

87. Ibid., 199.

88. Padilla, *Mission between the Times,* 160.

89. Ibid., 165.

90. For an account and evaluation of this process, see Padilla, "Latin American Evangelicals Enter the Public Square," *Transformation* 9/3 (1992), 2-7.

91. Mortimer Arias, *Announcing the Reign of God,* 15.

92. C. René Padilla, ed., *El Reino de Dios y América Latina* (El Paso, Tex.: Casa Bautista de Publicaciones, 1975).

93. Padilla, *The New Face of Evangelicalism,* 216.

94. Padilla, *El Reino de Dios y América Latina*; Pablo Deiros, ed., *Los evangélicos y el poder político en América Latina* (Buenos Aires: Nueva Creación; Grand Rapids, Mich.: Eerdmans, 1986).

95. Padilla, *Mission between the Times,* 127.

96. John Howard Yoder, *The Priestly Kingdom: Social Ethics as Gospel* (Notre Dame, Ind.: University of Notre Dame Press, 1984), 5.

97. Andrew Walls, *The Missionary Movement in Christian History* (Maryknoll, N.Y.: Orbis Books, 1996), 9-10.

98. Norberto Saracco, "The Liberating Options of Jesus," in Samuel and Sugden, *Sharing Jesus in the Two Thirds World,* 33-41.

99. Ibid., 33.

100. For a bibliography about the sources of this approach to the significance of Galilee for Jesus' mission, see Costas, *Liberating News,* 164.

101. Ibid., 67.

102. Padilla, *Mission between the Times,* 169.

11 Mission Theology from Pentecost to the Twenty-First Century

1. Walbert Bühlmann, *The Coming of the Third Church* (Maryknoll, N.Y.: Orbis Books, 1977), 217-18.

2. Justo L. González, "Today's Mission in the Land of *Mañana*," *Encounter* 29 (Summer 1972), 283.

3. Ibid., 286.

4. Karl-Wilhelm Westmeier, *Protestant Pentecostalism in Latin America* (Madison, N.J.: Fairleigh Dickinson University Press; London: Associated University Presses, 1999), 21.

5. Juan Sepúlveda, "Pentecostalism as Popular Religiosity," *International Review of Mission* 78/309 (January 1989), 80.

6. Ibid.

7. For a helpful distinction between these hermeneutics, see Richard Mouw, *Consulting the Faithful* (Grand Rapids, Mich.: Eerdmans, 1994), 10-14.

8. Douglas Petersen, "The Formation of Popular, National, Autonomous Pentecostal Churches in Central America," *Pneuma* 16/1 (Spring 1994), 32.

9. Ibid.

10. Florencio Galindo, *El Protestantismo fundamentalista: Una experiencia ambigua para America Latina* (Estela, Navarra: Verbo Divino, 1992).

11. José Míguez Bonino, *Faces of Latin American Protestantism* (Grand Rapids, Mich.: Eerdmans, 1995), ix-x.

12. Ibid., 131.

13. *Dictionary of Pentecostal and Charismatic Movements,* ed. Stanley Burgess, Gary McGee, and Patrick H. Alexander (Grand Rapids, Mich.: Zondervan, 1988).

14. *Pneuma* 16/1 (Spring 1994).

15. Gary B. McGee, "Pentecostal Missiology: Moving beyond Triumphalism to Face the Issues," *Pneuma* 16/3 (Fall 1994).

16. Russell P. Spittler, "Implicit Values in Pentecostal Missions," *Missiology* 16/4 (October 1988), 414.

17. Ibid., 416.

18. Melvin Hodges, quoted in Gary B. McGee, "Missions," in *Dictionary of Pentecostal and Charismatic Movements,* 621.

19. Melvin Hodges, *A Theology of the Church and Its Mission* (Springfield, Mo.: Gospel Publishing House, 1977), 9, 181-82.

20. Paul A. Pommerville, *The Third Force in Missions. A Pentecostal Contribution to Contemporary Mission Theology* (Peabody, Mass.: Hendrickson, 1985), 63.

21. Spittler, "Implicit Values in Pentecostal Missions," 422.

22. Eldin Villafañe, *The Liberating Spirit: Toward an Hispanic American Pentecostal Social Ethic* (Grand Rapids, Mich.: Eerdmans, 1993).

23. Samuel Solivan, *Orthopathos: Prolegomenon for a North American Hispanic Theology* (Ph.D. dissertation, Union Theological Seminary, 1993).

24. McGee, "Pentecostal Missiology," 281.

25. For Paul's missionary practice and missiological reflection, see the classic books of Roland Allen and the good summaries in Michael Green, *Evangelism in the Early Church* (Grand Rapids, Mich.: Eerdmans, 1970); David Bosch, *Transforming Mission* (Maryknoll, N.Y.: Orbis Books, 1991); and more recently, Peter Bolt and Mark Thompson, eds., *The Gospel to the Nations* (Downers Grove, Ill.: InterVarsity Press, 2000).

26. Lesslie Newbigin, *The Household of God* (New York: Friendship Press, 1954), 122.

27. Juan Sepúlveda, "Pentecostal Theology in the Context of the Struggle for Life," in *Faith Born in the Struggle for Life,* ed. Dow Kirkpatrick (Grand Rapids, Mich.: Eerdmans, 1988), 298.

28. Karl-Wilhelm Westmeier, *Reconciling Heaven and Earth: The Transcendental Enthusiasm and Growth of an Urban Protestant Community, Bogotá, Colombia* (Frankfurt: Peter Lang, 1986), esp. chap. 7.

29. For a purely sociological analysis that could take to missiological reflection, see, among others, Cecilia Loreto Mariz, "Deliverance and Ethics: An Analysis of the Discourse of Pentecostals Who Have Recovered from Alcholism," in *More Than Opium: An Anthropological Approach to Latin American and Caribbean Pentecostal Praxis,* ed. Barbara Boudewijnse et al. (Lanham, Md.: Scarecrow Press, 1998), 203-23.

30. See "Evangelism, Proselytism, and Common Witness: The Report from the Fourth Phase of the International Dialogue (1990-1997), between the Roman Catholic Church and Some Classic Pentecostal Churches and Leaders," *Pneuma* 21/1 (Spring 1999).

31. See Basil Meeking and John Stott, *The Evangelical-Roman Catholic Dialogue on Mission 1977-1984: A Report* (Grand Rapids, Mich.: Eerdmans, 1986).

32. Kilian McDonnell, O.S.B., "Pentecostals and Catholics on Evangelism and Sheep-Stealing," in *America* (March 6, 1999).

33. For my treatment of this question, see Samuel Escobar, "Missionary Dynamism in Search for Missiological Discernment," *Evangelical Review of Theology* 23/1 (January 1999), 70-91; also *One in Christ* 35/1 (1999), 69-92.

34. Orlando Costas, *Liberating News* (Grand Rapids, Mich.: Eerdmans, 1989), 148.

35. Here I have in mind the pioneering work of Edwin A. Judge in *The Social Pattern of Christian Groups in the New Testament* (London: Tyndale Press, 1960), and also the work of scholars such as Abraham J. Malherbe, Wayne Meeks, and Gerd Theissen.

36. An extensive bibliography on this matter is presented in Jean Duhaime, "Early Christianity and the Social Sciences: A Bibliography," *Social Compass* 39/2 (1992), 275-90. With regard to missiological use of this material, see Bosch, *Transforming Mission*, chap. 1.

37. Sepúlveda, "Pentecostal Theology in the Context of the Struggle for Life," 298.

38. The proceedings of CLADE III were published in CLADE III *Tercer Congreso Latinoamericano de Evangelizacion* (Quito: FTL, 1993).

39. Ricardo Gondim Rodrigues, "El Evangelio de Poder," in CLADE III *Tercer Congreso Latinoamericano de Evangelizacion*, 175.

40. Ibid., 176.

41. Ibid.

42. Norberto Saracco, "El Evangelio de Poder," 159.

43. Gondim Rodrigues, "El Evangelio de Poder," 182.

44. Spittler discusses this issue in relation to North American Pentecostalism and refers to "the tension between Spirit-born spontaneity and creeping organizational routinization" ("Implicit Values in Pentecostal Missions," 415).

45. Saracco, "El Evangelio de Poder," 183.

46. A starting point was C. René Padilla, ed., *El reino de Dios y América Latina* (El Paso, Tex.: Casa Bautista de Publicaciones, 1972).

47. See Pablo Deiros, ed., *Los evangélicos y el poder político* (Grand Rapids, Mich.: Eerdmans; Buenos Aires: Nueva Creación, 1985).

48. For a presentation and evaluation of this process, see my articles in the special edition of *Boletín Teológico* 42/43 (1991). C. René Padilla presents more recent developments in *De la marginación al compromiso* (Buenos Aires: FTL, 1994). Several chapters of this book were published in English in *Tranformation* 9/3 (1992).

49. See examples of testimonies and reflections in Padilla, *De la marginación al compromiso*.

50. Dario López, *Los Evangelicos y los Derechos Humanos* (Lima: CEMAA, 1998), 228-29.

51. Ibid., 289.

52. See my closing chapter in Padilla, *El Reino de Dios y América Latina*.

53. Sepúlveda, "Pentecostal Theology in the Context of the Struggle for Life," 300.

54. Ibid., 308.

55. On Chile, see Humberto Lagos Schuffeneger, *Crisis de la esperanza* (Santiago de Chile: Presor-Lar, 1988); see also Westmeier, *Reconciling Heaven and Earth*.

56. Freston's doctoral dissertation, *Protestantes e política no Brasil: da Constituinte ao Impeachment* (Universidade de Campinas, 1993), was the basis for his book *Evangélicos na política brasileira: Historia ambigua e desafío ético* (Curitiba: Encontrao Editora, 1994).

57. Paul Freston, "In Search of an Evangelical Project for Brazil: A Pentecostal 'Showvention,'" *Transformation* 9/3 (July-September 1992), 30.

58. Ibid., 31.

59. Ibid., 29. For a more detailed and sophisticated analysis, see Paul Freston, "Popular Protestants in Brazilian Politics: A Novel Turn in Sect-State Relations," *Social Compass* 41/4 (1994), 537-70.

60. Freston, *Evangélicos na política*, 138-40.

61. Freston, "In Search of an Evangelical Project for Brazil," 32.

62. Justo L. González, *Mañana: Christian Theology from a Hispanic Perspective* (Nashville, Tenn.: Abingdon Press, 1990).

63. Ibid., 157.

64. Ibid., 158.

65. Ibid., 160.

66. Ibid.

67. Ibid., 162.
68. Ibid., 163.
69. Ibid., 164.

12 Mission from Latin America

1. Rogelio Duarte, *El Desafío Protestante en el Paraguay* (Asunción, 1994), 81ff.
2. A. G. Tallon, *Historia del Metodismo en el Río de la Plata* (Buenos Aires: Imprenta Metodista, 1936).
3. *Historia del Avivamiento, Origen y Desarrollo de la Iglesia Evangélica Pentecostal* (Santiago: Corporación Iglesia Evangélic Pentecostal, 1977), 473ff.
4. Stephen Neill, *A History of Christian Missions*, rev. ed. (New York: Penguin Books, 1986), 99.
5. Lewis Hanke, *The Spanish Struggle for Justice in the Conquest of America* (Philadelphia: University of Pennsylvania Press, 1949).
6. See the classic work by Justo L. González, *Historia de las Misiones* (Buenos Aires: Methopress, 1970), 187-88; see also, Valdir Steuernagel, *Obediencia Misionera y Práctica Histórica* (Buenos Aires: Nueva Creación; Grand Rapids, Mich.: Eerdmans, 1996).
7. For a more extensive treatment of this subject, see Samuel Escobar, "Recruitment of Students for Mission," *Missiology* 15/4 (October 1987), 529-45.
8. Clarence P. Shedd, *Two Centuries of Student Christian Movements* (New York: Association Press, 1934), 32-90.
9. Angelyn Dries, *The Missionary Movement in American Catholic History* (Maryknoll, N.Y.: Orbis Books, 1998), 77.
10. Ibid., 87.
11. John R. Mott, *Strategic Points for the World Conquest* (New York: Fleming and Revell, 1897), 211.
12. For a recent history of the movement that gives a good account of its context and projection, see Michael Parker, *The Kingdom of Character: The Student Volunteer Movement for Foreign Missions* (Lanham, Md.: University Press of America and American Society of Missiology, 1998).
13. David M. Howard, *Moving Out: The Story of Student Initiative in World Missions* (Downers Grove, Ill.: InterVarsity Press, 1984); see also a brief missiological evaluation in Samuel Escobar, "The Two-Party System and the Missionary Enterprise," in *Re-Forming the Center: American Protestantism 1900 to the Present*, ed. Douglas Jacobsen and William Vance Trollinger (Grand Rapids, Mich.: Eerdmans, 1998), 341-60.
14. For a brief history of the origins and missionary projections of these movements, see Samuel Escobar, *La Chispa y la Llama* (Buenos Aires: Certeza, 1978).
15. *Jesus Cristo: Senhorio, propósito, missão* (São Paulo: ABU Editora, 1978).
16. For an interpretative account of the event, see Samuel Escobar, *Una década en tiempo de misión* (Lima: Comunidad Internacional de Estudiantes Evangélicos, 1987).
17. This gathering took place in Huampaní, Lima, Peru, December 1-6, 1987. An interpretative account of the event may be found in Washington Padilla, *Hacia una Transformación Integral* (Buenos Aires: FTL, 1989).
18. William D. Taylor and Emilio A. Núñez, *Crisis and Hope in Latin America* (Pasadena, Calif.: William Carey Library, 1996), 41.
19. Luis Bush and Rudy Giron, quoted in Sharon E. Mumper, "Latin America: Called to Missions," *Evangelical Missions Quarterly* (April 1988), 168-69.
20. Luis Bush offers a brief account of the establishment of the movement in *Introducción al Atlas de COMIBAM* (no date or other publication information); see also, Federico Bertuzzi, "El esfuerzo missionero desde América Latina," in CLADE III, *Tercer Congreso Latinoamericano de Evangelizacion* (Quito: FTL, 1993), 359-61.
21. See, for example, the testimonies and brief histories of mission in Muslim countries gathered in Federico Bertuzzi, ed., *Rios en la soledad* (Santa Fe, Argentina: Proyecto Magreb, 1991).

22. Ted Limpic, ed., *Iberoamerican Missions Handbook 1997* (Acapulco: COMIBAM, 1997).

23. Pablo A. Deiros, *Diccionario Hispano-Americano de la Mision* (Miami, Fla.: COMIBAM/UNILIT, 1998).

24. Emilio A. Núñez, *Hacia una Misionología Evangélica Latinoamericana* (Miami, Fla.: COMIBAM/UNILIT, 1997).

25. Larry Pate, *From Every People: A Handbook of Two-Thirds World Missions with Directory/Histories/Analysis* (Monrovia, Calif.: MARC, 1989).

26. Ted Limpic, *Catálogo de Organizaciones Misioneras Iberoamericanas* (Miami, Fla.: COMIBAM/UNILIT, 1997), 171.

27. *Memorias del COMLA-4*, minutes of the Fourth Latin American Missionary Congress, Lima, February 3-8, 1991 (Lima: Ediciones Paulinas y Obras Misionales Pontifícias, 1991), 267.

28. Jeffrey Klaiber, S.J., *The Catholic Church in Peru—1821-1985* (Washington, D.C.: Catholic University of America Press, 1992), 38. The figures are for 1973, but the situation has not changed much and is the same in several other countries.

29. *Puebla Document,* par. 368; see English text in John Eagleson and Philip Scharper, eds., *Puebla and Beyond: Documentation and Commentary* (Maryknoll, N.Y.: Orbis Books, 1979), 175.

30. *Memorias del COMLA-4*, 247.

31. Fernando Galbiati, "The Intense Missionary Experience of a Continent," *Omnis Terra* [Pontifical Missionary Union, Rome] 301 (November 1999), 362.

32. Roger Aubry, *La Misión: Siguiendo a Jesús por los Caminos de América Latina* (Buenos Aires: Editorial Guadalupe, 1990), 132-33.

33. Galbiati, "The Intense Missionary Experience of a Continent," 363.

34. González, *Historia de las Misiones,* 49.

35. José Míguez Bonino, *Faces of Latin American Protestantism* (Grand Rapids, Mich.: Eerdmans, 1997), 50-51.

36. Valdir Steuernagel, "La universalidad de la misión," in CLADE III, *Tercer Congreso Latinoamericano de Evangelización,* 345.

37. Ibid., 347.

13 Formation of the Transcultural Missionary

1. Eduardo Hoornaert, *The Memory of the Christian People* (Maryknoll, N.Y.: Orbis Books, 1988); see a brief evaluation in Samuel Escobar, "Mission Studies: Past, Present and Future," *Missiology* 25/1 (January 1996), 3-29.

2. Eugene A. Nida, *Understanding Latin Americans* (Pasadena, Calif.: William Carey Library, 1974); idem, *Message and Mission: the Communication of the Christian Faith*, rev. ed. (Pasadena, Calif.: William Carey Library, 1990).

3. Jacob A. Loewen, *Culture and Human Values: Christian Intervention in Anthropological Perspective* (Pasadena, Calif.: William Carey Library, 1975).

4. Paul G. Hiebert, *Anthropological Reflections on Missiological Issues* (Grand Rapids, Mich.: Baker, 1994); idem, *Missiological Implications of Epistemological Shifts* (Harrisburg, Pa.: Trinity Press International, 1998).

5. Samuel Escobar, *Paulo Freire: Una Pedagogía Latinoamericana* (Mexico: CUPSA-Kyrios, 1993).

6. Stephen Neill, *A History of Christian Missions* (Harmondsworth, England: Penguin Books, 1964), 25.

7. For an example close to our situation, see the letters of James Thomson and the autobiographical notes of Francisco Penzotti in *Precursores Evangélicos*, ed. Samuel Escobar (Lima: Ediciones Presencia, 1984).

8. Valdir Steuernagel, *Obediencia misionera y práctica histórica* (Buenos Aires: Nueva Creación, 1996), 112.

9. Donald Senior and Carroll Stuhlmueller, *Biblia y misión* (Estella: Verbo Divino, 1985), translated from *The Biblical Foundations for Mission* (Maryknoll, N.Y.: Orbis Books, 1983).

10. C. René Padilla, ed., *Bases bíblicas de la misión: Perspectivas latinoamericanas* (Buenos Aires: Nueva Creación; Grand Rapids, Mich.: Eerdmans, 1998).

11. Paul S. Minear, *The Obedience of Faith: The Purpose of Paul in the Epistle to the Romans* (London: SCM Press, 1971).

12. On the educational process in the churches in relation to mission, see Roberto W. Pazmiño, *Principles and Practices of Christian Education: An Evangelical Perspective* (Grand Rapids, Mich.: Baker, 1992).

13. For the best study of this issue, see Lamin Sanneh, *Translating the Message: The Missionary Impact on Culture* (Maryknoll, N.Y.: Orbis Books, 1989).

Index

Adventist work in education, 51
affiliation, changing religious, 27, 44, 88
Africa, 85–86
Agrarian Reform, 52–53
Alianca Biblica Universitaria (ABU), 157
alternative societies, creation of, 54–58
Anabaptists, 106, 146
Anglo Pentecostal missiology, 136
anthropology, 126, 141
Antichrist, 127–128, 144
Assemblies of God, 77, 79, 134
atonement, 116–117
attitude changes, 132–133, 175–176
Australia, 10
authority, 74, 114
Báez-Camargo, Gonzalo, 24–25, 26
Base Ecclesial Communities, 60, 71–72
beliefs/doctrines, 82
Bible: distribution of/impact of use of, 69–
    70; effects of reading on the poor, 109;
    fresh reading of, 113; reading in one's
    own language, 48; small-group study of,
    169; translations of, 49, 85–86, 168, 174
Bible-centered theology, 70
biblical authority, 114
biblical formation for mission, 167–168
biblical model of mission, 19–20
"black legend," 37
Boer, Harry, 105
Bolivia, 52
Brazil, 146, 156–158
Brazilian Baptist Convention, 156–157
Brunner, Emil, 103
Canadian missionaries, 52, 64
Catholic Action movement, 29–30
Catholic approach to mission: Catholic sec-
    tor of mission, 10; conflict of, with evan-

gelical policies, 73–74; development of,
28–32; influence of Protestantism on,
169; missionary concern in, 160–162;
objective of, versus Protestant, 38–41;
versus police approach, 90–91; versus
Protestant, 121, 138, 168. *See also* methodology; Protestant approach to mission
Catholicism/Catholic Church: arrival of, in
    Latin America, 23; changes in, 96–98;
    crisis of, in Europe, 67; differences in
    forms of, 61; exodus to Protestant
    Church from, 88; modernization of
    Catholic church, 40–41; nominal Catho-
    lics, 59; Pentacostalism and, agreements
    between, 139–140; problems of Roman
    Catholic Church, 72–73; versus Protes-
    tantism, 97–98; Protestant presence as
    incentive for renewal of, 59–60; rate of
    change in, 169; relationship of, to Bra-
    zil politics, 16; Roman Catholic Church,
    117–118, 162; structural differences be-
    tween Protestantism and, 74; weak-
    nesses of Latin American, 39
caudillo-style leadership, 42, 142
CELAM (Latin American Bishops' Confer-
    ences), 28–29, 30–31, 62, 63, 65–67, 90;
    Missions Department, 93
charismatic movements, 44, 78, 80, 136
Chile, 71–72, 142
Christendom: mentality, 40; model of mis-
    sion, 165; without Christ, 116
Christian faith, 173
Christian identity, 128
Christianity/Christian Church: central truths
    of, 116–117; character of popular, 85;
    growth of, 7–9; loss of strength of, 84;
    message of, new understanding of, 69–